TITAN COMICS

EDITOR
Andrew James

ASSISTANT EDITOR
Jessica Burton

COLLECTION DESIGNER
Rob Farmer

SENIOR EDITOR
Steve White

TITAN COMICS EDITORIAL
Lizzie Kaye, Tom Williams

PRODUCTION SUPERVISORS
Maria Pearson, Jackie Flook

PRODUCTION MANAGER
Obi Onuora

STUDIO MANAGER
Selina Juneja

SENIOR SALES MANAGER
Steve Tothill

SENIOR MARKETING & PRESS OFFICER
Owen Johnson

DIRECT SALES & MARKETING MANAGER
Ricky Claydon

COMMERCIAL MANAGER
Michelle Fairlamb

PUBLISHING MANAGER
Darryl Tothill

PUBLISHING DIRECTOR
Chris Teather

OPERATIONS DIRECTOR
Leigh Baulch

EXECUTIVE DIRECTOR
Vivian Cheung

PUBLISHER
Nick Landau

Special thanks to Steven Moffat, Brian Minchin, Mandy Thwaites, Matt Nicholls, James Dudley, Edward Russell, Derek Ritchie, Scott Handcock, Kirsty Mullan, Kate Bush, Julia Nocciolino, and Ed Casey, for their invaluable assistance.

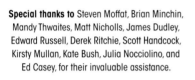

BBC WORLDWIDE

DIRECTOR OF EDITORIAL GOVERNANCE
Nicolas Brett

DIRECTOR OF CONSUMER PRODUCTS AND PUBLISHING
Andrew Moultrie

HEAD OF UK PUBLISHING
Chris Kerwin

PUBLISHER
Mandy Thwaites

PUBLISHING CO-ORDINATOR
Eva Abramik

DOCTOR WHO: THE NINTH DOCTOR VOL 1:
WEAPONS OF PAST DESTRUCTION
HB ISBN: 9781782763369 SB ISBN: 9781785851056
Published by Titan Comics, a division of
Titan Publishing Group, Ltd. 144 Southwark Street,
London, SE1 0UP.

A CIP catalogue record for this title is available from the British Library. First
edition: March 2016.

10 9 8 7 6 5 4 3 2 1

Printed in China. TC0777

Titan Comics does not read or accept unsolicited DOCTOR WHO submissions of
ideas, stories or artwork.

www.titan-comics.com

DOCTOR WHO
THE NINTH DOCTOR

VOL 1: WEAPONS OF PAST DESTRUCTION

WRITER: CAVAN SCOTT

**ARTIST: BLAIR SHEDD
WITH RACHAEL STOTT**

**COLORISTS: BLAIR SHEDD
AND ANANG SETYAWAN**

**LETTERS: RICHARD STARKINGS AND
COMICRAFT'S JIMMY BETANCOURT**

BBC

DOCTOR WHO

THE NINTH DOCTOR

THE DOCTOR

Last of the Time Lords of Gallifrey. Believes himself to be the sole survivor of the Time War, which ravaged the universe until he put a stop to it, at the cost of his entire species. He is just beginning to have his rough edges sanded off by Rose.

CAPTAIN JACK

A roguish ex-Time Agent from the 51st Century, Jack was working as an interstellar con man when the Doctor and Rose ran into him during the Blitz. Brash, brave – and willing to hit on anything with a pulse – Jack has now joined the TARDIS crew full-time!

ROSE TYLER

A former shop assistant from London, Rose became the Doctor's companion when she helped him save London from an Auton invasion. She's been traveling with him ever since – from the last days of Earth to Victorian London and beyond!

PREVIOUSLY...

Having just saved Blitz-stricken London from the threat of a damaged Chula warship and its runaway nanogenes – and with Jack having revealed his inner heroism by nearly blowing himself up while towing a German bomb into space – the Doctor, Rose and Jack are taking a tour of the universe, hoping for more sightseeing opportunities and less occasions of near-certain death...

This adventure happens between 'The Doctor Dances' and 'Boom Town'.

When you've finished reading this collection, please email your thoughts to doctorwhocomic@titanemail.com

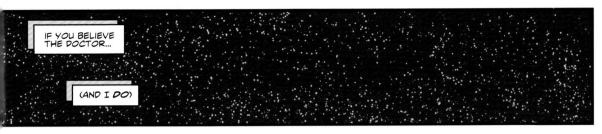

IF YOU BELIEVE THE DOCTOR...

(AND I *DO*)

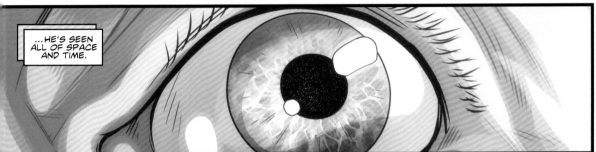

...HE'S SEEN ALL OF SPACE AND TIME.

STARS BORN...

AND STARS DIE.

EVERY LIFE FORM UNDER EVERY SUN.

NO.

I DON'T BELIEVE IT.

YOU'D THINK *NOTHING* WOULD SURPRISE HIM ANY MORE.

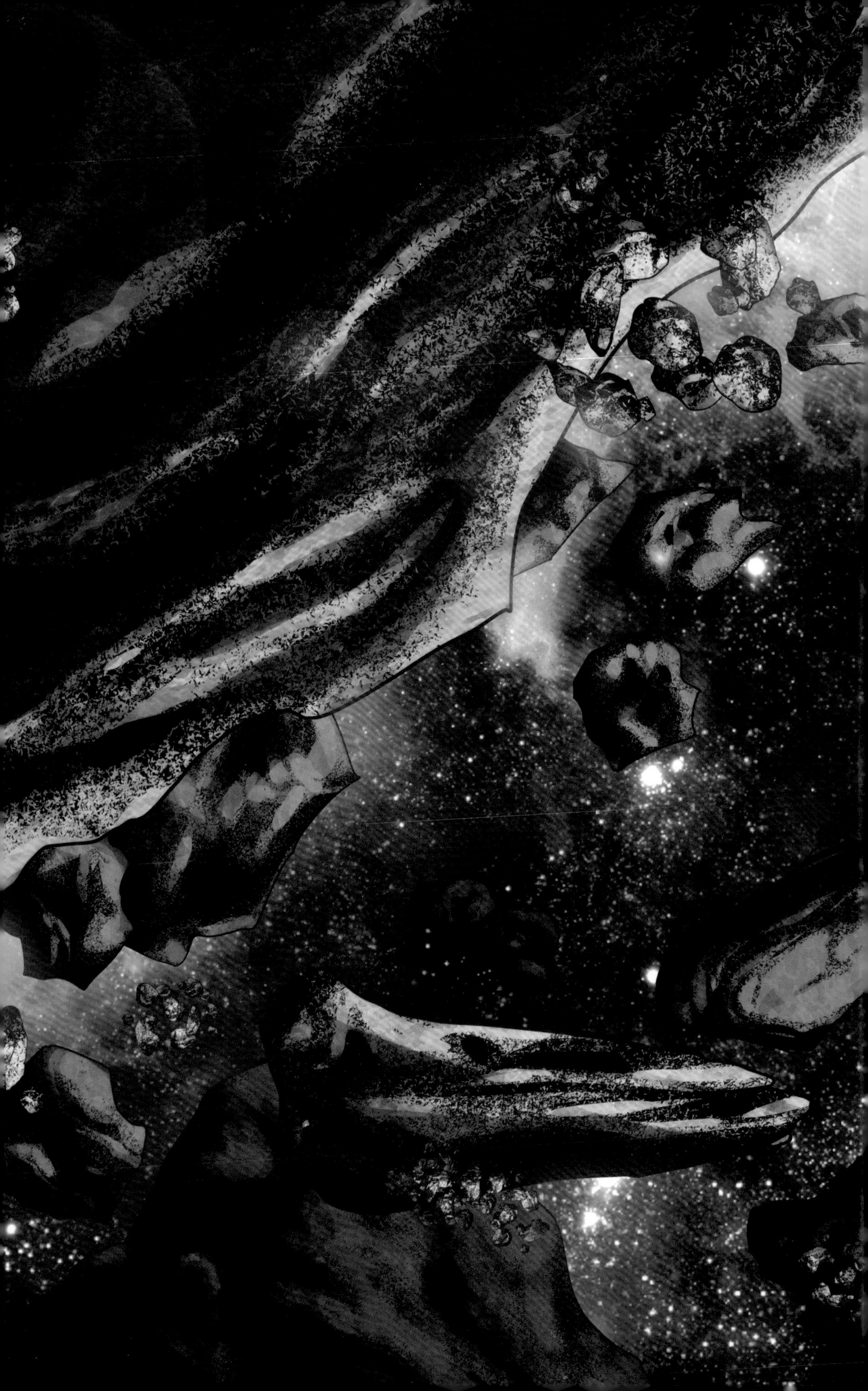

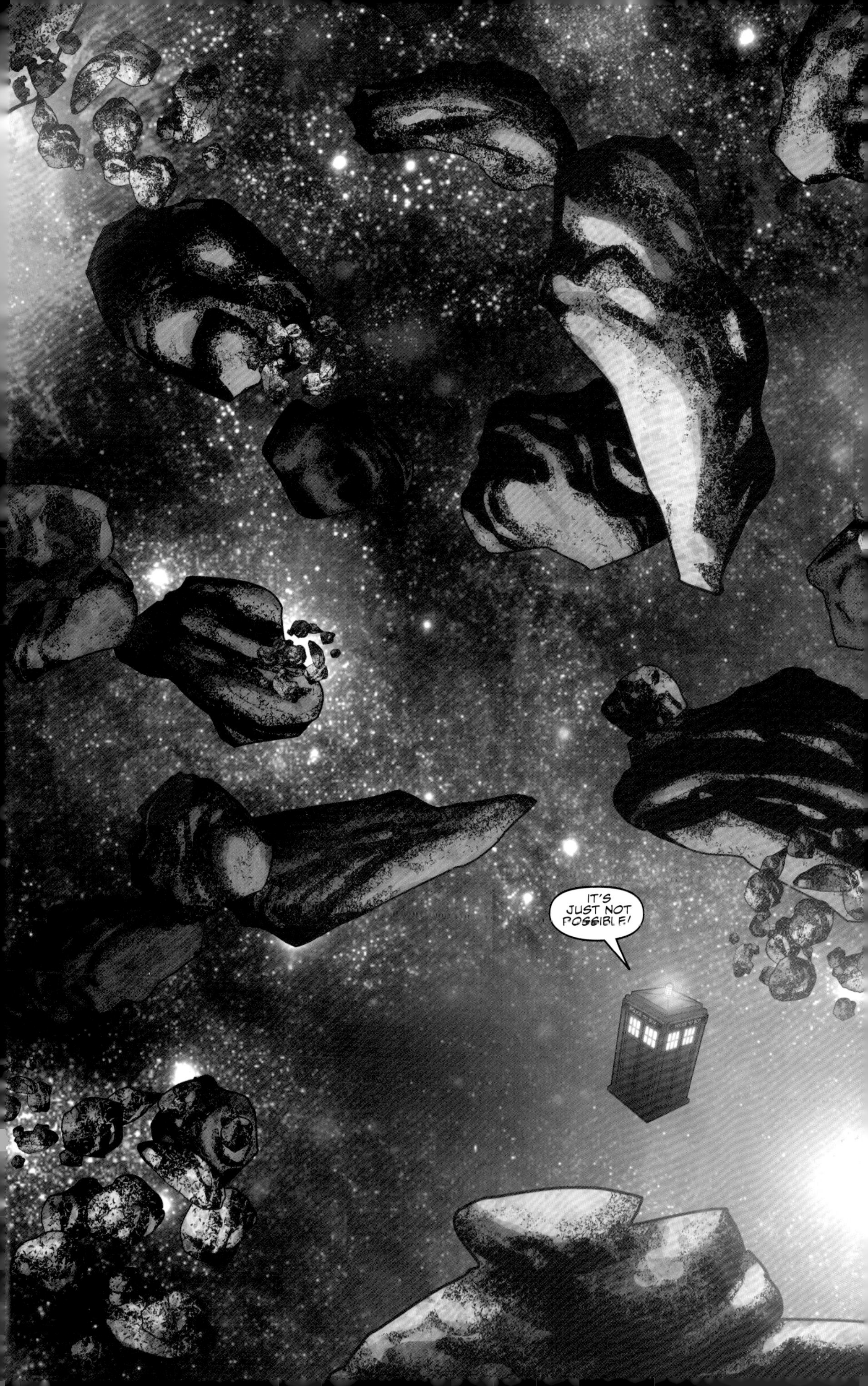
IT'S JUST NOT POSSIBLE!

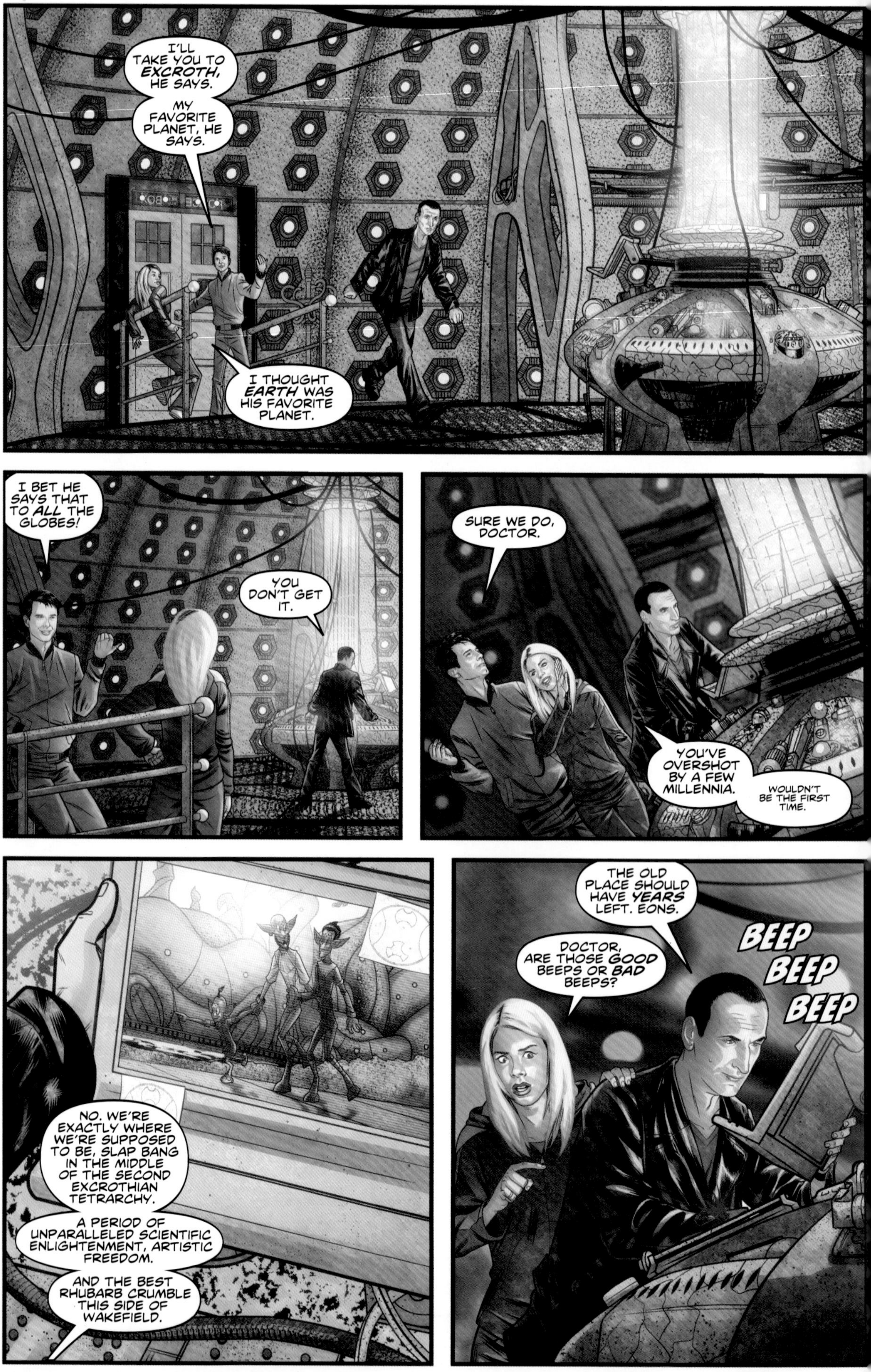
I'LL TAKE YOU TO *EXCROTH,* HE SAYS.
MY FAVORITE PLANET, HE SAYS.
I THOUGHT *EARTH* WAS HIS FAVORITE PLANET.
I BET HE SAYS THAT TO *ALL* THE GLOBES!
YOU DON'T GET IT.
SURE WE DO, DOCTOR.
YOU'VE OVERSHOT BY A FEW MILLENNIA.
WOULDN'T BE THE FIRST TIME.
NO. WE'RE EXACTLY WHERE WE'RE SUPPOSED TO BE, SLAP BANG IN THE MIDDLE OF THE SECOND EXCROTHIAN TETRARCHY.
A PERIOD OF UNPARALLELED SCIENTIFIC ENLIGHTENMENT, ARTISTIC FREEDOM.
AND THE BEST RHUBARB CRUMBLE THIS SIDE OF WAKEFIELD.
THE OLD PLACE SHOULD HAVE *YEARS* LEFT. EONS.
DOCTOR, ARE THOSE *GOOD* BEEPS OR *BAD* BEEPS?
BEEP
BEEP
BEEP

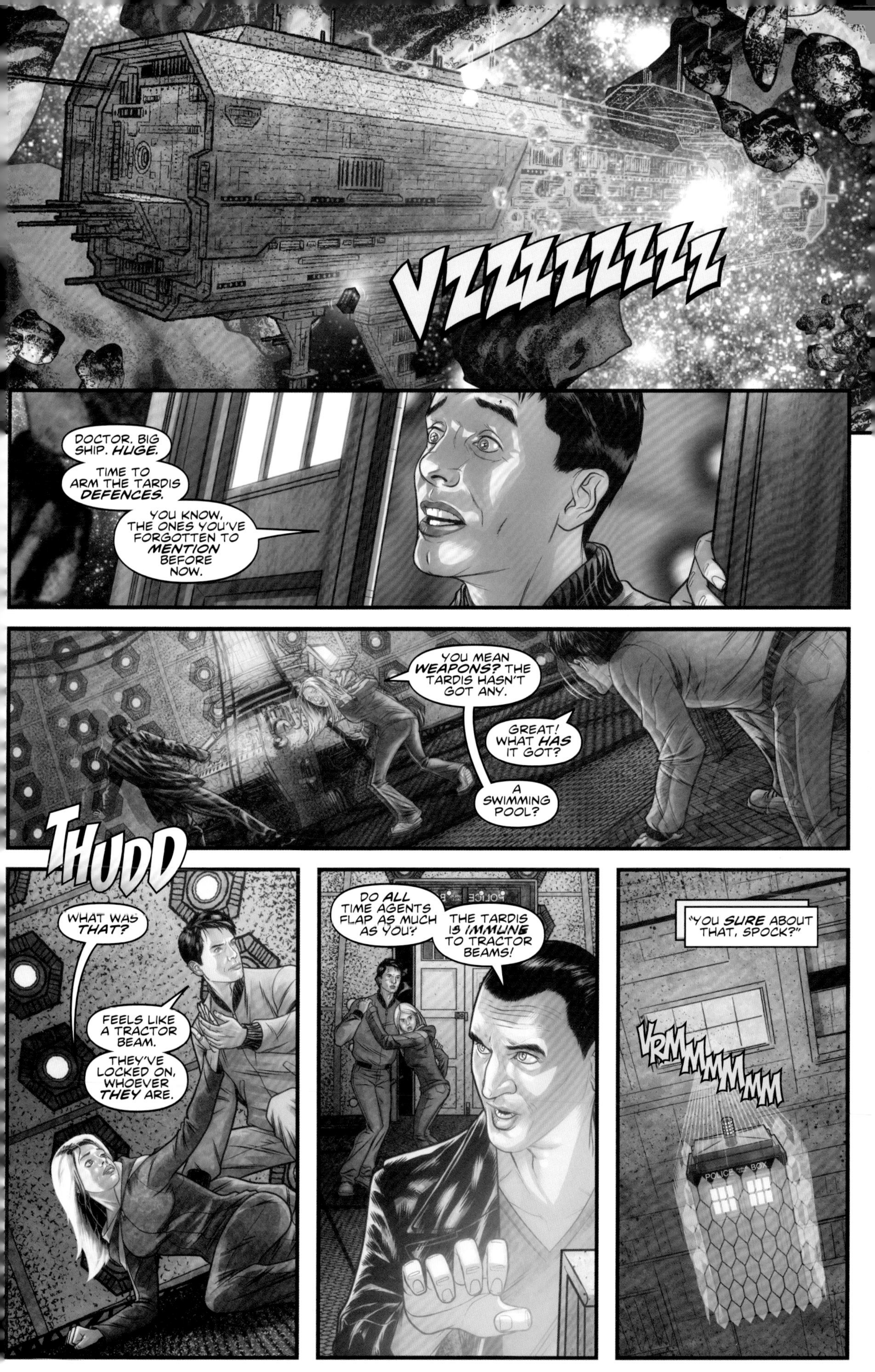
VZZZZZZZZZ
DOCTOR. BIG SHIP. HUGE.
TIME TO ARM THE TARDIS DEFENCES.
YOU KNOW, THE ONES YOU'VE FORGOTTEN TO MENTION BEFORE NOW.
YOU MEAN WEAPONS? THE TARDIS HASN'T GOT ANY.
GREAT! WHAT HAS IT GOT?
A SWIMMING POOL?
THUDD
WHAT WAS THAT?
FEELS LIKE A TRACTOR BEAM.
THEY'VE LOCKED ON, WHOEVER THEY ARE.
DO ALL TIME AGENTS FLAP AS MUCH AS YOU?
THE TARDIS IS IMMUNE TO TRACTOR BEAMS!
"YOU SURE ABOUT THAT, SPOCK?"
VRMMMMMMM

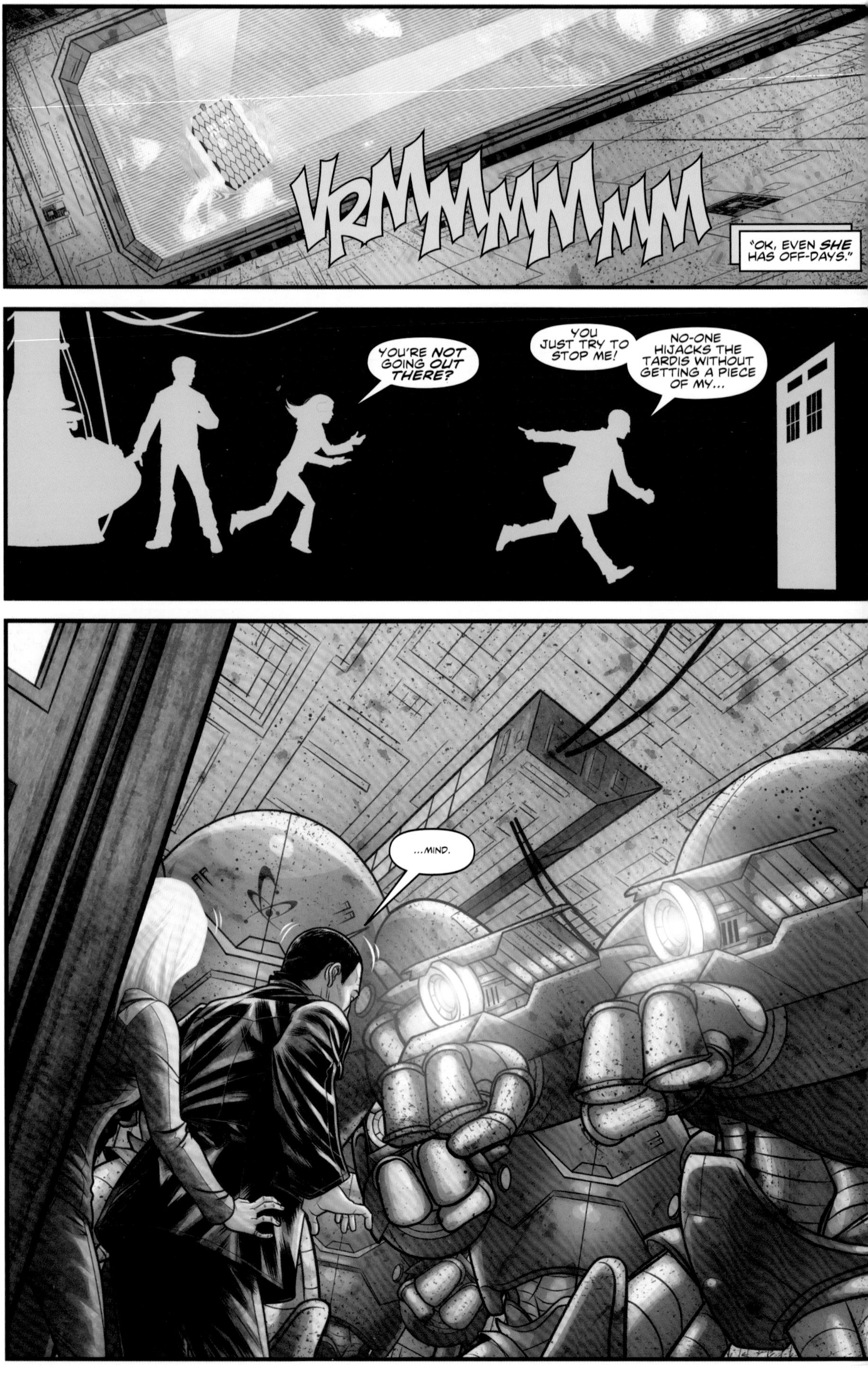
VRMMMMMMM
"OK, EVEN SHE HAS OFF-DAYS."
YOU'RE NOT GOING OUT THERE?
YOU JUST TRY TO STOP ME!
NO-ONE HIJACKS THE TARDIS WITHOUT GETTING A PIECE OF MY...
...MIND.

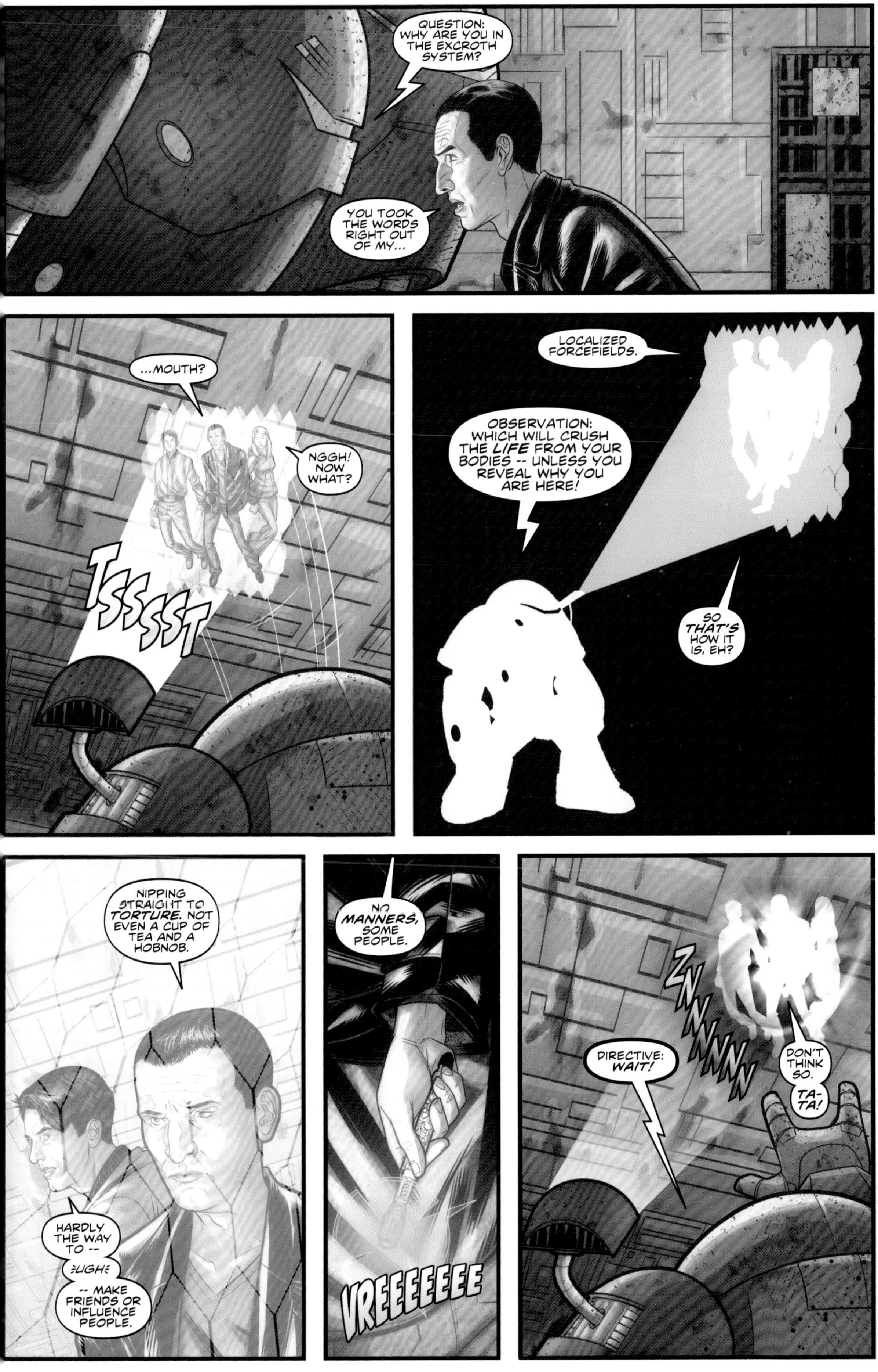
QUESTION: WHY ARE YOU IN THE EXCROTH SYSTEM?
YOU TOOK THE WORDS RIGHT OUT OF MY...
...MOUTH?
NGGH! NOW WHAT?
TSSSSST
LOCALIZED FORCEFIELDS.
OBSERVATION: WHICH WILL CRUSH THE *LIFE* FROM YOUR BODIES -- UNLESS YOU REVEAL WHY YOU ARE HERE!
SO *THAT'S* HOW IT IS, EH?
NIPPING STRAIGHT TO *TORTURE.* NOT EVEN A CUP OF TEA AND A HOBNOB.
HARDLY THE WAY TO --
UGH
-- MAKE FRIENDS OR INFLUENCE PEOPLE.
NO *MANNERS,* SOME PEOPLE.
VREEEEEEE
ZNNNNNN
DIRECTIVE: *WAIT!*
DON'T THINK SO.
TA-TA!

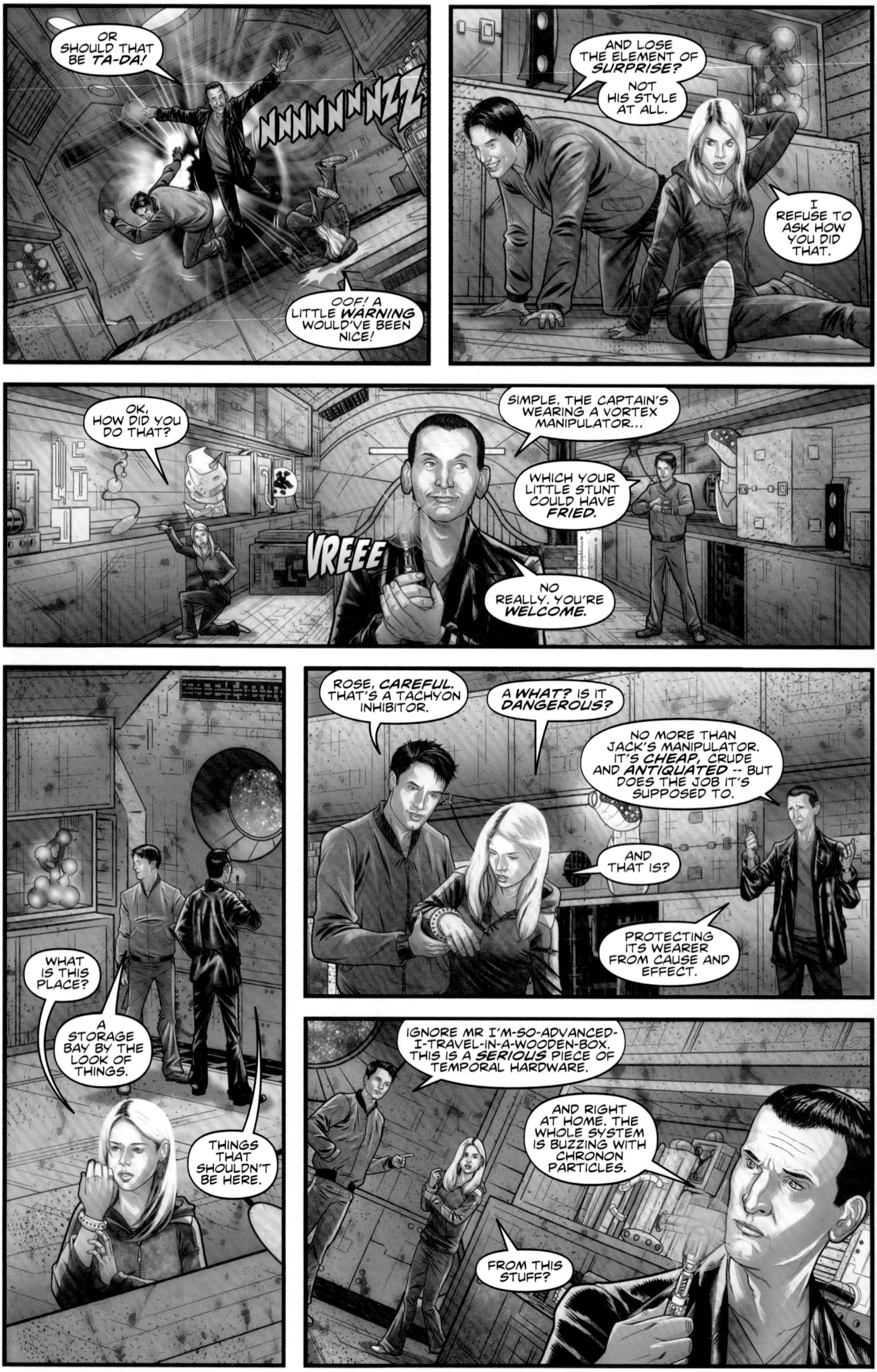
OR SHOULD THAT BE TA-DA!
NNNNNNNZZ
OOF! A LITTLE WARNING WOULD'VE BEEN NICE!
AND LOSE THE ELEMENT OF SURPRISE?
NOT HIS STYLE AT ALL.
I REFUSE TO ASK HOW YOU DID THAT.
OK, HOW DID YOU DO THAT?
SIMPLE. THE CAPTAIN'S WEARING A VORTEX MANIPULATOR...
WHICH YOUR LITTLE STUNT COULD HAVE FRIED.
VREEE
NO REALLY. YOU'RE WELCOME.
WHAT IS THIS PLACE?
A STORAGE BAY BY THE LOOK OF THINGS.
THINGS THAT SHOULDN'T BE HERE.
ROSE, CAREFUL. THAT'S A TACHYON INHIBITOR.
A WHAT? IS IT DANGEROUS?
NO MORE THAN JACK'S MANIPULATOR. IT'S CHEAP, CRUDE AND ANTIQUATED -- BUT DOES THE JOB IT'S SUPPOSED TO.
AND THAT IS?
PROTECTING ITS WEARER FROM CAUSE AND EFFECT.
IGNORE MR I'M-SO-ADVANCED-I-TRAVEL-IN-A-WOODEN-BOX. THIS IS A SERIOUS PIECE OF TEMPORAL HARDWARE.
AND RIGHT AT HOME. THE WHOLE SYSTEM IS BUZZING WITH CHRONON PARTICLES.
FROM THIS STUFF?

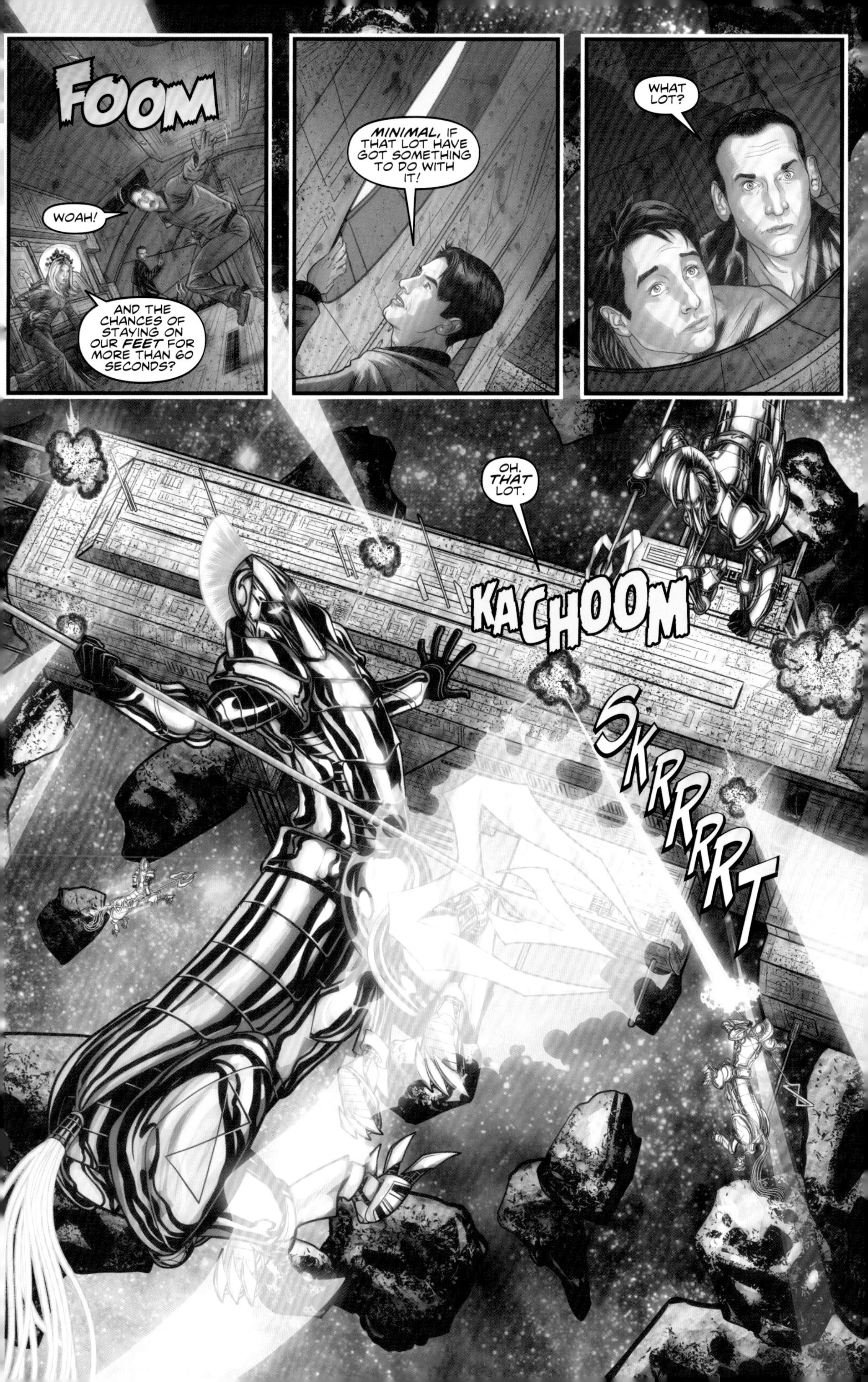
FOOM
WOAH!
AND THE CHANCES OF STAYING ON OUR FEET FOR MORE THAN 60 SECONDS?
MINIMAL, IF THAT LOT HAVE GOT SOMETHING TO DO WITH IT!
WHAT LOT?
OH. THAT LOT.
KACHOOM
SKRRRRRT

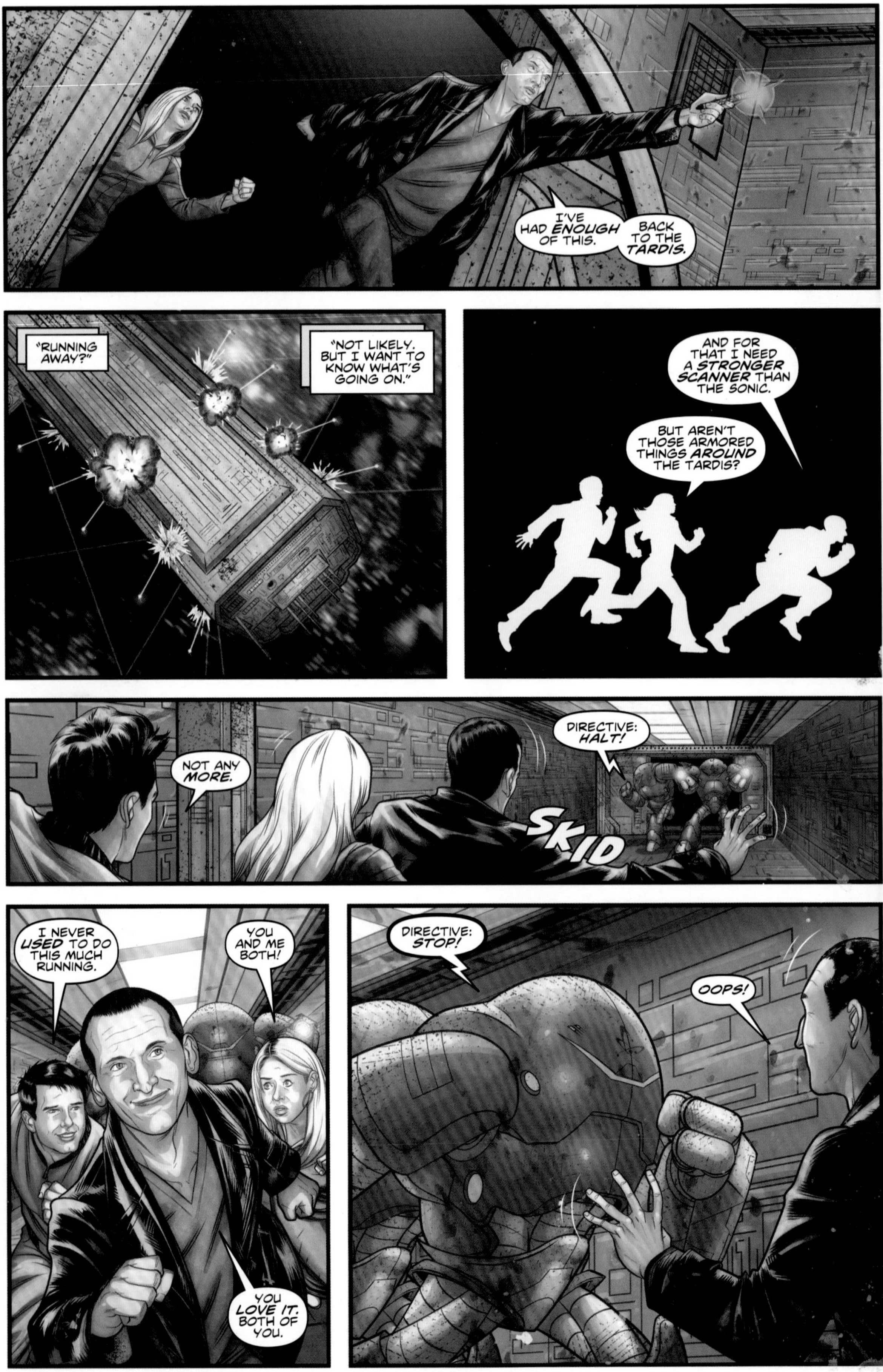
I'VE HAD ENOUGH OF THIS.
BACK TO THE TARDIS.
"RUNNING AWAY?"
"NOT LIKELY. BUT I WANT TO KNOW WHAT'S GOING ON."
AND FOR THAT I NEED A STRONGER SCANNER THAN THE SONIC.
BUT AREN'T THOSE ARMORED THINGS AROUND THE TARDIS?
NOT ANY MORE.
DIRECTIVE: HALT!
SKID
I NEVER USED TO DO THIS MUCH RUNNING.
YOU AND ME BOTH!
YOU LOVE IT. BOTH OF YOU.
DIRECTIVE: STOP!
OOPS!

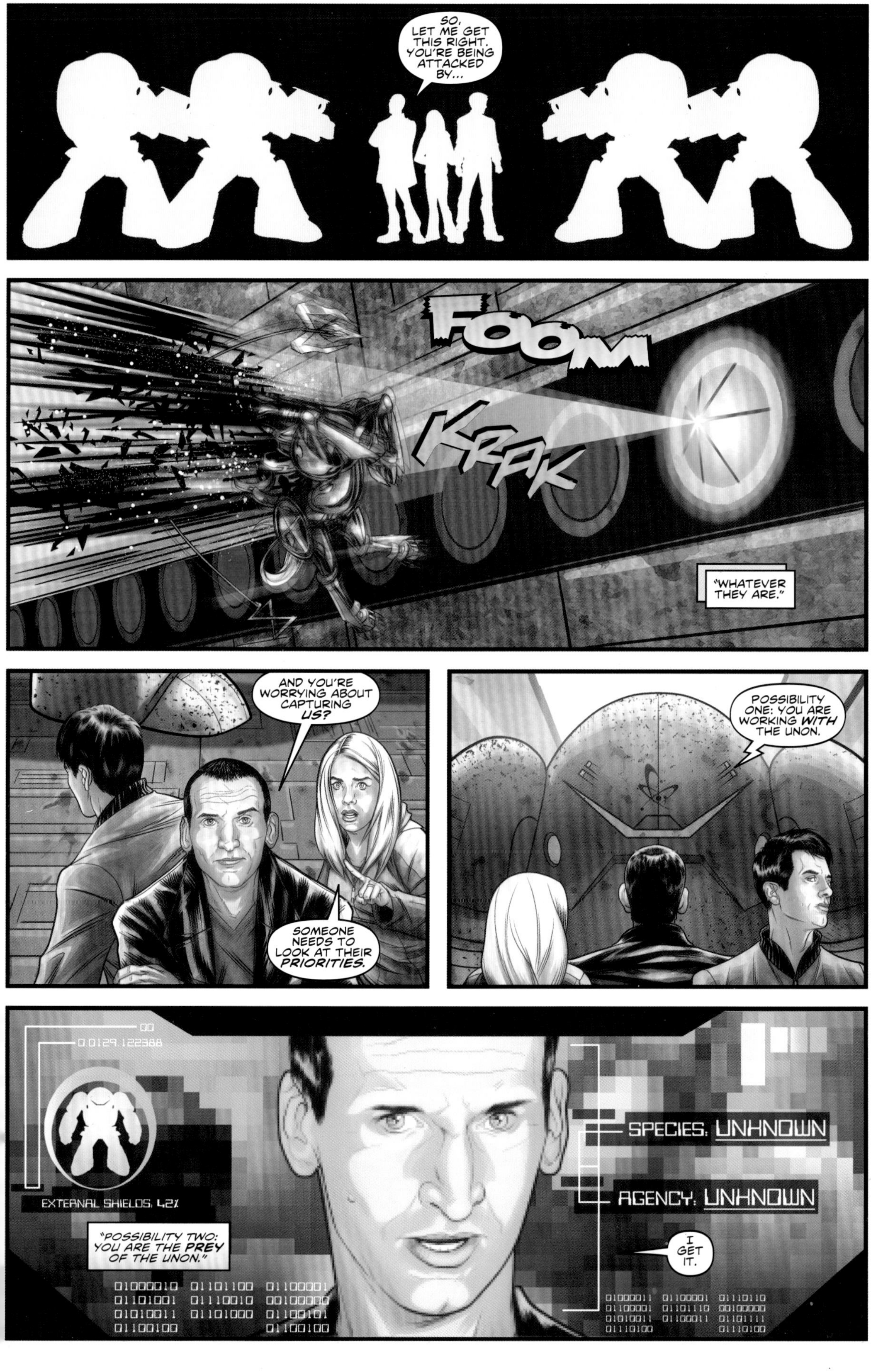
SO, LET ME GET THIS RIGHT. YOU'RE BEING ATTACKED BY...
FOOM
KRAK
"WHATEVER THEY ARE."
AND YOU'RE WORRYING ABOUT CAPTURING *US*?
SOMEONE NEEDS TO LOOK AT THEIR *PRIORITIES*.
POSSIBILITY ONE: YOU ARE WORKING *WITH* THE UNON.
00
0.0129.122388
EXTERNAL SHIELDS: 42%
SPECIES: UNKNOWN
AGENCY: UNKNOWN
"POSSIBILITY TWO: YOU ARE THE *PREY* OF THE UNON."
I GET IT.
01000010 01101100 01100001
01101001 01110010 00100000
01010011 01101000 01100101
01100100 01100100
01000011 01100001 01110110
01100001 01101110 00100000
01010011 01100011 01101111
01110100 01110100

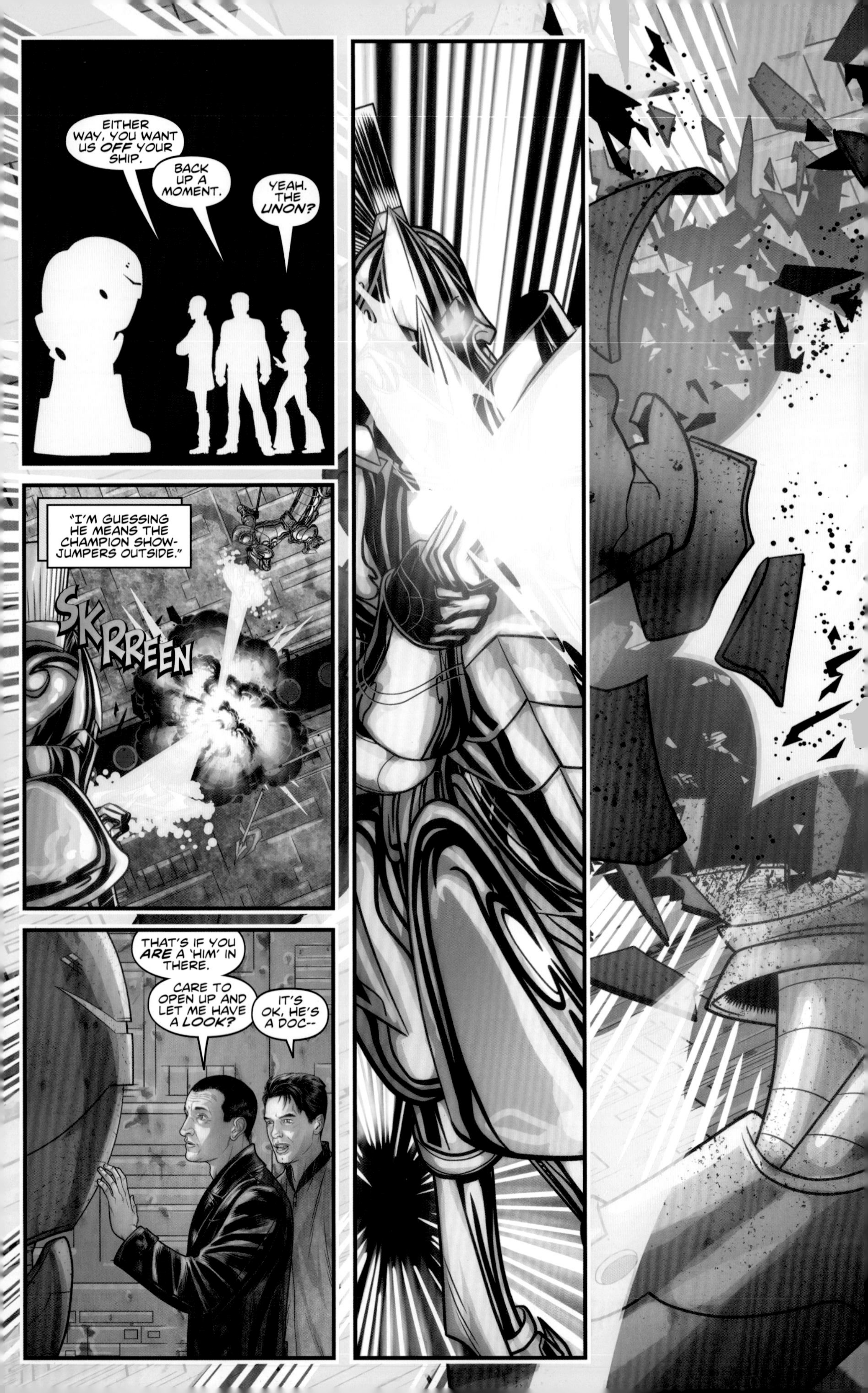
EITHER WAY, YOU WANT US OFF YOUR SHIP.
BACK UP A MOMENT.
YEAH. THE UNON?
"I'M GUESSING HE MEANS THE CHAMPION SHOW-JUMPERS OUTSIDE."
SKRREEN
THAT'S IF YOU ARE A 'HIM' IN THERE.
CARE TO OPEN UP AND LET ME HAVE A LOOK?
IT'S OK, HE'S A DOC--

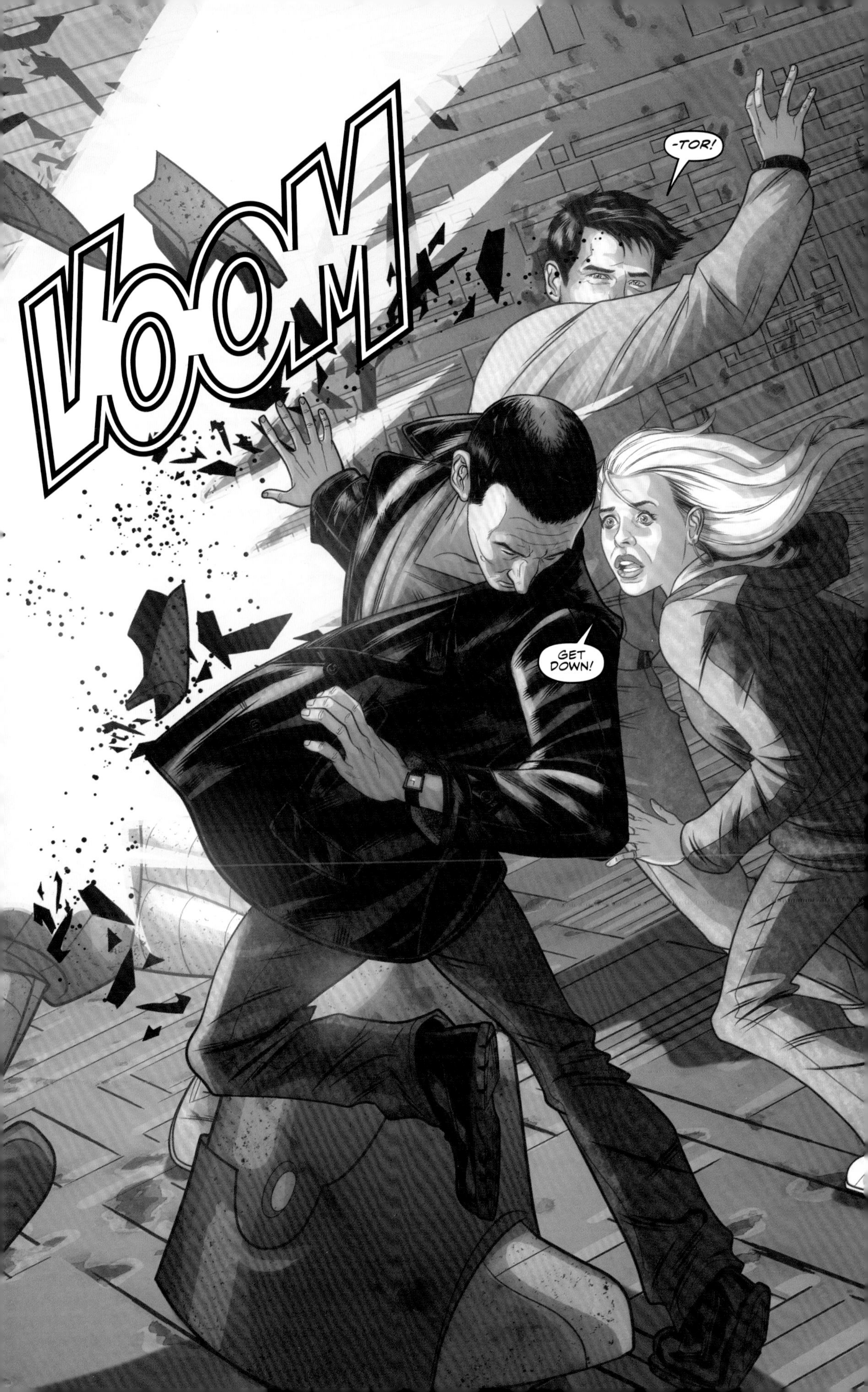
VOOM
-TOR!
GET DOWN!

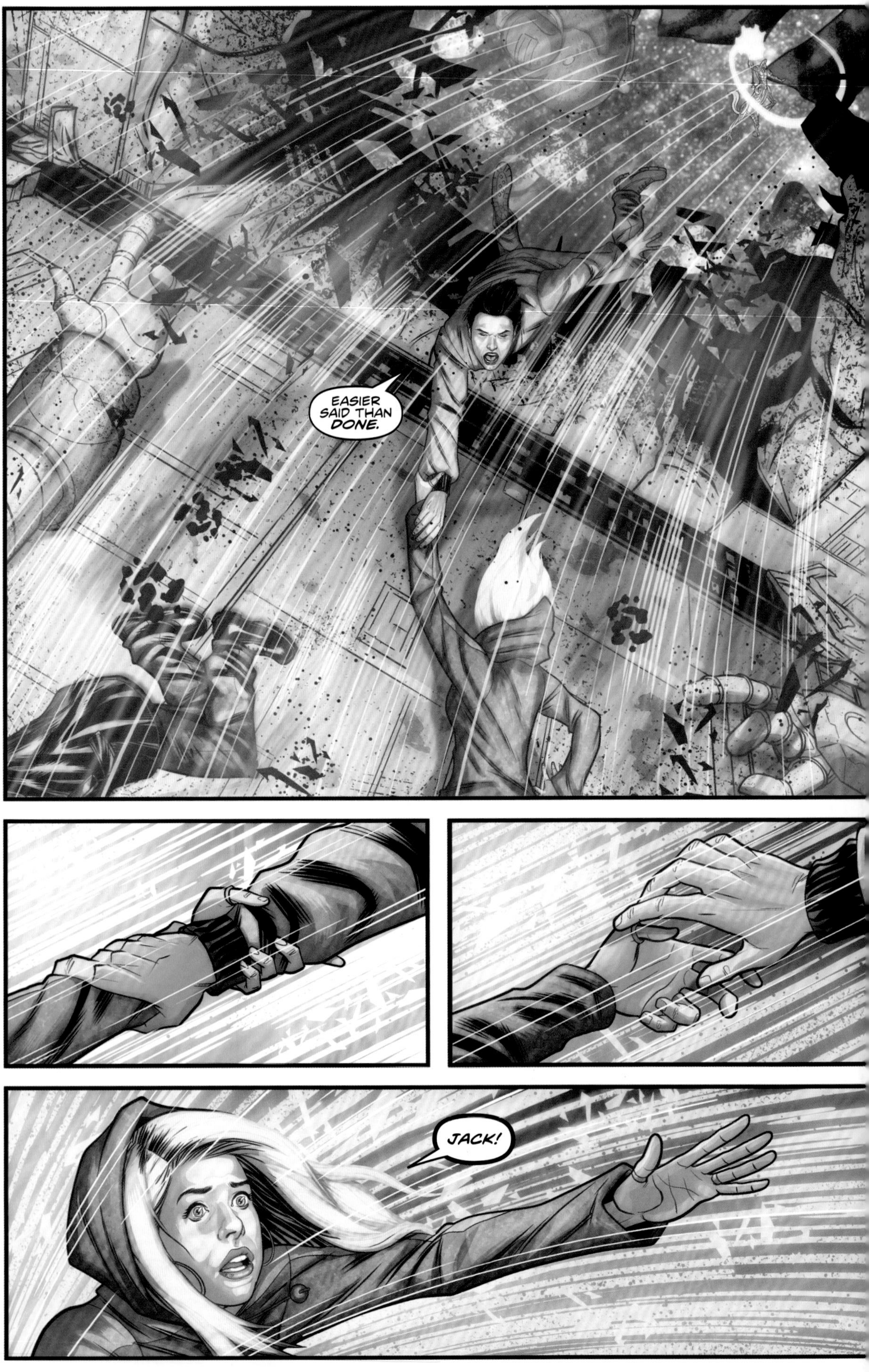
EASIER SAID THAN DONE.
JACK!

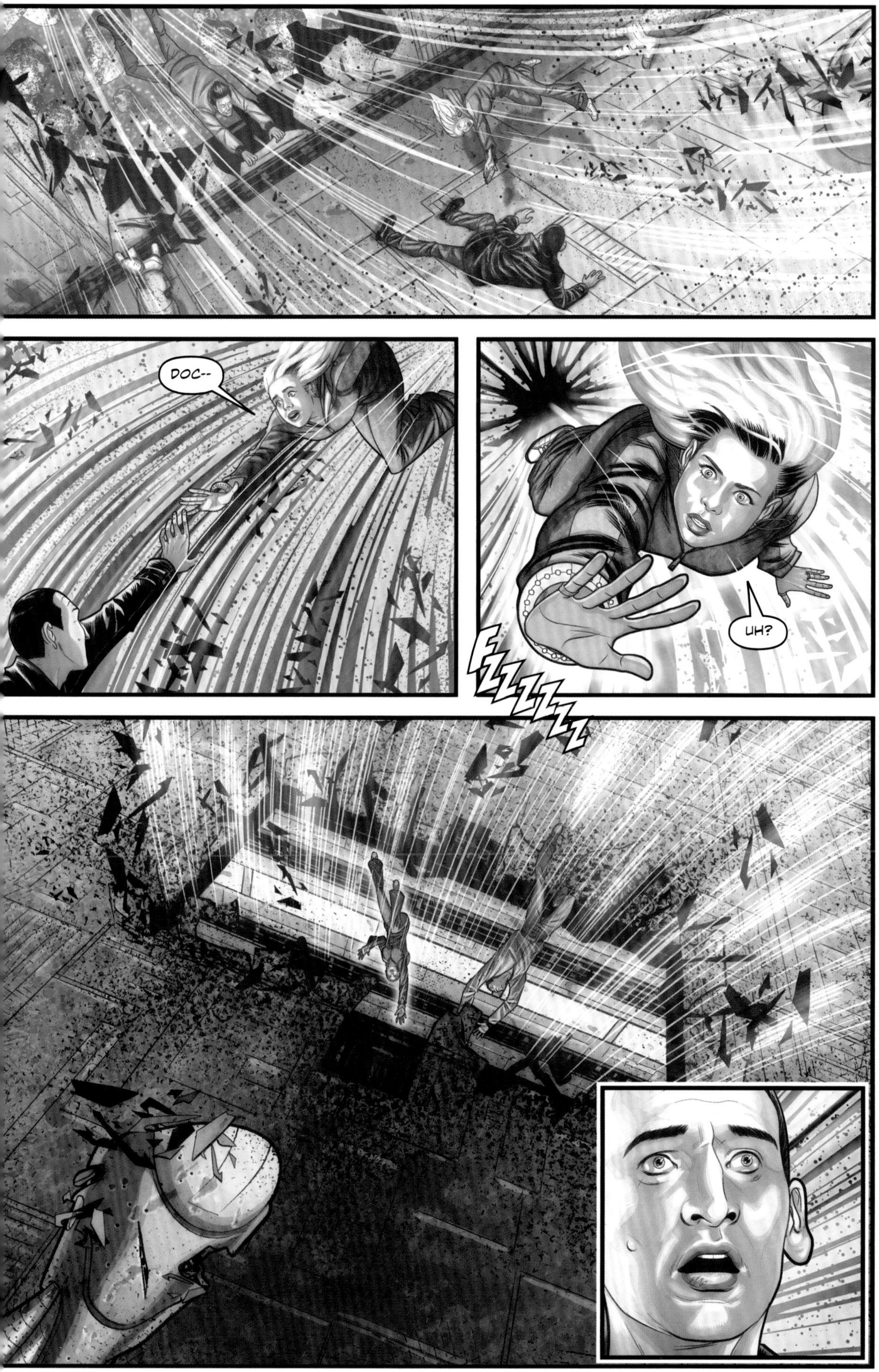
DOC--
UH?
FZZZZZZZ

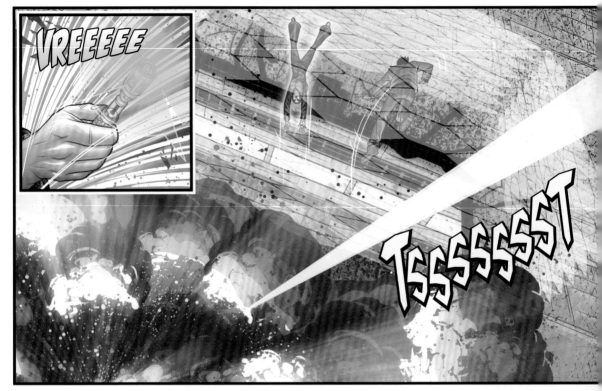

VREEEE

TSSSSSSST

SSSKT

AGH!

THUD

≨KOFF≨
≨KOFF≨

GUESS I SHOULD *THANK* YOU, DOCTOR.

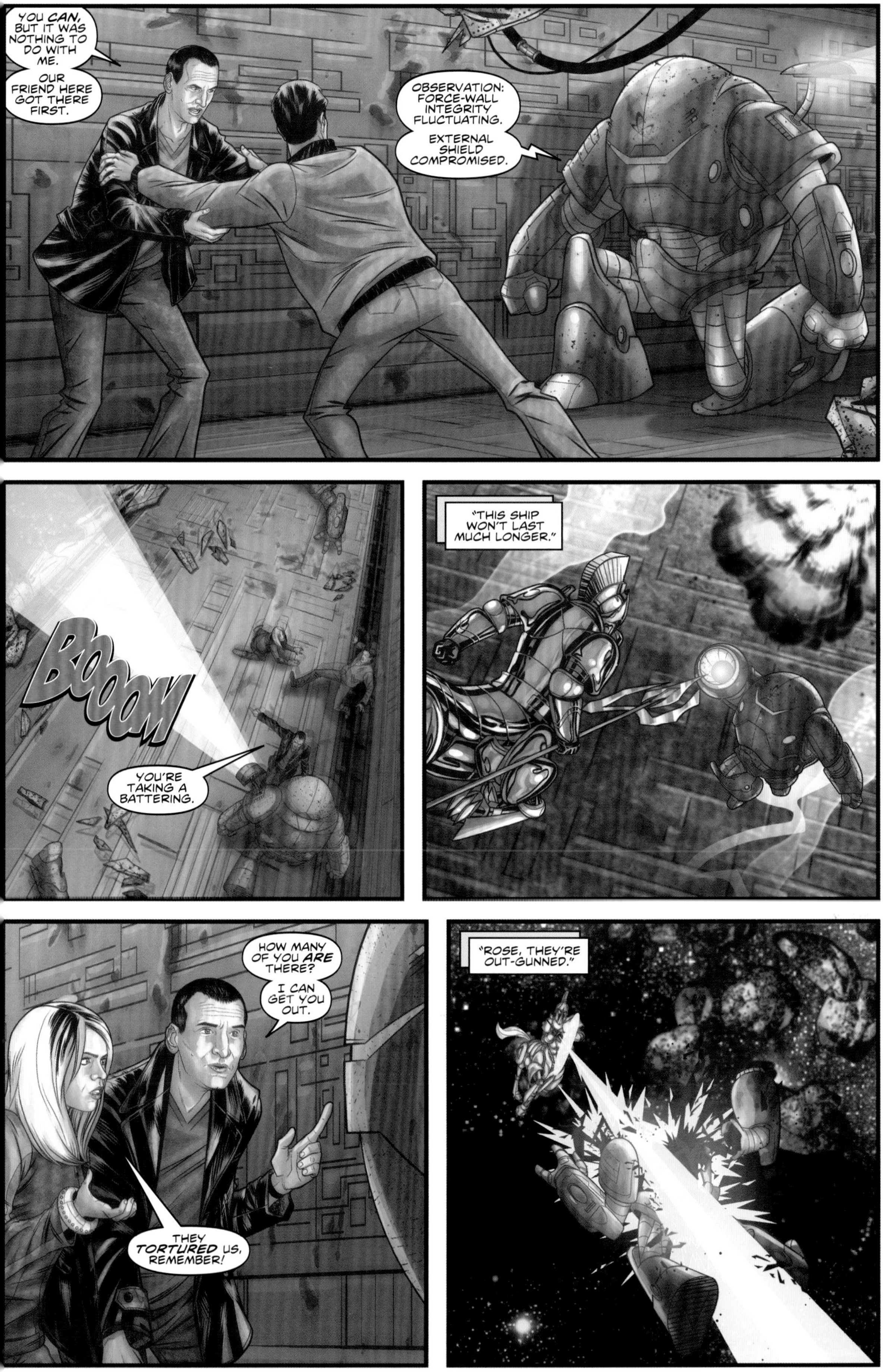
YOU CAN, BUT IT WAS NOTHING TO DO WITH ME.
OUR FRIEND HERE GOT THERE FIRST.
OBSERVATION: FORCE-WALL INTEGRITY FLUCTUATING.
EXTERNAL SHIELD COMPROMISED.
BOOOM
YOU'RE TAKING A BATTERING.
"THIS SHIP WON'T LAST MUCH LONGER."
HOW MANY OF YOU ARE THERE?
I CAN GET YOU OUT.
THEY TORTURED US, REMEMBER!
"ROSE, THEY'RE OUT-GUNNED."

AND I CAN *NEVER* RESIST AN UNDERDOG.

AGENCY: UNKNOWN

ORDERS: TERMINATE

EXTERNAL SHIELDS: 0%

INFORMATION: LECT NEVER RUN FROM BATTLE.

DOCTOR!

VOOSH

SHAKKT

OBSERVATION: UNIT DAMAGED.

YEAH, GOOD THINKING, *EINSTEIN.* BLAST THE NICE MANIAC WHO'S SINGLE-HANDEDLY KEEPING THE *HULL* SEALED.

AND WHO JUST TRIED TO *KILL* YOU. COME ON!

YOUR BOYFRIEND KNOWS WHAT I THINK ABOUT GUNS!

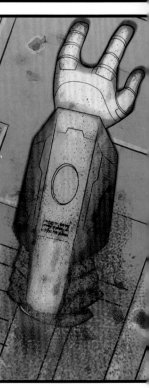

YOU CAN TELL ME AGAIN. WHEN WE'RE BACK IN THE TARDIS.

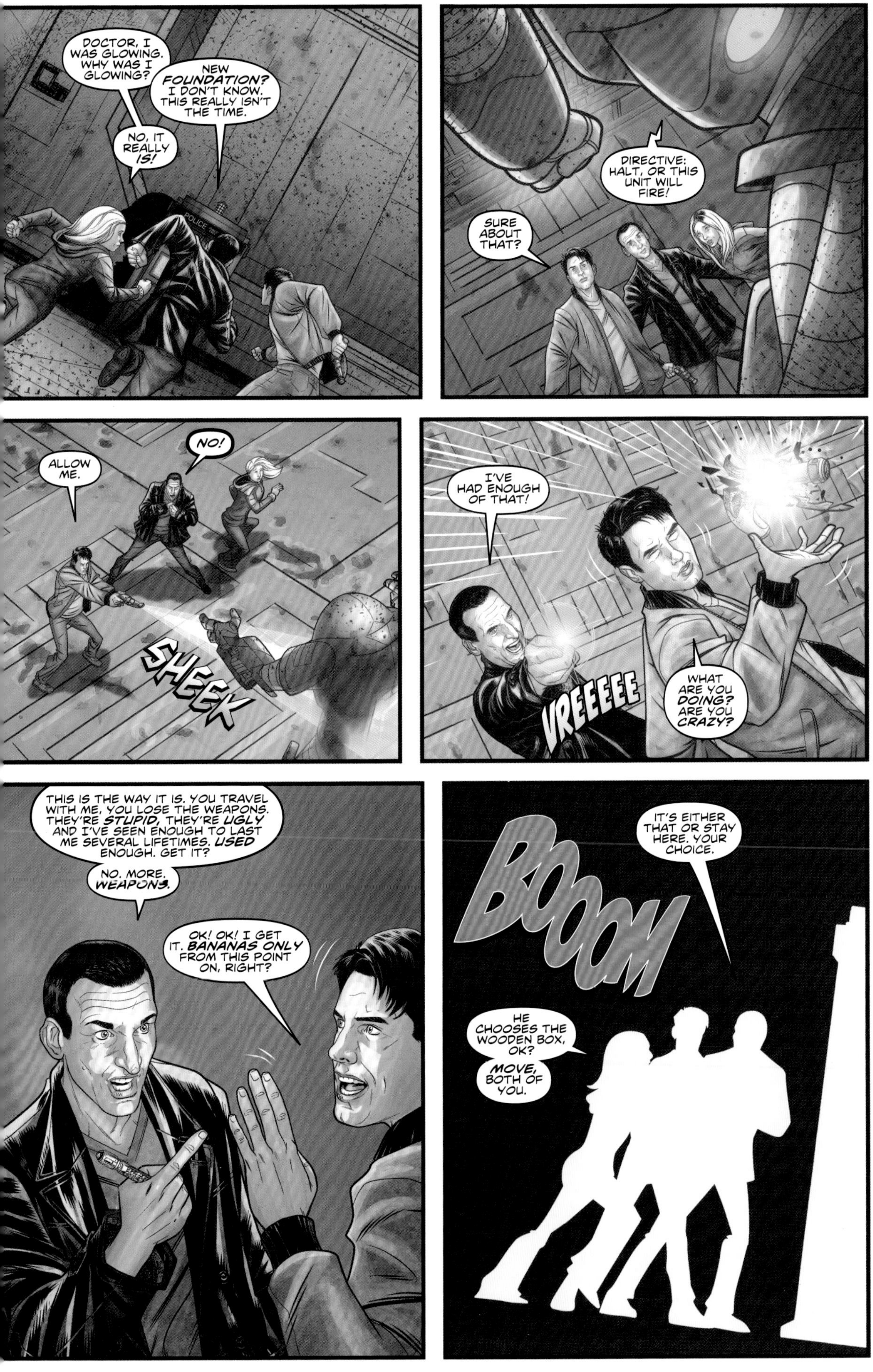
DOCTOR, I WAS GLOWING. WHY WAS I GLOWING?
NEW FOUNDATION? I DON'T KNOW. THIS REALLY ISN'T THE TIME.
NO, IT REALLY IS!
POLICE
DIRECTIVE: HALT, OR THIS UNIT WILL FIRE!
SURE ABOUT THAT?
ALLOW ME.
NO!
SHEEK
I'VE HAD ENOUGH OF THAT!
VREEEEE
WHAT ARE YOU DOING? ARE YOU CRAZY?
THIS IS THE WAY IT IS. YOU TRAVEL WITH ME, YOU LOSE THE WEAPONS. THEY'RE STUPID, THEY'RE UGLY AND I'VE SEEN ENOUGH TO LAST ME SEVERAL LIFETIMES. USED ENOUGH. GET IT?
NO. MORE. WEAPONS.
OK! OK! I GET IT. BANANAS ONLY FROM THIS POINT ON, RIGHT?
BOOOM
IT'S EITHER THAT OR STAY HERE. YOUR CHOICE.
HE CHOOSES THE WOODEN BOX, OK?
MOVE, BOTH OF YOU.

IN!

YOU SAID, USED.

WHAT?

BACK THEN, YOU SAID YOU'VE *USED* WEAPONS.

"SO?"

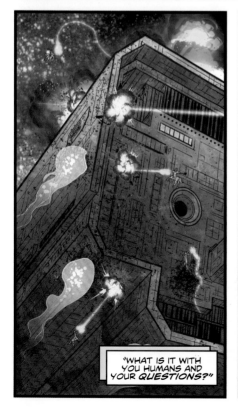

"WHAT IS IT WITH YOU HUMANS AND YOUR *QUESTIONS?*"

"I'M TRYING TO MAKE A *GETAWAY* HERE."

POLICE BOX

SLAMM

DOCTOR!

TRYING TO KEEP YOU SAFE.

VWOORRRP

VWOORRRP

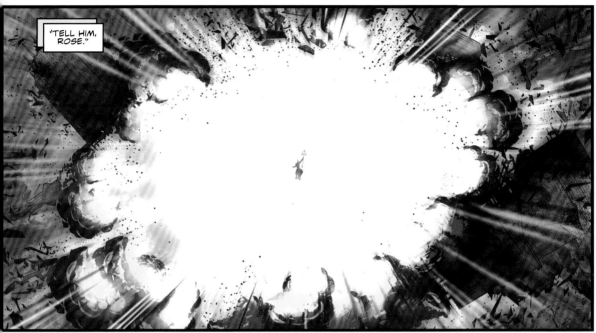

"TELL HIM, ROSE."

THAT'S ODD. THE SHIP'S GONE. FLASH, BANG, WALLOP. BYE BYE LECT.

BUT IF THESE READINGS ARE CORRECT, IT WAS BLASTED STRAIGHT INTO THE VORTEX ITSELF.

WE NEED TO GO BACK!

BACK? NOW WHO'S THE CRAZY ONE?

SHE WASN'T ON BOARD, DOCTOR. WHEN YOU DEMATERIALIZED.

SHE NEVER MADE IT THROUGH THE DOOR.

"DO YOU HEAR ME DOCTOR?"

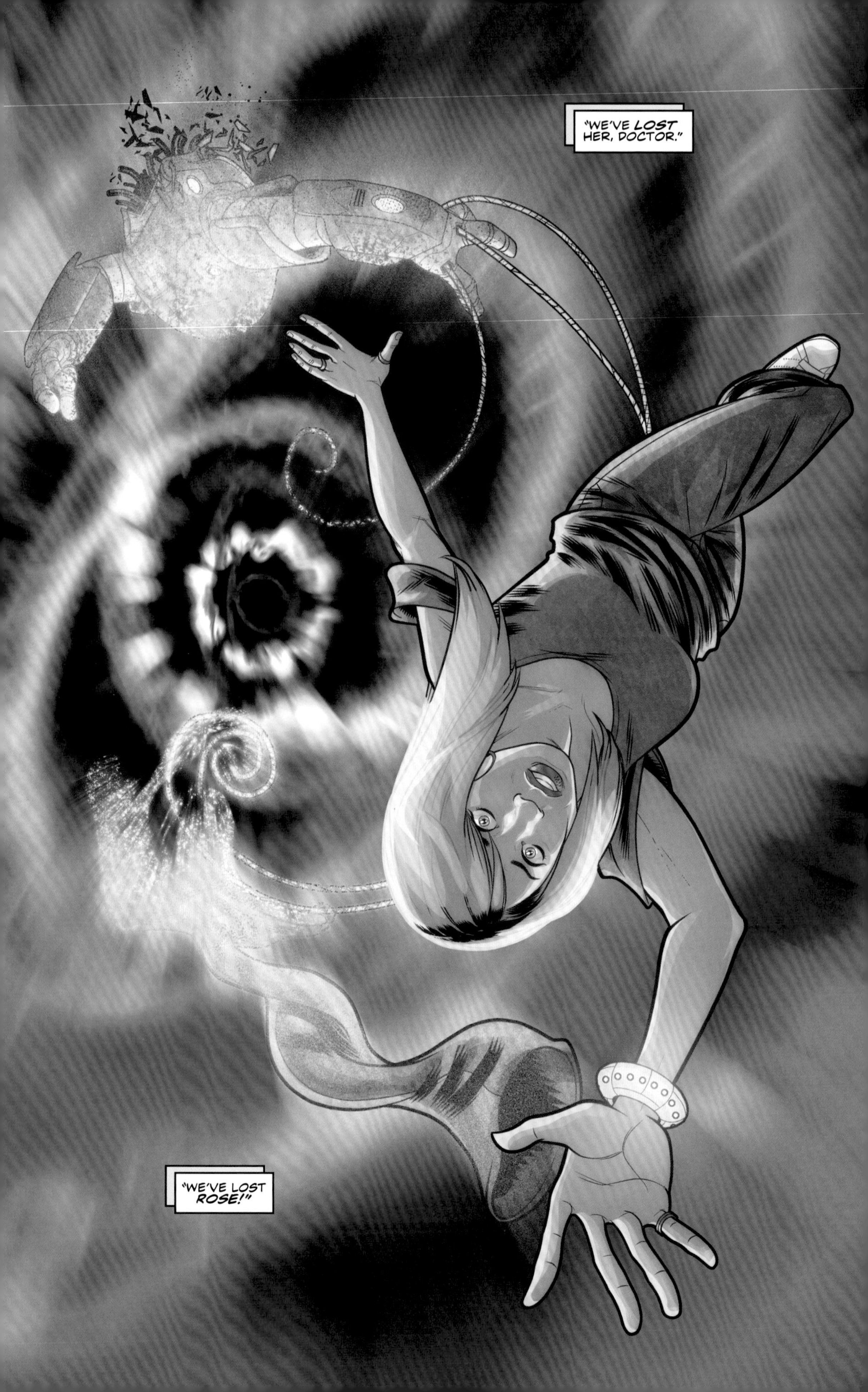
"WE'VE LOST HER, DOCTOR."
"WE'VE LOST ROSE!"

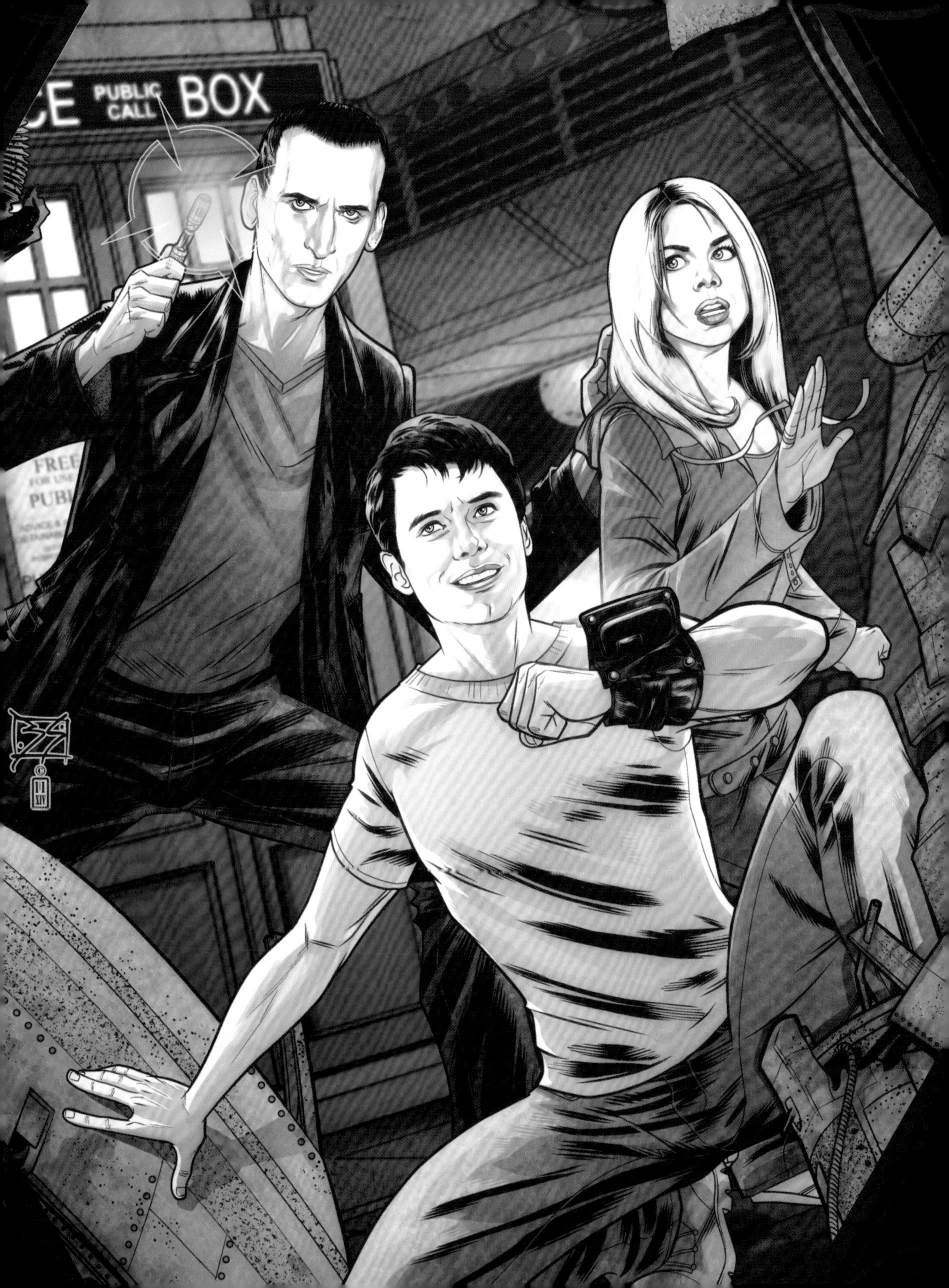

CE PUBLIC CALL BOX
FREE
PUBL

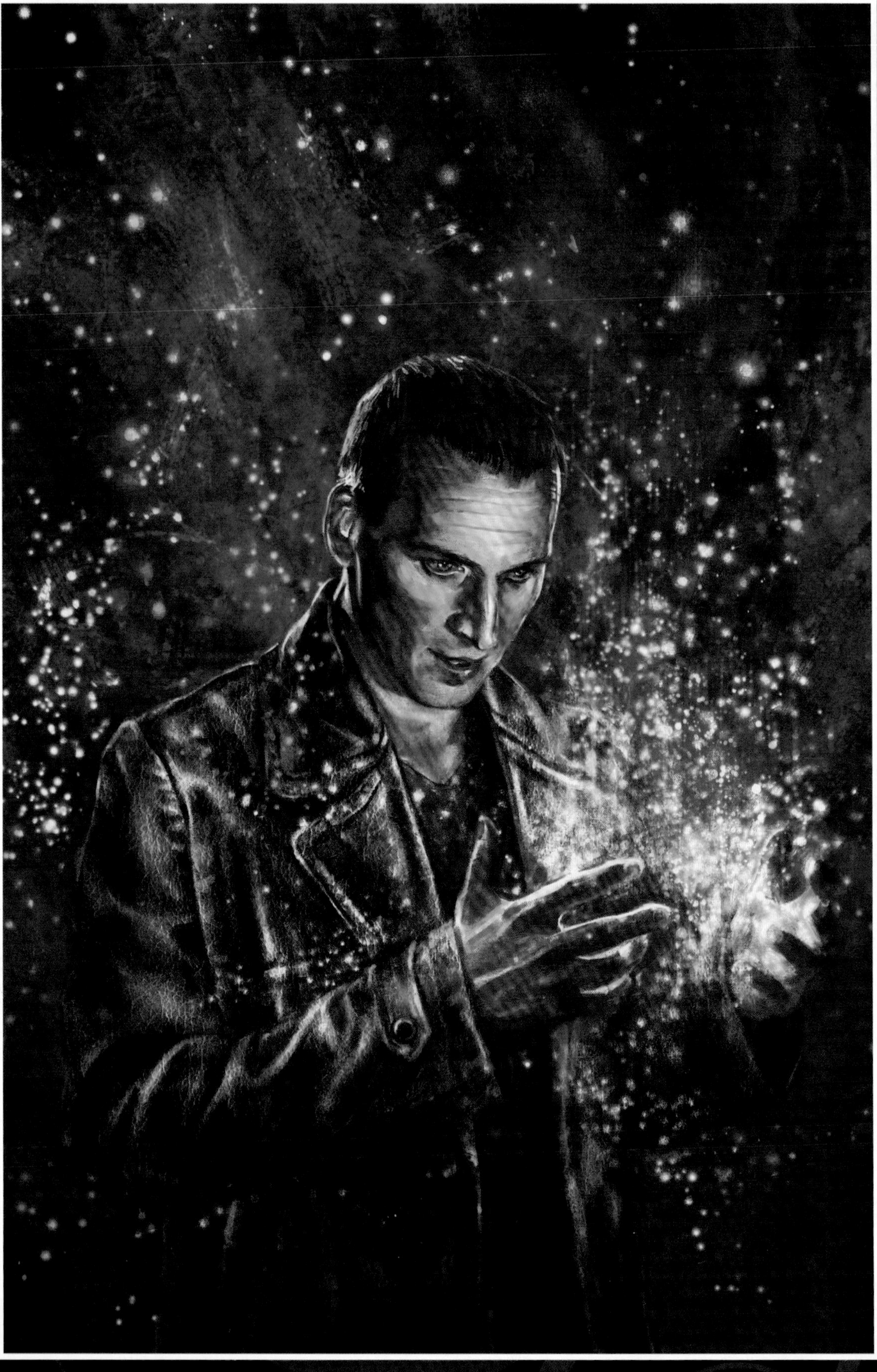

9D #2 Cover A: ALICE X. ZHANG

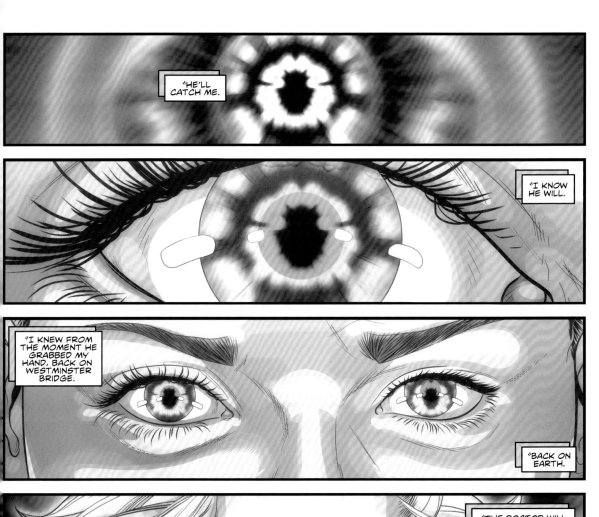

"HE'LL CATCH ME.

"I KNOW HE WILL.

"I KNEW FROM THE MOMENT HE GRABBED MY HAND, BACK ON WESTMINSTER BRIDGE.

"BACK ON EARTH.

"THE DOCTOR WILL CATCH ME IF I FALL.

"HE'LL NEVER LET ME GO."

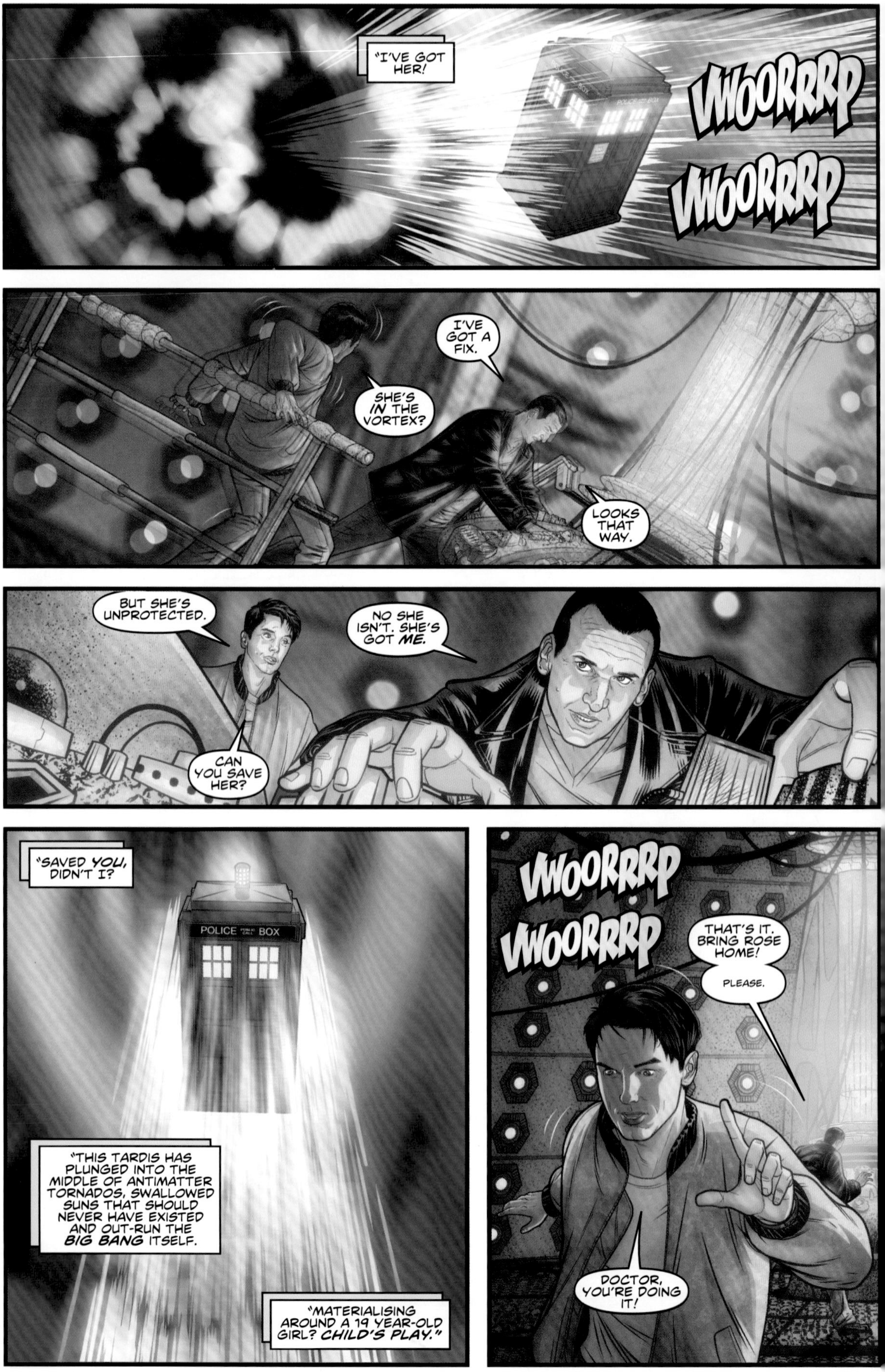
"I'VE GOT HER!
VWOORRRP
VWOORRRP
I'VE GOT A FIX.
SHE'S *IN* THE VORTEX?
LOOKS THAT WAY.
BUT SHE'S UNPROTECTED.
NO SHE ISN'T. SHE'S GOT *ME*.
CAN YOU SAVE HER?
"SAVED *YOU*, DIDN'T I?
POLICE BOX
"THIS TARDIS HAS PLUNGED INTO THE MIDDLE OF ANTIMATTER TORNADOS, SWALLOWED SUNS THAT SHOULD NEVER HAVE EXISTED AND OUT-RUN THE *BIG BANG* ITSELF.
"MATERIALISING AROUND A 19 YEAR-OLD GIRL? *CHILD'S PLAY*."
VWOORRRP
VWOORRRP
THAT'S IT. BRING ROSE HOME!
PLEASE.
DOCTOR, YOU'RE DOING IT!

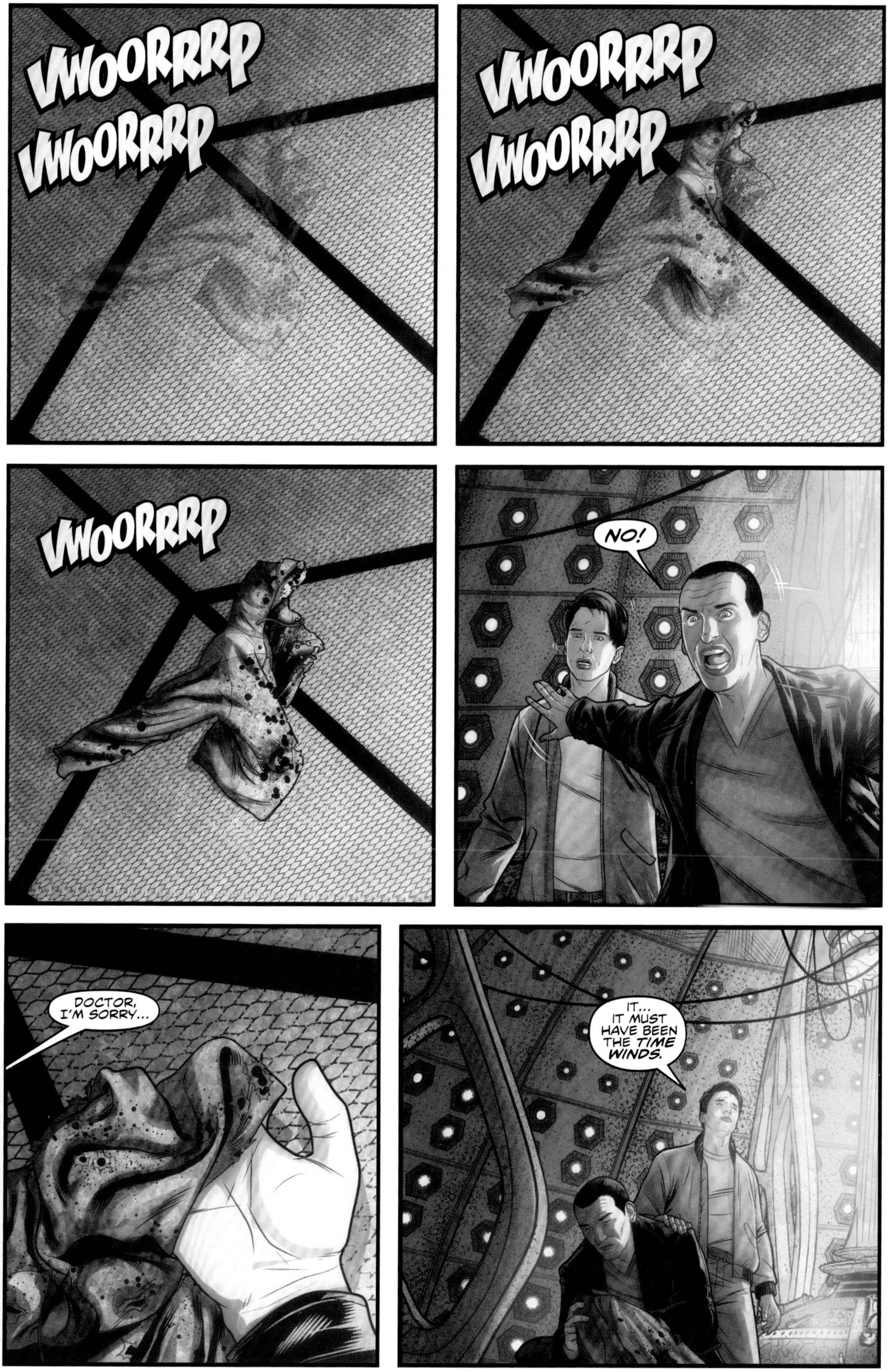
VWOORRRP
VWOORRRP
VWOORRRP
VWOORRRP
VWOORRRP
NO!
DOCTOR, I'M SORRY...
IT... IT MUST HAVE BEEN THE TIME WINDS.

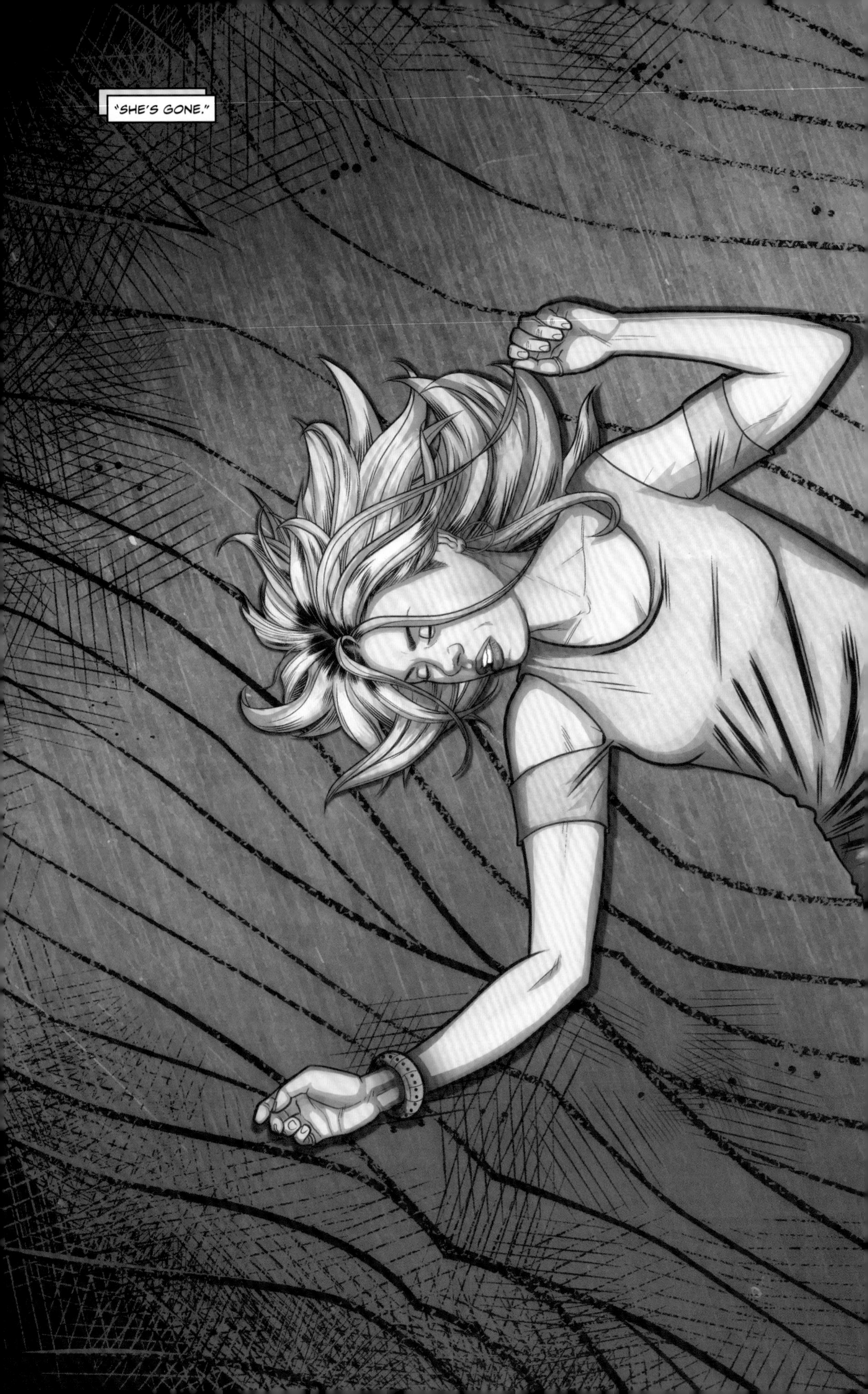
"SHE'S GONE."

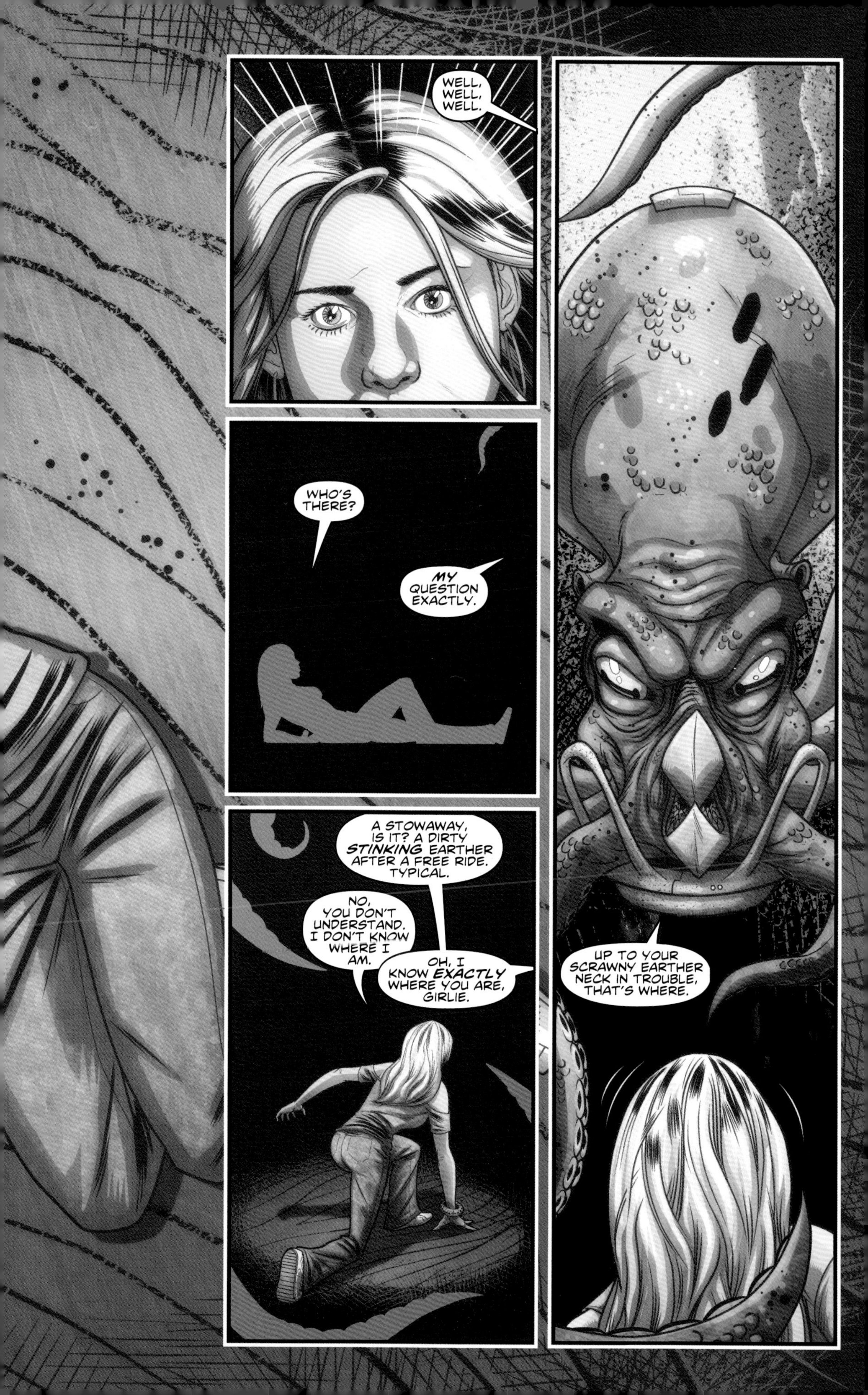
WELL, WELL, WELL.
WHO'S THERE?
MY QUESTION EXACTLY.
A STOWAWAY, IS IT? A DIRTY STINKING EARTHER AFTER A FREE RIDE. TYPICAL.
NO, YOU DON'T UNDERSTAND. I DON'T KNOW WHERE I AM.
OH, I KNOW EXACTLY WHERE YOU ARE, GIRLIE.
UP TO YOUR SCRAWNY EARTHER NECK IN TROUBLE, THAT'S WHERE.

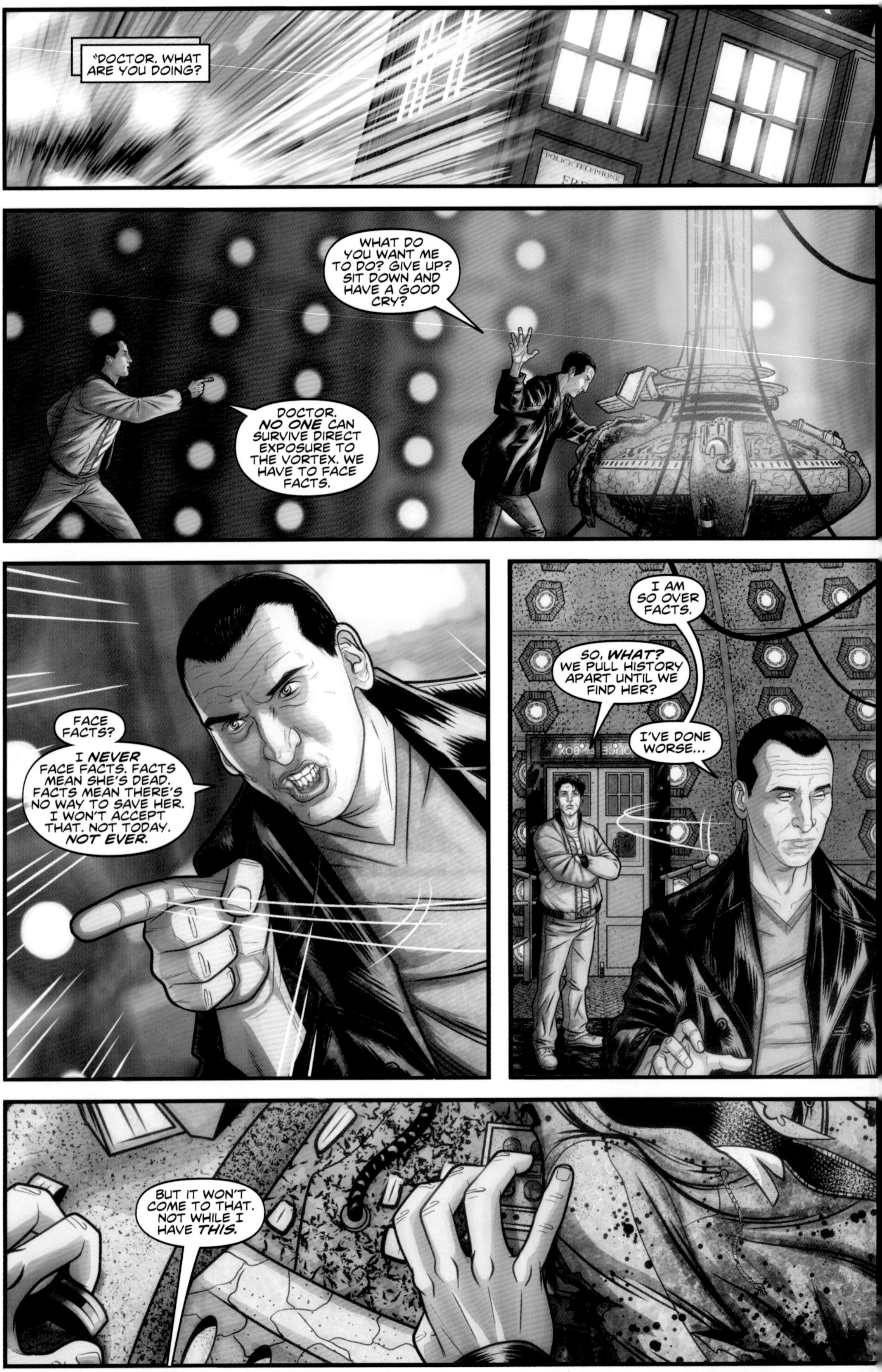
"DOCTOR. WHAT ARE YOU DOING?
POLICE TELEPHONE
WHAT DO YOU WANT ME TO DO? GIVE UP? SIT DOWN AND HAVE A GOOD CRY?
DOCTOR. NO ONE CAN SURVIVE DIRECT EXPOSURE TO THE VORTEX. WE HAVE TO FACE FACTS.
FACE FACTS?
I NEVER FACE FACTS. FACTS MEAN SHE'S DEAD. FACTS MEAN THERE'S NO WAY TO SAVE HER. I WON'T ACCEPT THAT. NOT TODAY. NOT EVER.
I AM SO OVER FACTS.
SO, WHAT? WE PULL HISTORY APART UNTIL WE FIND HER?
I'VE DONE WORSE...
BUT IT WON'T COME TO THAT. NOT WHILE I HAVE THIS.

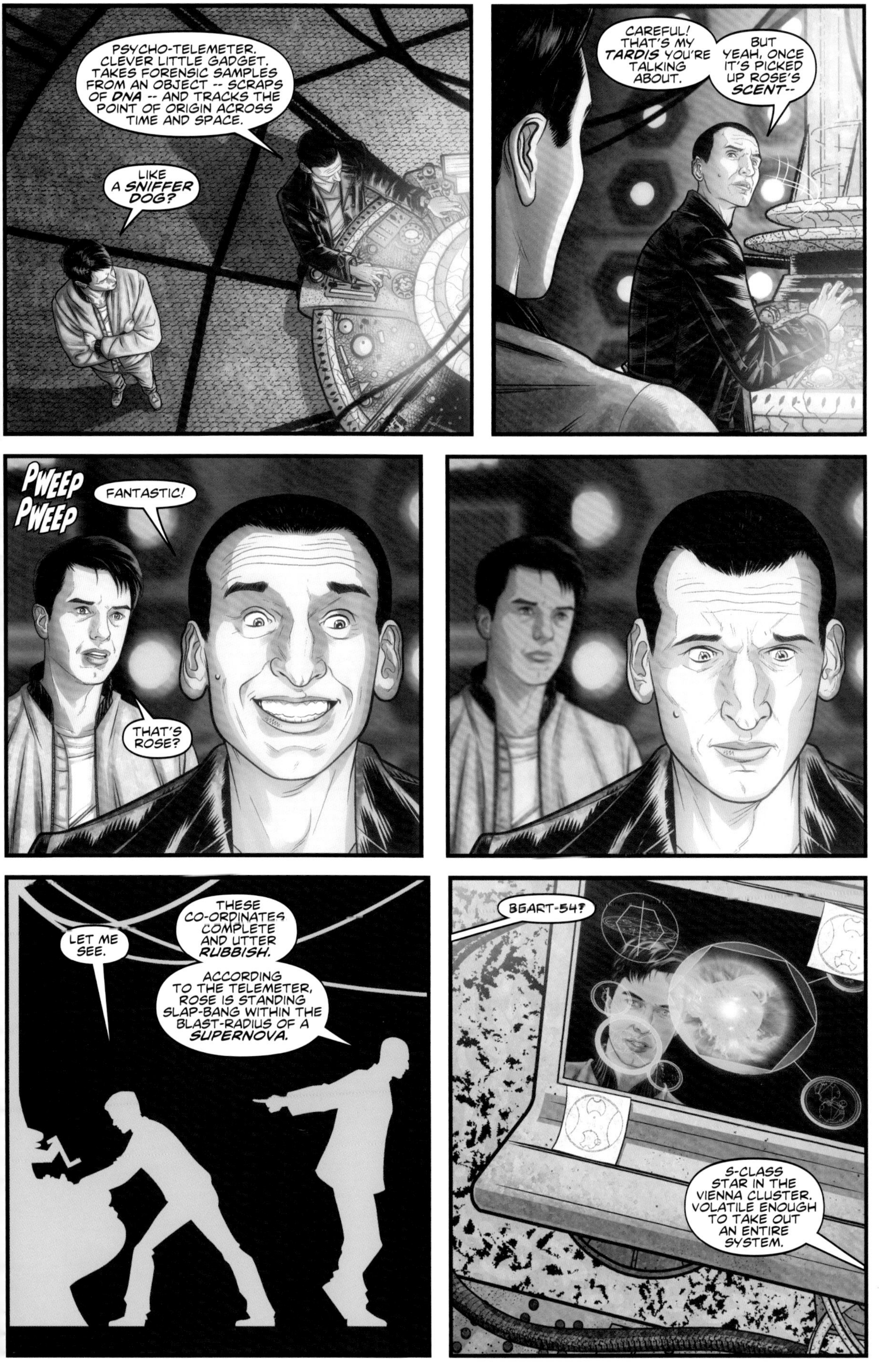
PSYCHO-TELEMETER. CLEVER LITTLE GADGET. TAKES FORENSIC SAMPLES FROM AN OBJECT -- SCRAPS OF DNA -- AND TRACKS THE POINT OF ORIGIN ACROSS TIME AND SPACE.
LIKE A SNIFFER DOG?
CAREFUL! THAT'S MY TARDIS YOU'RE TALKING ABOUT.
BUT YEAH, ONCE IT'S PICKED UP ROSE'S SCENT--
PWEEP PWEEP
FANTASTIC!
THAT'S ROSE?
LET ME SEE.
THESE CO-ORDINATES COMPLETE AND UTTER RUBBISH.
ACCORDING TO THE TELEMETER, ROSE IS STANDING SLAP-BANG WITHIN THE BLAST-RADIUS OF A SUPERNOVA.
BEART-54?
S-CLASS STAR IN THE VIENNA CLUSTER. VOLATILE ENOUGH TO TAKE OUT AN ENTIRE SYSTEM.

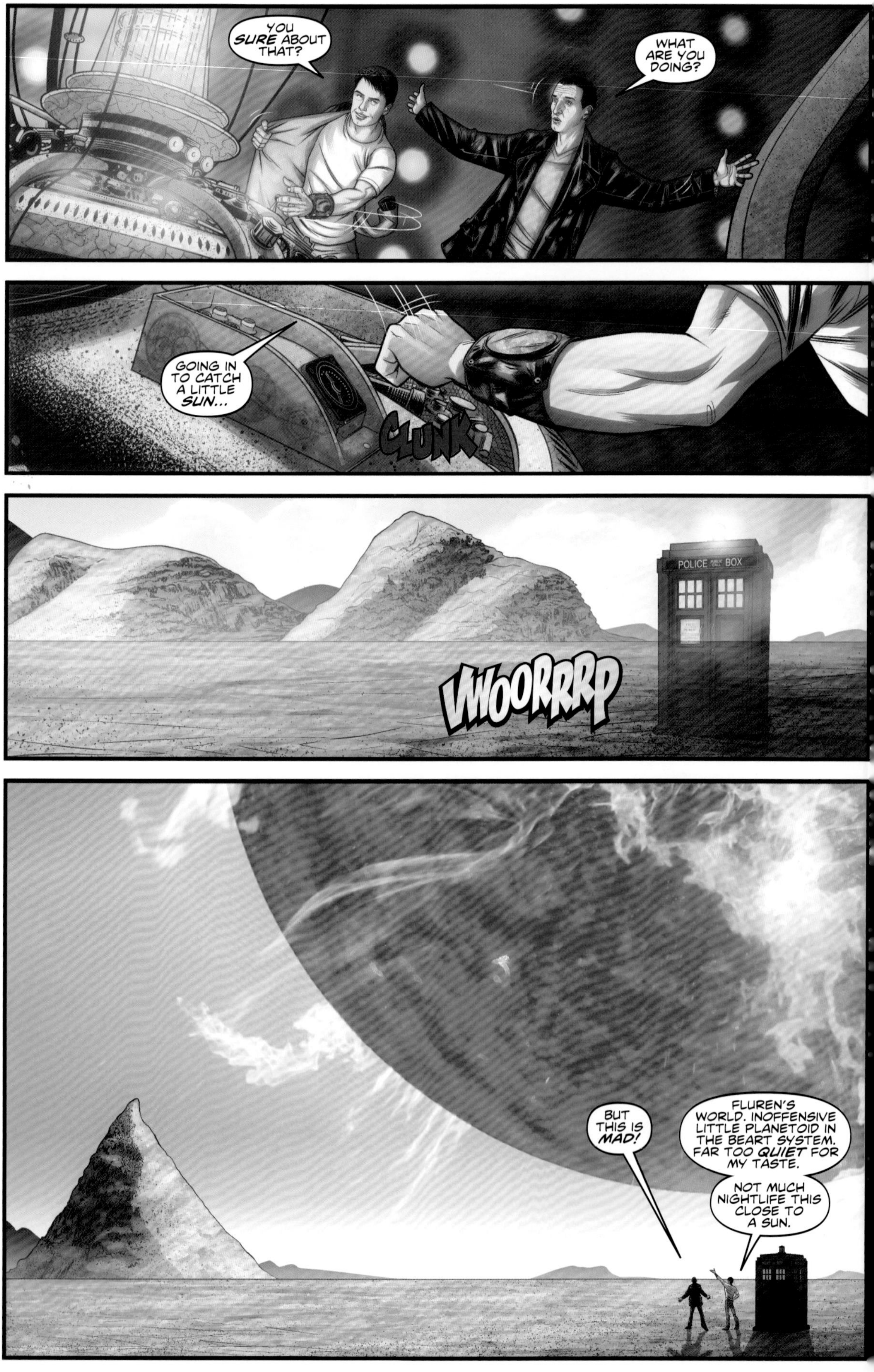
YOU SURE ABOUT THAT?
WHAT ARE YOU DOING?
GOING IN TO CATCH A LITTLE SUN...
CLUNK
POLICE PUBLIC CALL BOX
VWOORRRP
BUT THIS IS MAD!
FLUREN'S WORLD. INOFFENSIVE LITTLE PLANETOID IN THE BEART SYSTEM. FAR TOO QUIET FOR MY TASTE.
NOT MUCH NIGHTLIFE THIS CLOSE TO A SUN.

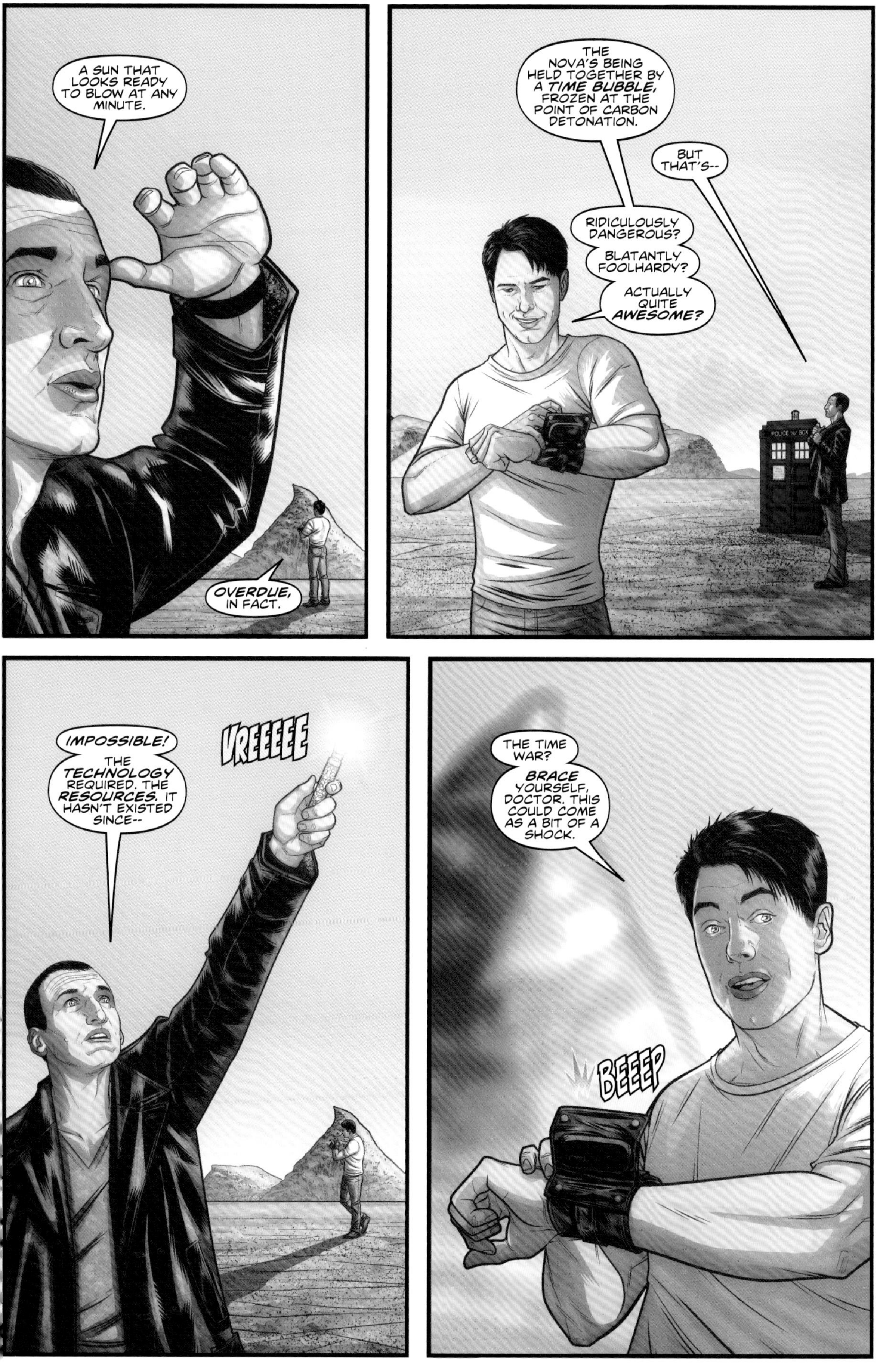
A SUN THAT LOOKS READY TO BLOW AT ANY MINUTE.
OVERDUE, IN FACT.
THE NOVA'S BEING HELD TOGETHER BY A TIME BUBBLE, FROZEN AT THE POINT OF CARBON DETONATION.
BUT THAT'S--
RIDICULOUSLY DANGEROUS?
BLATANTLY FOOLHARDY?
ACTUALLY QUITE AWESOME?
IMPOSSIBLE!
THE TECHNOLOGY REQUIRED. THE RESOURCES. IT HASN'T EXISTED SINCE--
VREEEEE
THE TIME WAR?
BRACE YOURSELF, DOCTOR. THIS COULD COME AS A BIT OF A SHOCK.
BEEEP

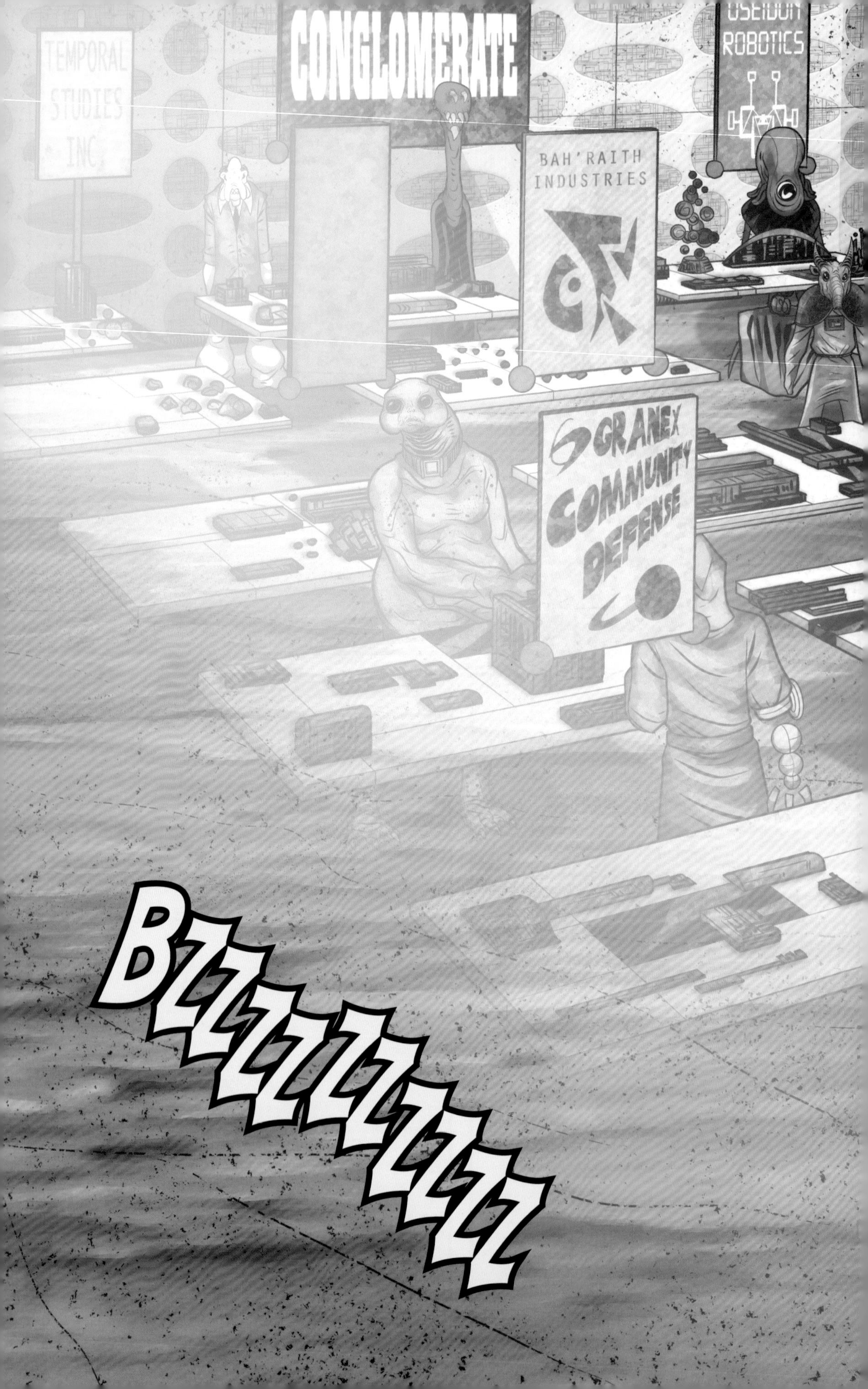
TEMPORAL STUDIES INC
CONGLOMERATE
ROBOTICS
BAH'RAITH INDUSTRIES
GRANEX COMMUNITY DEFENSE
BZZZZZZZZZZ

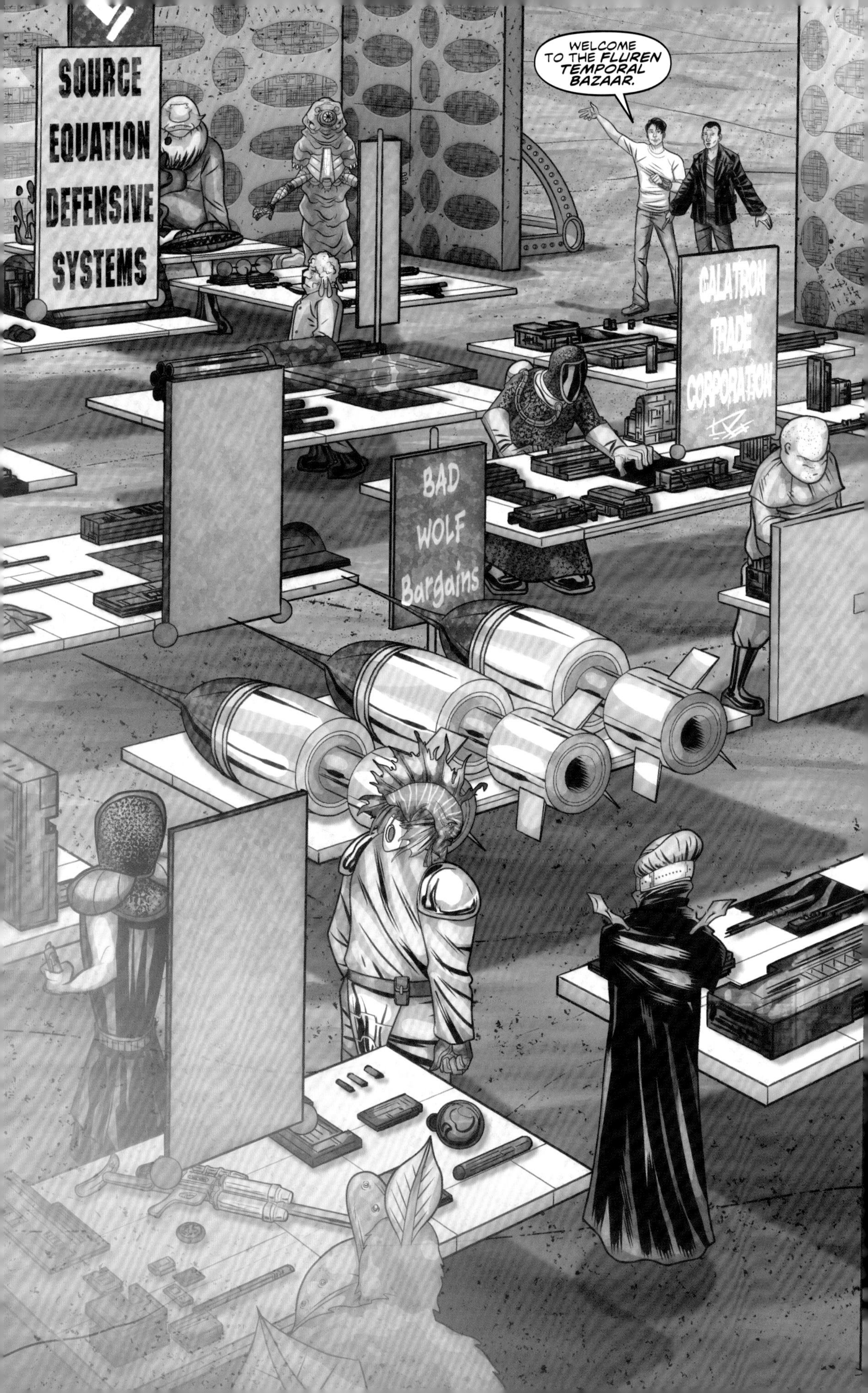
WELCOME TO THE *FLUREN TEMPORAL BAZAAR.*
SOURCE EQUATION DEFENSIVE SYSTEMS
GALATRON TRADE CORPORATION
BAD WOLF Bargains

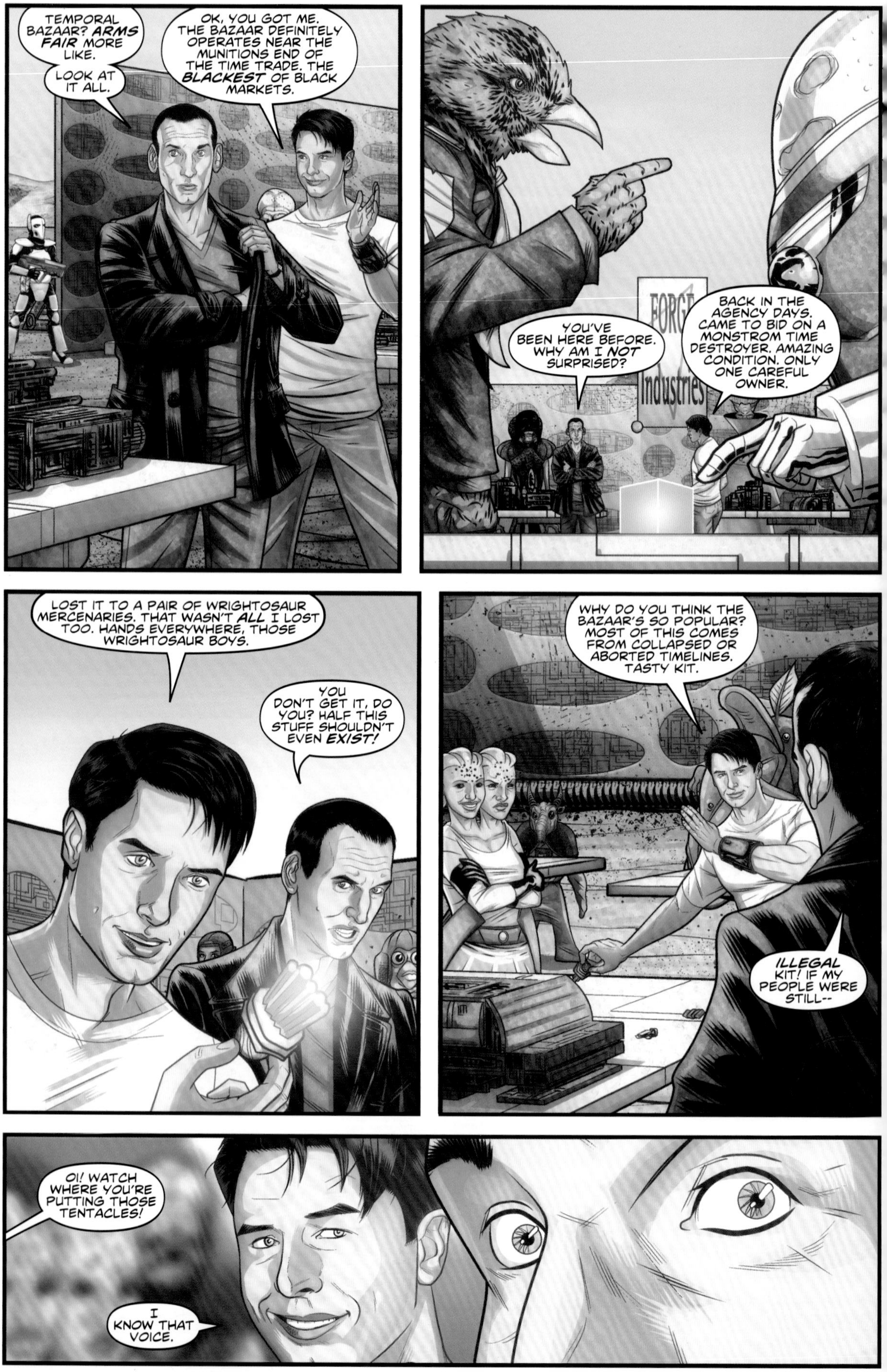
TEMPORAL BAZAAR? ARMS FAIR MORE LIKE.
LOOK AT IT ALL.
OK, YOU GOT ME. THE BAZAAR DEFINITELY OPERATES NEAR THE MUNITIONS END OF THE TIME TRADE. THE BLACKEST OF BLACK MARKETS.
YOU'VE BEEN HERE BEFORE. WHY AM I NOT SURPRISED?
BACK IN THE AGENCY DAYS. CAME TO BID ON A MONSTROM TIME DESTROYER. AMAZING CONDITION. ONLY ONE CAREFUL OWNER.
FORGE Industries
LOST IT TO A PAIR OF WRIGHTOSAUR MERCENARIES. THAT WASN'T ALL I LOST TOO. HANDS EVERYWHERE, THOSE WRIGHTOSAUR BOYS.
YOU DON'T GET IT, DO YOU? HALF THIS STUFF SHOULDN'T EVEN EXIST!
WHY DO YOU THINK THE BAZAAR'S SO POPULAR? MOST OF THIS COMES FROM COLLAPSED OR ABORTED TIMELINES. TASTY KIT.
ILLEGAL KIT! IF MY PEOPLE WERE STILL--
OI! WATCH WHERE YOU'RE PUTTING THOSE TENTACLES!
I KNOW THAT VOICE.

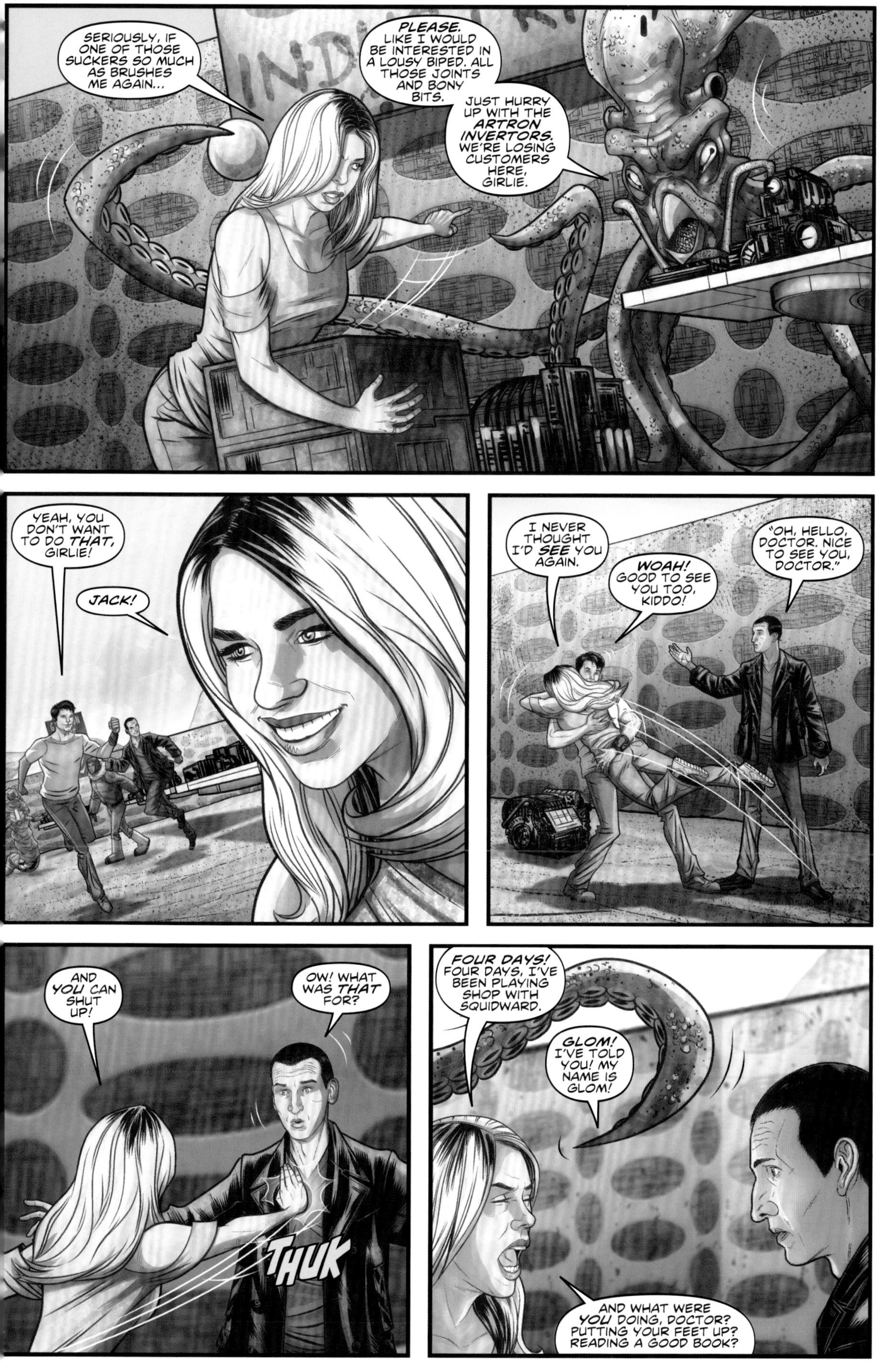
SERIOUSLY, IF ONE OF THOSE SUCKERS SO MUCH AS BRUSHES ME AGAIN...
PLEASE. LIKE I WOULD BE INTERESTED IN A LOUSY BIPED. ALL THOSE JOINTS AND BONY BITS.
JUST HURRY UP WITH THE ARTRON INVERTORS. WE'RE LOSING CUSTOMERS HERE, GIRLIE.
YEAH, YOU DON'T WANT TO DO THAT, GIRLIE!
JACK!
I NEVER THOUGHT I'D SEE YOU AGAIN.
WOAH! GOOD TO SEE YOU TOO, KIDDO!
"OH, HELLO, DOCTOR. NICE TO SEE YOU, DOCTOR."
AND YOU CAN SHUT UP!
OW! WHAT WAS THAT FOR?
THUK
FOUR DAYS! FOUR DAYS, I'VE BEEN PLAYING SHOP WITH SQUIDWARD.
GLOM! I'VE TOLD YOU! MY NAME IS GLOM!
AND WHAT WERE YOU DOING, DOCTOR? PUTTING YOUR FEET UP? READING A GOOD BOOK?

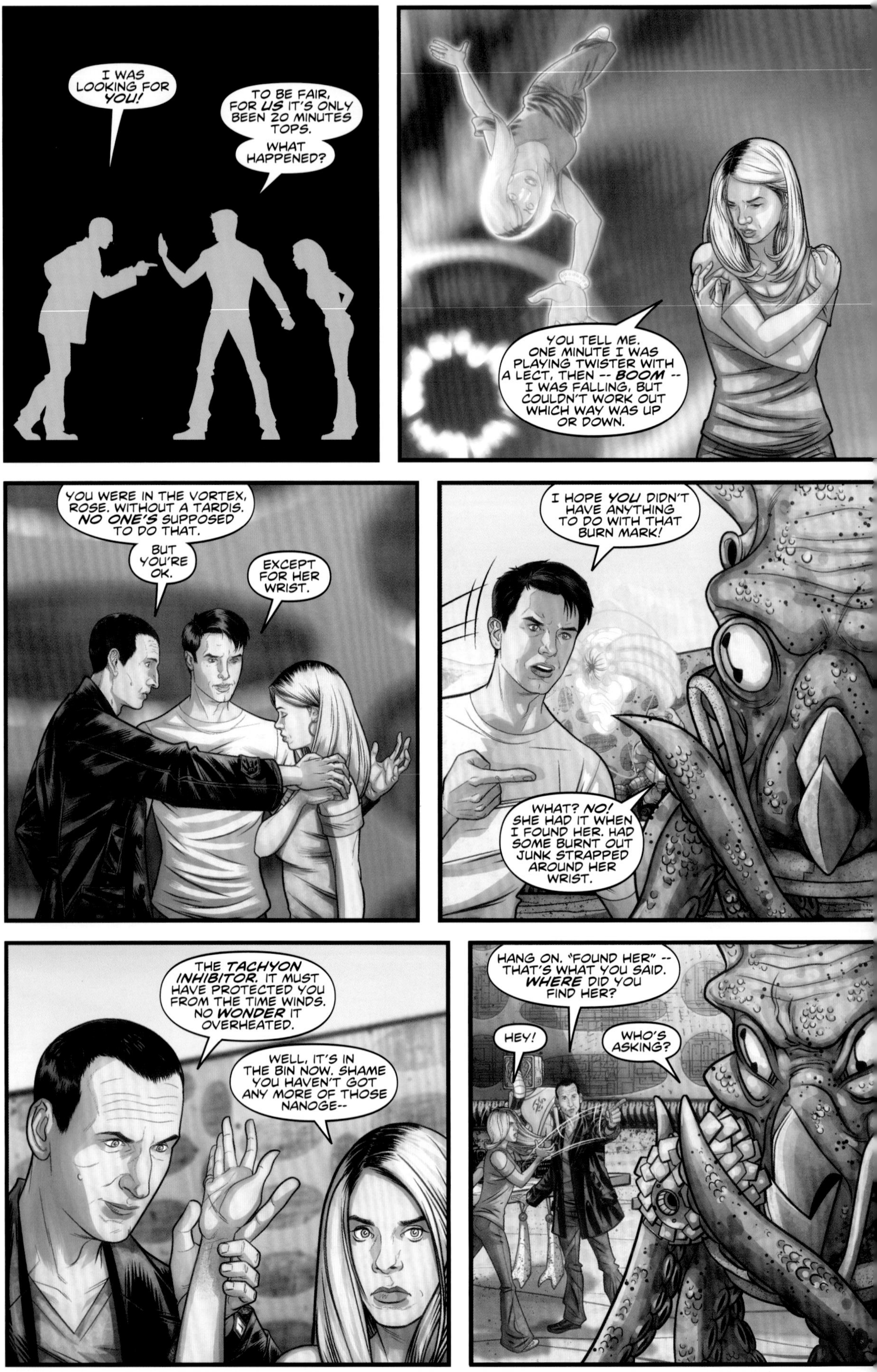
I WAS LOOKING FOR YOU!
TO BE FAIR, FOR US IT'S ONLY BEEN 20 MINUTES TOPS.
WHAT HAPPENED?
YOU TELL ME. ONE MINUTE I WAS PLAYING TWISTER WITH A LECT, THEN -- BOOM -- I WAS FALLING, BUT COULDN'T WORK OUT WHICH WAY WAS UP OR DOWN.
YOU WERE IN THE VORTEX, ROSE. WITHOUT A TARDIS. NO ONE'S SUPPOSED TO DO THAT.
BUT YOU'RE OK.
EXCEPT FOR HER WRIST.
I HOPE YOU DIDN'T HAVE ANYTHING TO DO WITH THAT BURN MARK!
WHAT? NO! SHE HAD IT WHEN I FOUND HER. HAD SOME BURNT OUT JUNK STRAPPED AROUND HER WRIST.
THE TACHYON INHIBITOR. IT MUST HAVE PROTECTED YOU FROM THE TIME WINDS. NO WONDER IT OVERHEATED.
WELL, IT'S IN THE BIN NOW. SHAME YOU HAVEN'T GOT ANY MORE OF THOSE NANOGE--
HANG ON. "FOUND HER" -- THAT'S WHAT YOU SAID. WHERE DID YOU FIND HER?
HEY!
WHO'S ASKING?

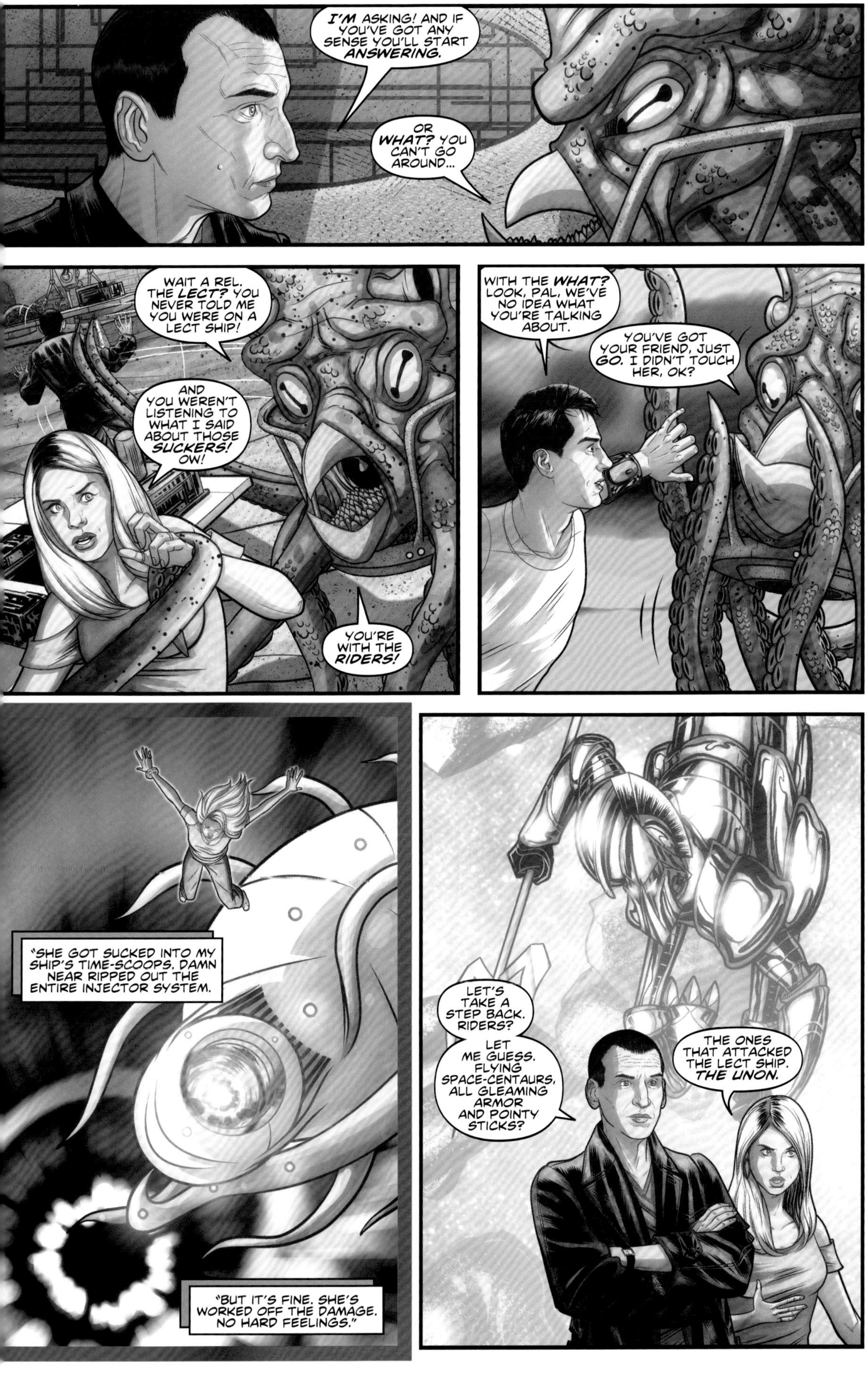
I'M ASKING! AND IF YOU'VE GOT ANY SENSE YOU'LL START ANSWERING.
OR WHAT? YOU CAN'T GO AROUND...
WAIT A REL. THE LECT? YOU NEVER TOLD ME YOU WERE ON A LECT SHIP!
AND YOU WEREN'T LISTENING TO WHAT I SAID ABOUT THOSE SUCKERS! OW!
YOU'RE WITH THE RIDERS!
WITH THE WHAT? LOOK, PAL, WE'VE NO IDEA WHAT YOU'RE TALKING ABOUT.
YOU'VE GOT YOUR FRIEND, JUST GO. I DIDN'T TOUCH HER, OK?
"SHE GOT SUCKED INTO MY SHIP'S TIME-SCOOPS. DAMN NEAR RIPPED OUT THE ENTIRE INJECTOR SYSTEM.
"BUT IT'S FINE. SHE'S WORKED OFF THE DAMAGE. NO HARD FEELINGS."
LET'S TAKE A STEP BACK. RIDERS?
LET ME GUESS. FLYING SPACE-CENTAURS, ALL GLEAMING ARMOR AND POINTY STICKS?
THE ONES THAT ATTACKED THE LECT SHIP. THE UNON.

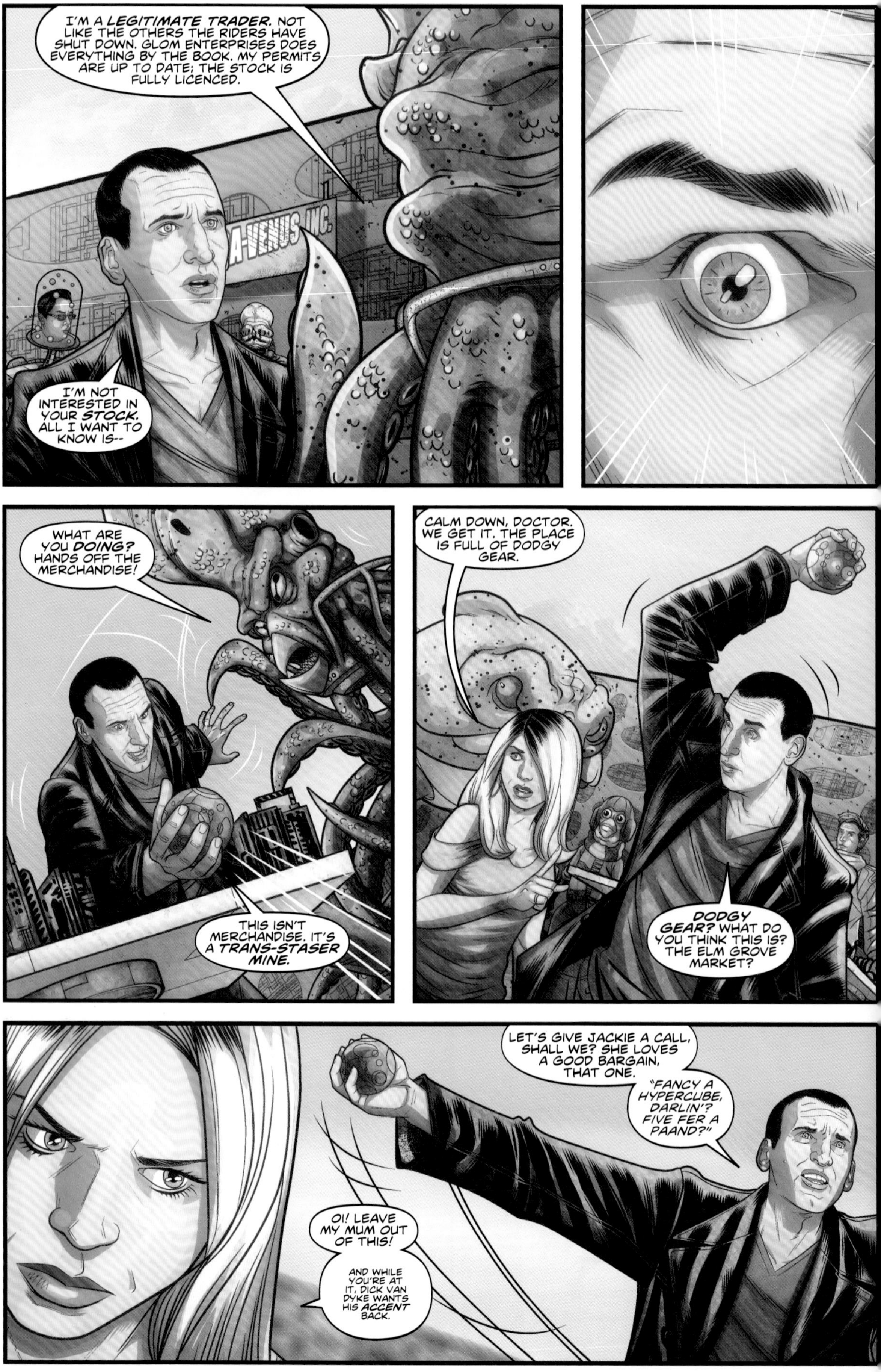
I'M A LEGITIMATE TRADER. NOT LIKE THE OTHERS THE RIDERS HAVE SHUT DOWN. GLOM ENTERPRISES DOES EVERYTHING BY THE BOOK. MY PERMITS ARE UP TO DATE; THE STOCK IS FULLY LICENCED.
A-VENUS INC.
I'M NOT INTERESTED IN YOUR STOCK. ALL I WANT TO KNOW IS--
WHAT ARE YOU DOING? HANDS OFF THE MERCHANDISE!
THIS ISN'T MERCHANDISE. IT'S A TRANS-STASER MINE.
CALM DOWN, DOCTOR. WE GET IT. THE PLACE IS FULL OF DODGY GEAR.
DODGY GEAR? WHAT DO YOU THINK THIS IS? THE ELM GROVE MARKET?
LET'S GIVE JACKIE A CALL, SHALL WE? SHE LOVES A GOOD BARGAIN, THAT ONE.
"FANCY A HYPERCUBE, DARLIN'? FIVE FER A PAAND?"
OI! LEAVE MY MUM OUT OF THIS!
AND WHILE YOU'RE AT IT, DICK VAN DYKE WANTS HIS ACCENT BACK.

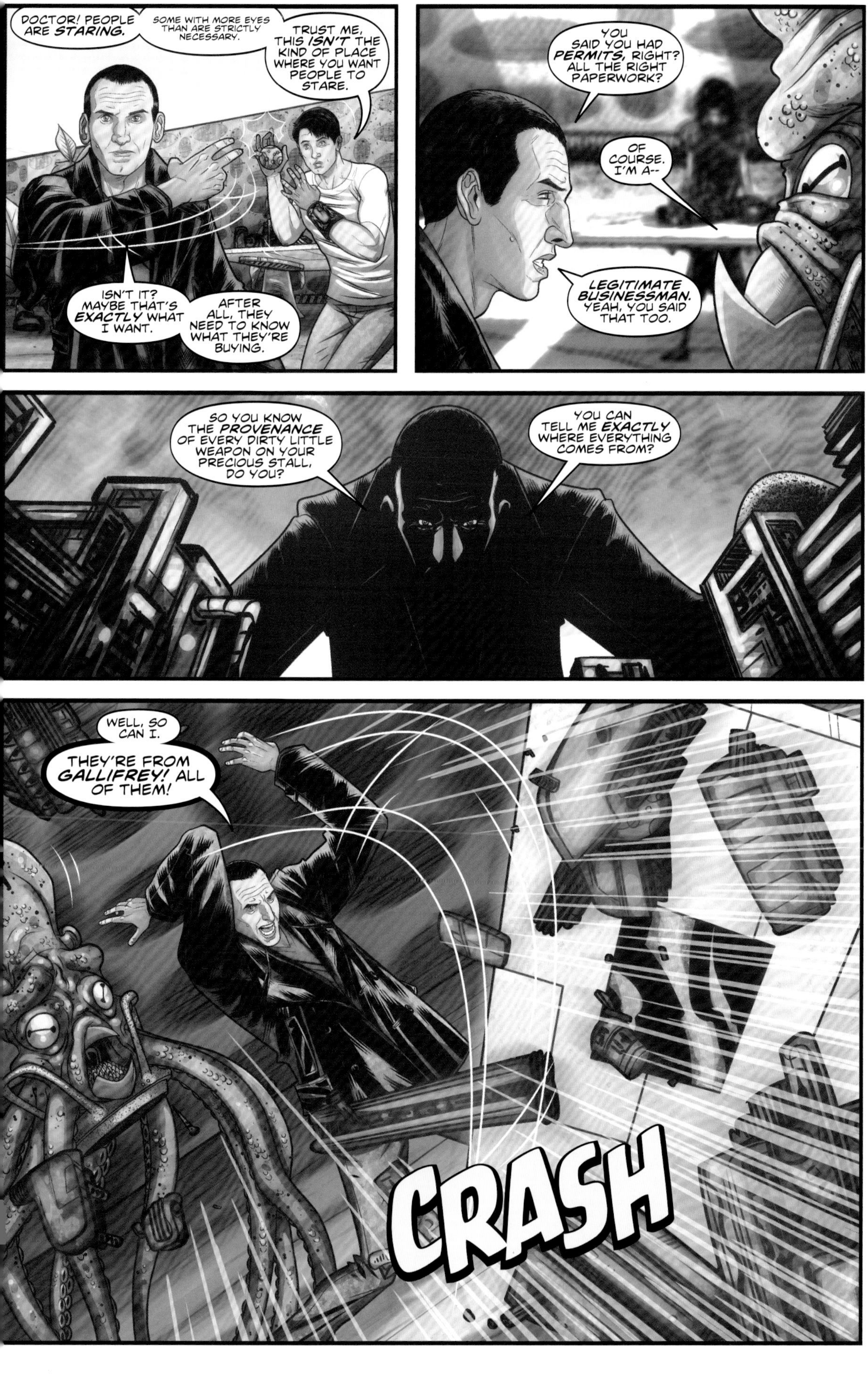
DOCTOR! PEOPLE ARE STARING.
SOME WITH MORE EYES THAN ARE STRICTLY NECESSARY.
TRUST ME, THIS ISN'T THE KIND OF PLACE WHERE YOU WANT PEOPLE TO STARE.
ISN'T IT? MAYBE THAT'S EXACTLY WHAT I WANT.
AFTER ALL, THEY NEED TO KNOW WHAT THEY'RE BUYING.
YOU SAID YOU HAD PERMITS, RIGHT? ALL THE RIGHT PAPERWORK?
OF COURSE. I'M A--
LEGITIMATE BUSINESSMAN. YEAH, YOU SAID THAT TOO.
SO YOU KNOW THE PROVENANCE OF EVERY DIRTY LITTLE WEAPON ON YOUR PRECIOUS STALL, DO YOU?
YOU CAN TELL ME EXACTLY WHERE EVERYTHING COMES FROM?
WELL, SO CAN I.
THEY'RE FROM GALLIFREY! ALL OF THEM!
CRASH

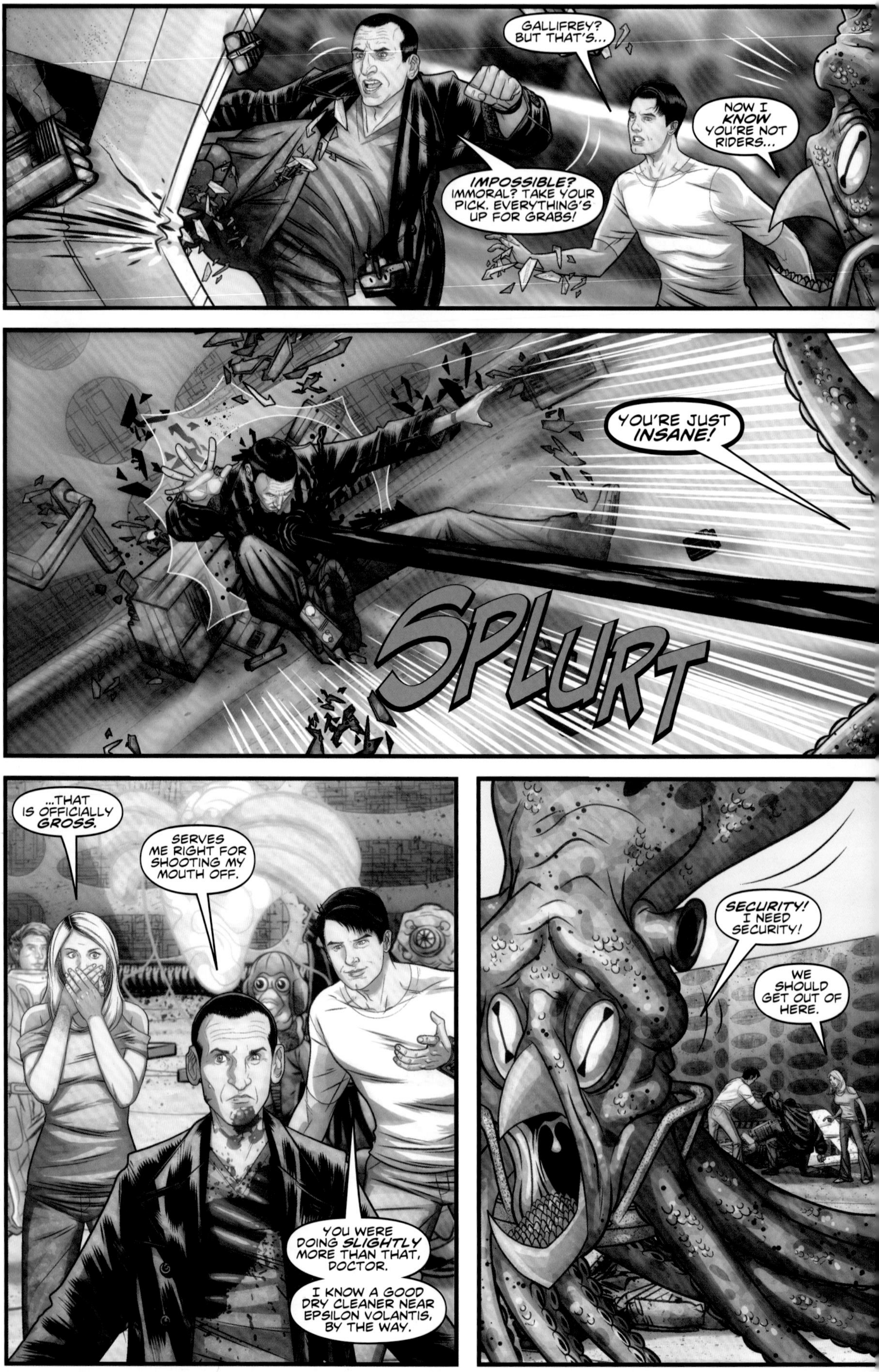
GALLIFREY? BUT THAT'S...
IMPOSSIBLE? IMMORAL? TAKE YOUR PICK. EVERYTHING'S UP FOR GRABS!
NOW I KNOW YOU'RE NOT RIDERS...
YOU'RE JUST INSANE!
SPLURT
...THAT IS OFFICIALLY GROSS.
SERVES ME RIGHT FOR SHOOTING MY MOUTH OFF.
YOU WERE DOING SLIGHTLY MORE THAN THAT, DOCTOR.
I KNOW A GOOD DRY CLEANER NEAR EPSILON VOLANTIS, BY THE WAY.
SECURITY! I NEED SECURITY!
WE SHOULD GET OUT OF HERE.

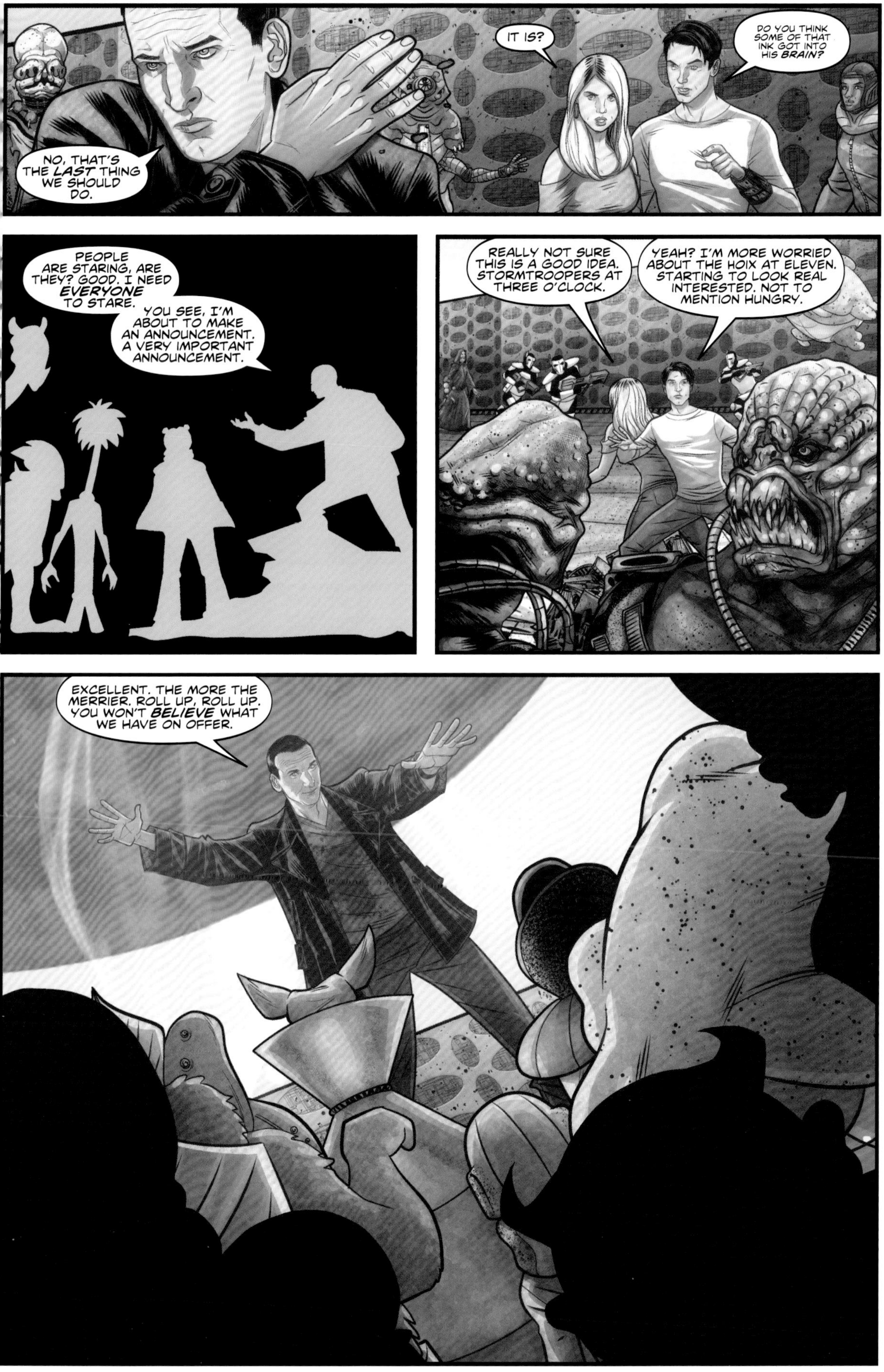
NO, THAT'S THE *LAST* THING WE SHOULD DO.
IT IS?
DO YOU THINK SOME OF THAT INK GOT INTO HIS *BRAIN?*
PEOPLE ARE STARING, ARE THEY? GOOD. I NEED *EVERYONE* TO STARE.
YOU SEE, I'M ABOUT TO MAKE AN ANNOUNCEMENT. A VERY IMPORTANT ANNOUNCEMENT.
REALLY NOT SURE THIS IS A GOOD IDEA. STORMTROOPERS AT THREE O'CLOCK.
YEAH? I'M MORE WORRIED ABOUT THE HOIX AT ELEVEN. STARTING TO LOOK REAL INTERESTED. NOT TO MENTION HUNGRY.
EXCELLENT. THE MORE THE MERRIER. ROLL UP, ROLL UP. YOU WON'T *BELIEVE* WHAT WE HAVE ON OFFER.

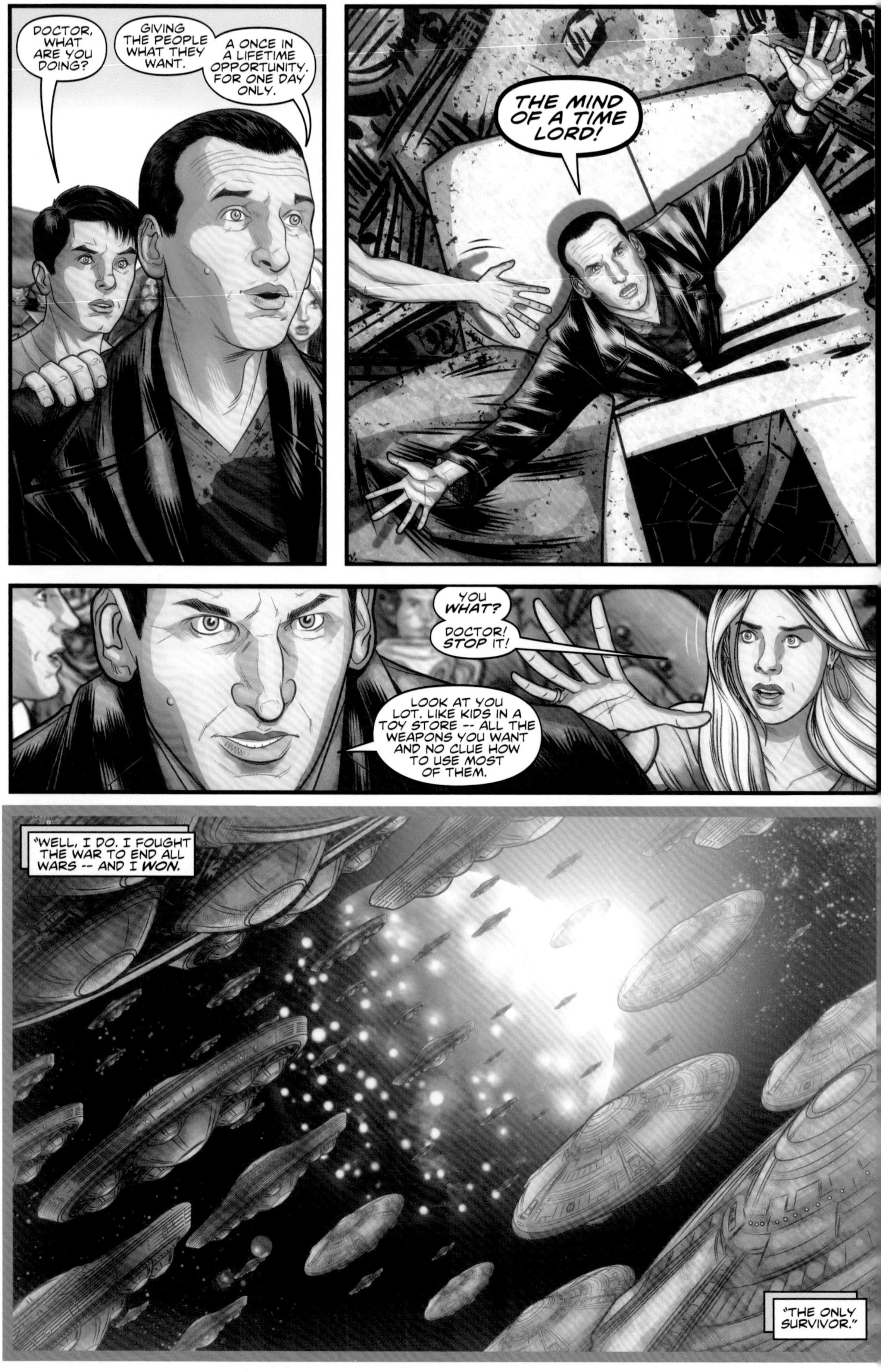
DOCTOR, WHAT ARE YOU DOING?
GIVING THE PEOPLE WHAT THEY WANT.
A ONCE IN A LIFETIME OPPORTUNITY. FOR ONE DAY ONLY.
THE MIND OF A TIME LORD!
YOU WHAT?
DOCTOR! STOP IT!
LOOK AT YOU LOT. LIKE KIDS IN A TOY STORE -- ALL THE WEAPONS YOU WANT AND NO CLUE HOW TO USE MOST OF THEM.
"WELL, I DO. I FOUGHT THE WAR TO END ALL WARS -- AND I WON.
"THE ONLY SURVIVOR."

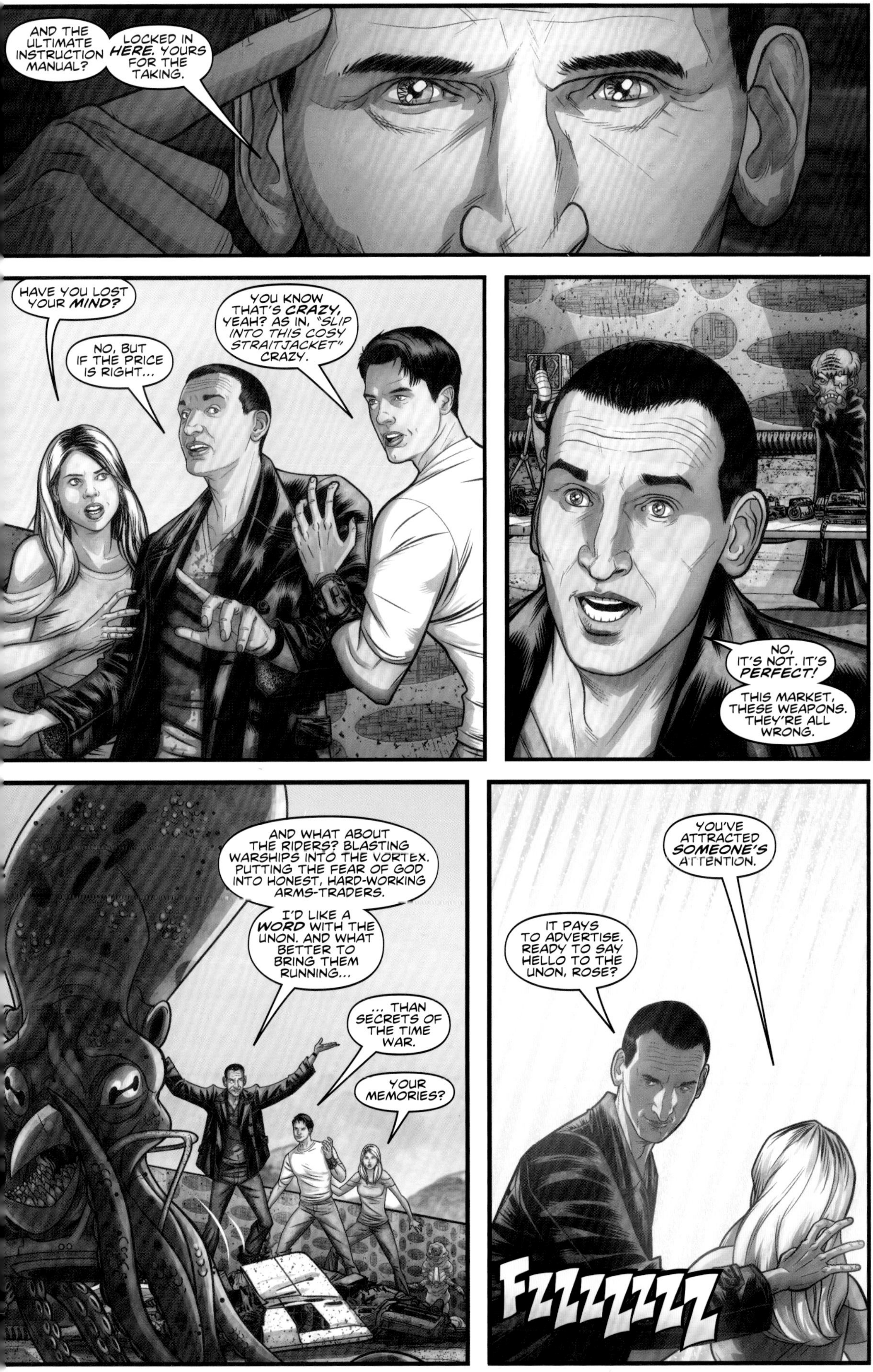
AND THE ULTIMATE INSTRUCTION MANUAL?
LOCKED IN HERE. YOURS FOR THE TAKING.
HAVE YOU LOST YOUR MIND?
NO, BUT IF THE PRICE IS RIGHT...
YOU KNOW THAT'S CRAZY, YEAH? AS IN, "SLIP INTO THIS COSY STRAITJACKET" CRAZY.
NO, IT'S NOT. IT'S PERFECT!
THIS MARKET, THESE WEAPONS. THEY'RE ALL WRONG.
AND WHAT ABOUT THE RIDERS? BLASTING WARSHIPS INTO THE VORTEX. PUTTING THE FEAR OF GOD INTO HONEST, HARD-WORKING ARMS-TRADERS.
I'D LIKE A WORD WITH THE UNION. AND WHAT BETTER TO BRING THEM RUNNING...
... THAN SECRETS OF THE TIME WAR.
YOUR MEMORIES?
YOU'VE ATTRACTED SOMEONE'S ATTENTION.
IT PAYS TO ADVERTISE. READY TO SAY HELLO TO THE UNION, ROSE?
FZZZZZZZ

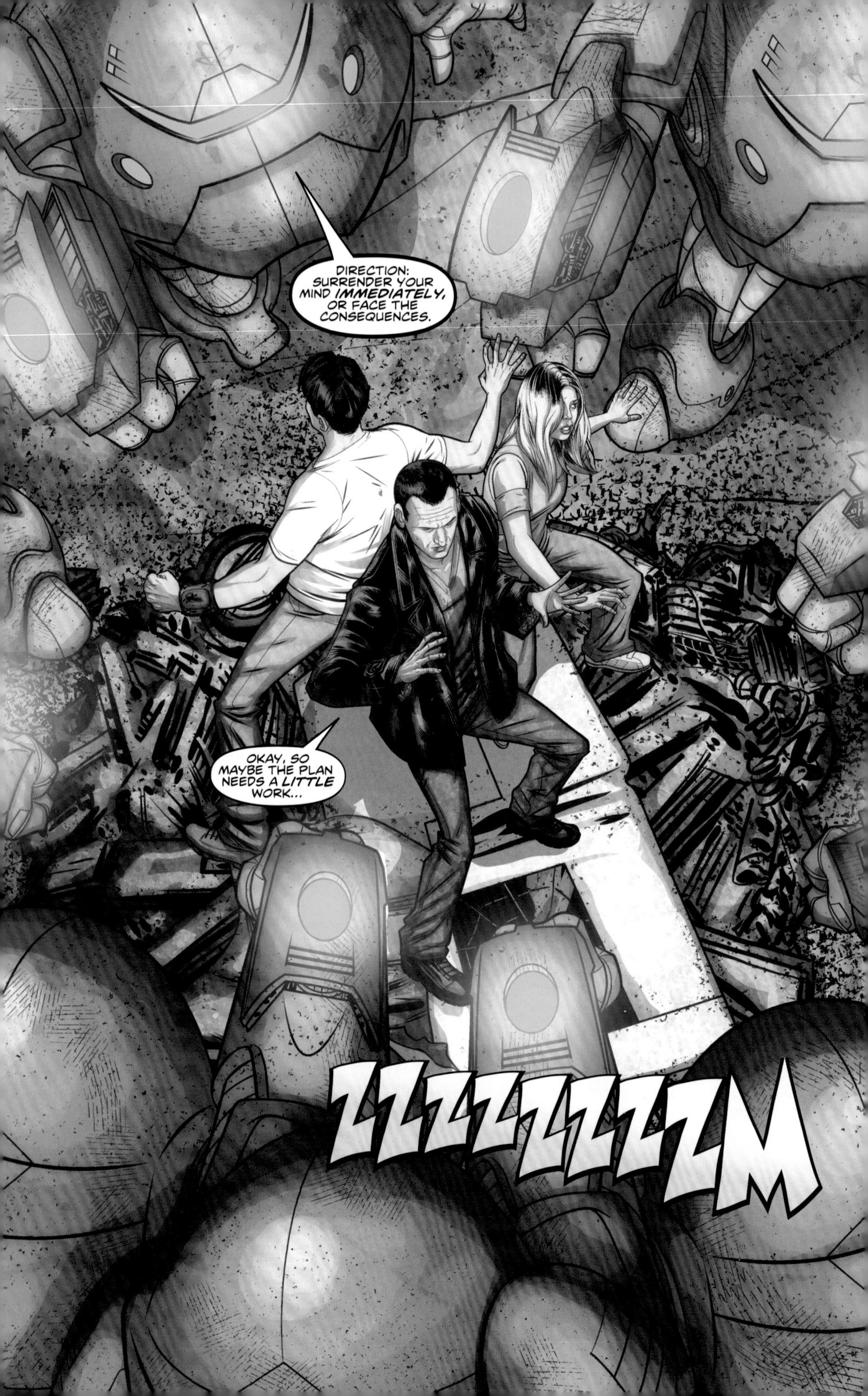
DIRECTION: SURRENDER YOUR MIND *IMMEDIATELY*, OR FACE THE CONSEQUENCES.
OKAY, SO MAYBE THE PLAN NEEDS A *LITTLE* WORK...
ZZZZZZZZZM

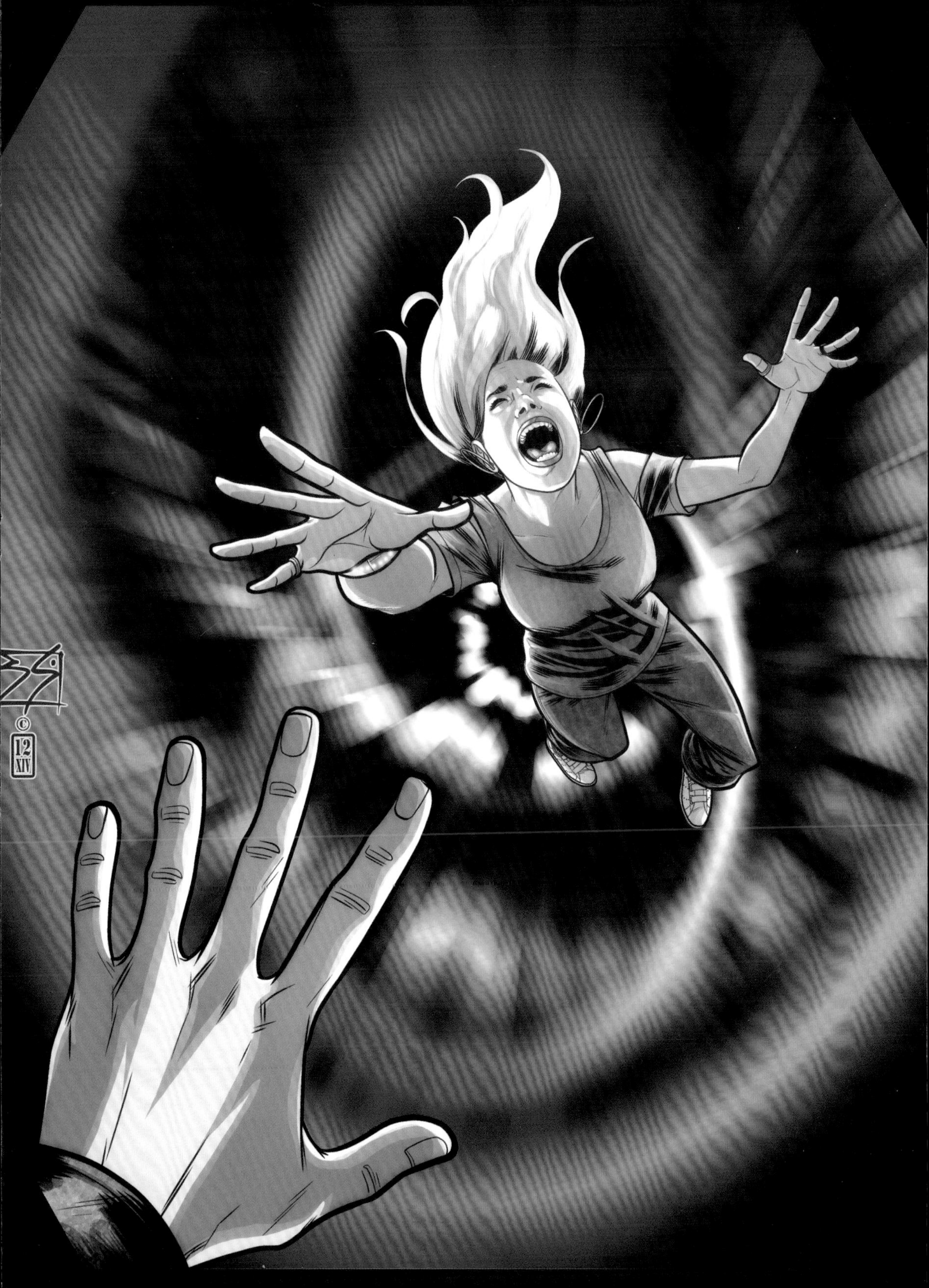

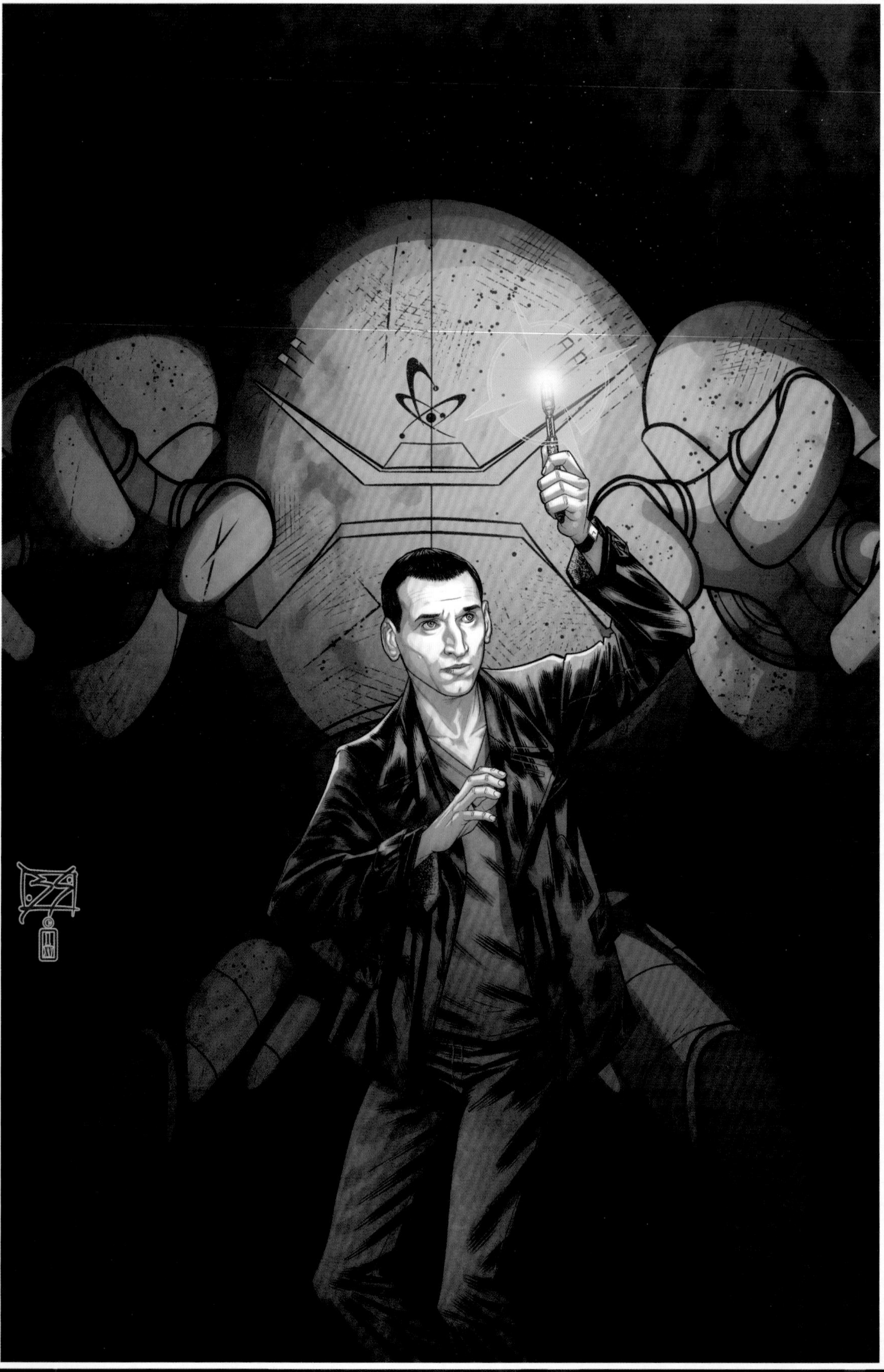

9D #3 Cover A: BLAIR SHEDD

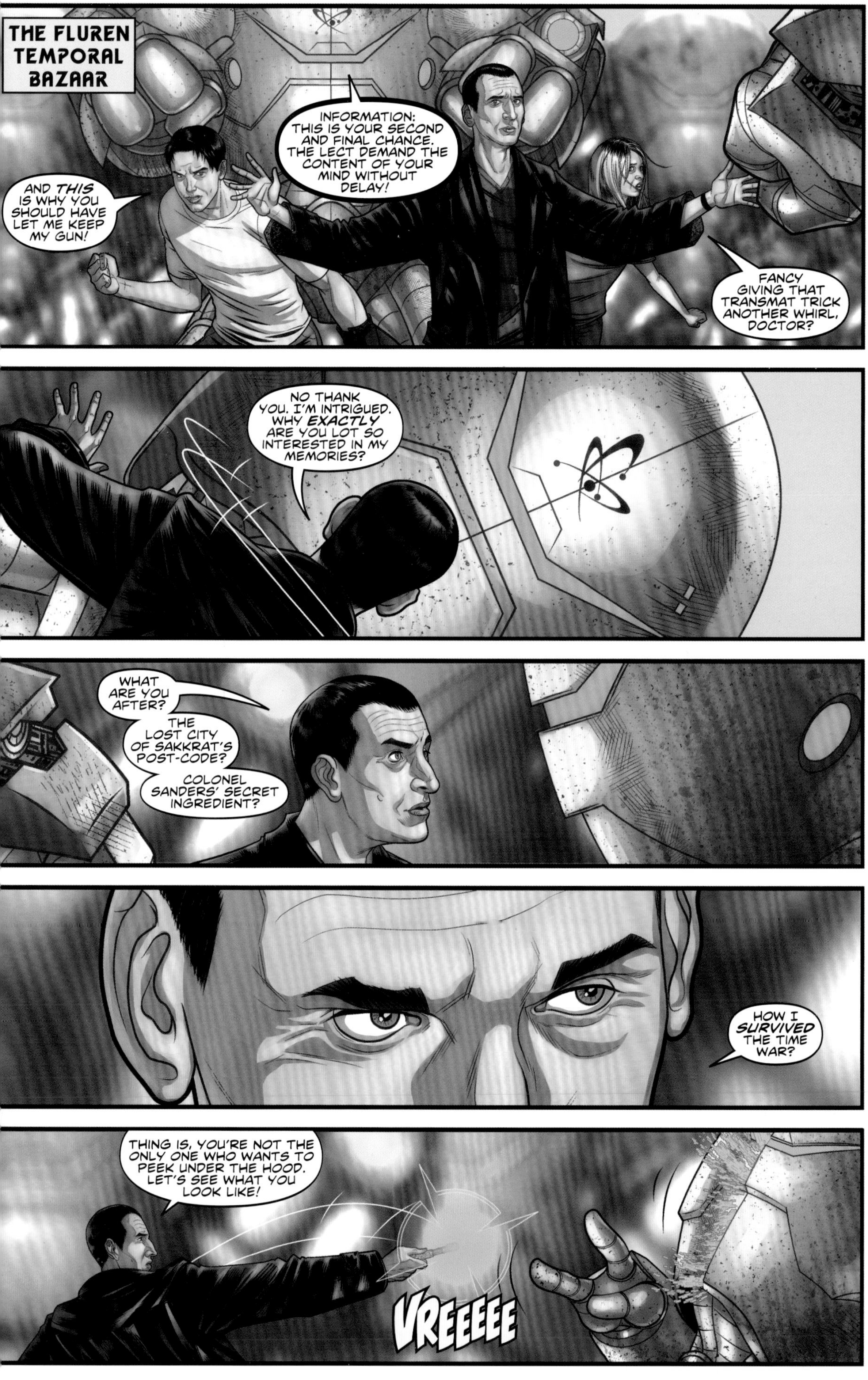
THE FLUREN TEMPORAL BAZAAR
INFORMATION: THIS IS YOUR SECOND AND FINAL CHANCE. THE LECT DEMAND THE CONTENT OF YOUR MIND WITHOUT DELAY!
AND THIS IS WHY YOU SHOULD HAVE LET ME KEEP MY GUN!
FANCY GIVING THAT TRANSMAT TRICK ANOTHER WHIRL, DOCTOR?
NO THANK YOU. I'M INTRIGUED. WHY EXACTLY ARE YOU LOT SO INTERESTED IN MY MEMORIES?
WHAT ARE YOU AFTER?
THE LOST CITY OF SAKKRAT'S POST-CODE?
COLONEL SANDERS' SECRET INGREDIENT?
HOW I SURVIVED THE TIME WAR?
THING IS, YOU'RE NOT THE ONLY ONE WHO WANTS TO PEEK UNDER THE HOOD. LET'S SEE WHAT YOU LOOK LIKE!
VREEEEE

DIRECTIVE: DESIST. YOU WILL COME WITH US OR DIE!
YEAH? AND HOW WILL YOU GET YOUR PRECIOUS MEMORIES IF I'M DEAD?
GET OFF HIM!
ROSE! DON'T...
BOK
NO, WAIT!
CHK

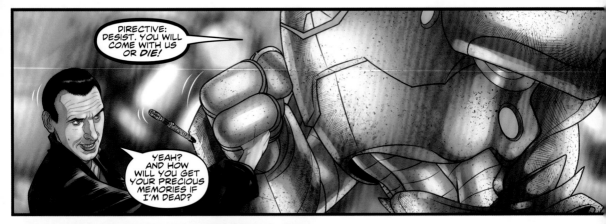

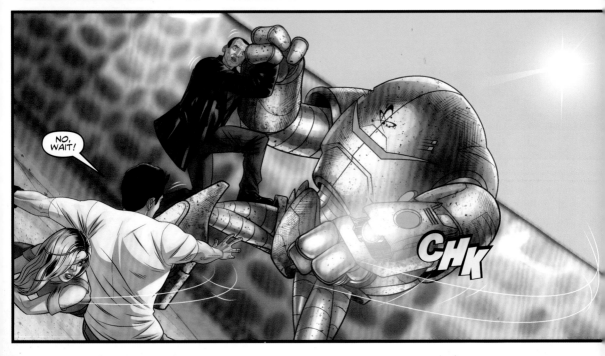

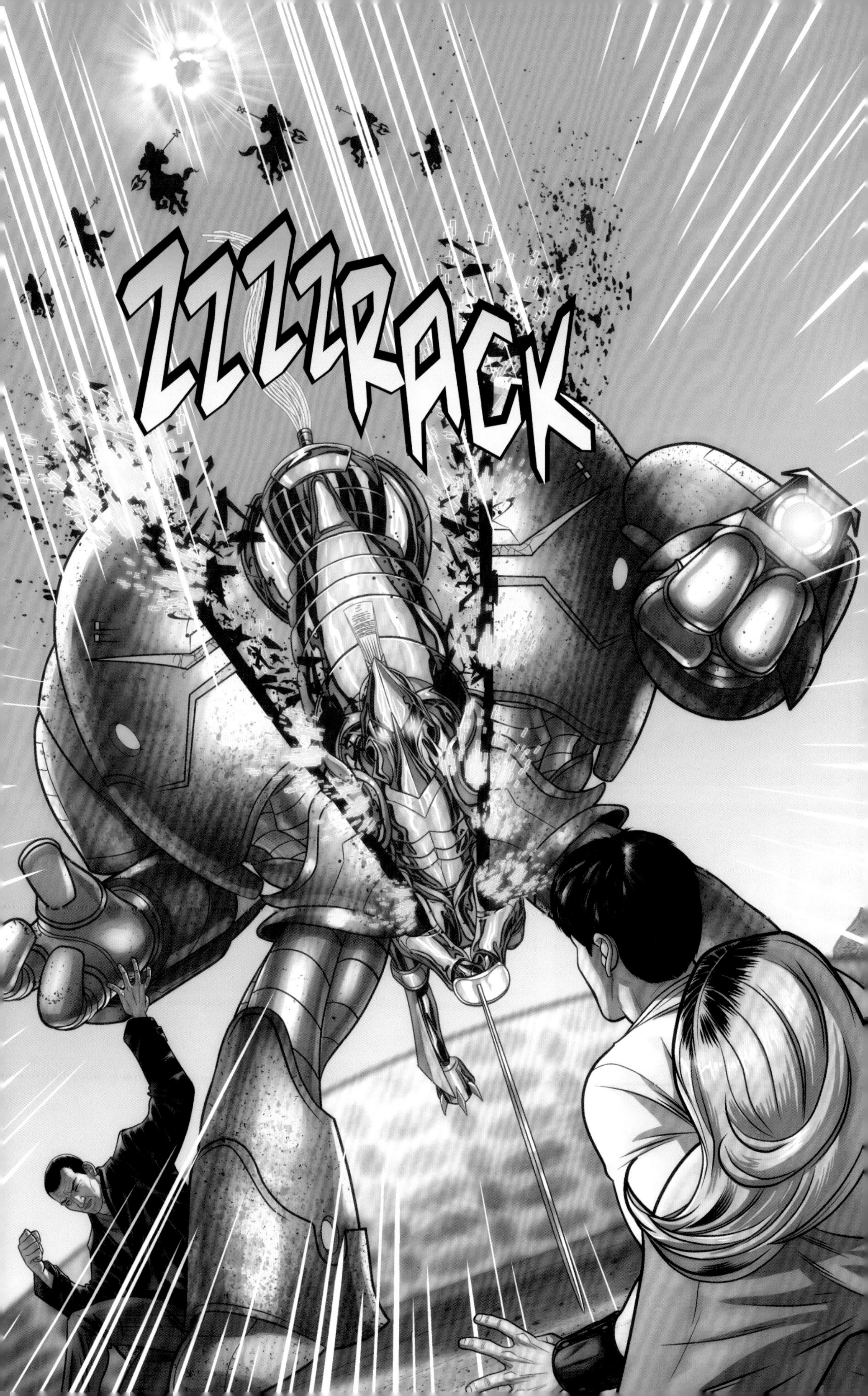
ZZZZRACK

LOOKS LIKE YOU GOT YOUR WISH. GOOD OLD UNON, EH?

BETTER LATE THAN NEVER. THEY *REALLY* DON'T LIKE THE LECT, DO THEY?

IT SEEMS THE FEELING'S MUTUAL. GET EVERYONE CLEAR!

THE FRIENDLY-NEIGHBOURHOOD *ARMS* DEALERS, YOU MEAN?

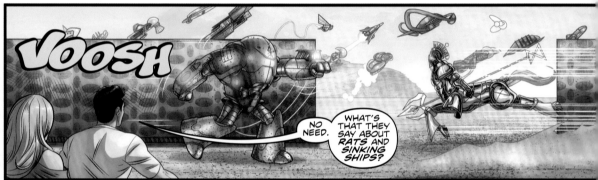

VOOSH

NO NEED. WHAT'S THAT THEY SAY ABOUT *RATS* AND SINKING SHIPS?

VOOM

WEAPONS NOT SO CLEVER NOW *THE RATS* ARE THE ONES UNDER ATTACK!

IF YOU'VE *ANY* SENSE IN THAT BONY SKULL OF YOURS, YOU'LL FOLLOW THEIR EXAMPLE. GET OUT OF HERE BEFORE THE *EMERGENCY PROTOCOL* IS TRIGGERED.

HEY, *WATCH IT*, INKY! DON'T BARGE WHAT YOU CAN'T AFFORD!

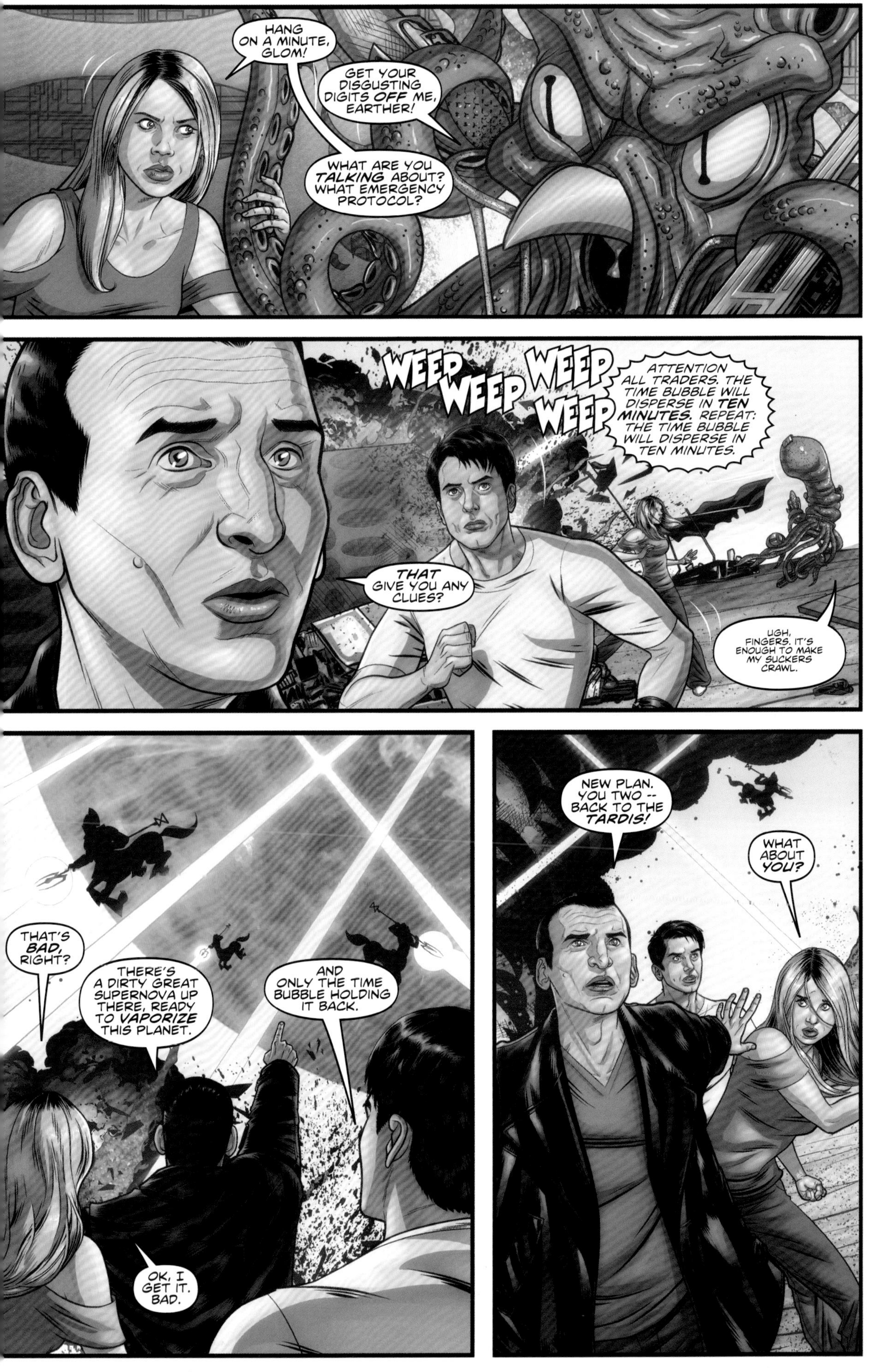

HANG ON A MINUTE, GLOM!
GET YOUR DISGUSTING DIGITS OFF ME, EARTHER!
WHAT ARE YOU TALKING ABOUT? WHAT EMERGENCY PROTOCOL?
WEEP WEEP WEEP WEEP
ATTENTION ALL TRADERS. THE TIME BUBBLE WILL DISPERSE IN TEN MINUTES. REPEAT: THE TIME BUBBLE WILL DISPERSE IN TEN MINUTES.
THAT GIVE YOU ANY CLUES?
UGH, FINGERS. IT'S ENOUGH TO MAKE MY SUCKERS CRAWL.
THAT'S BAD, RIGHT?
THERE'S A DIRTY GREAT SUPERNOVA UP THERE, READY TO VAPORIZE THIS PLANET.
AND ONLY THE TIME BUBBLE HOLDING IT BACK.
OK, I GET IT. BAD.
NEW PLAN. YOU TWO -- BACK TO THE TARDIS!
WHAT ABOUT YOU?

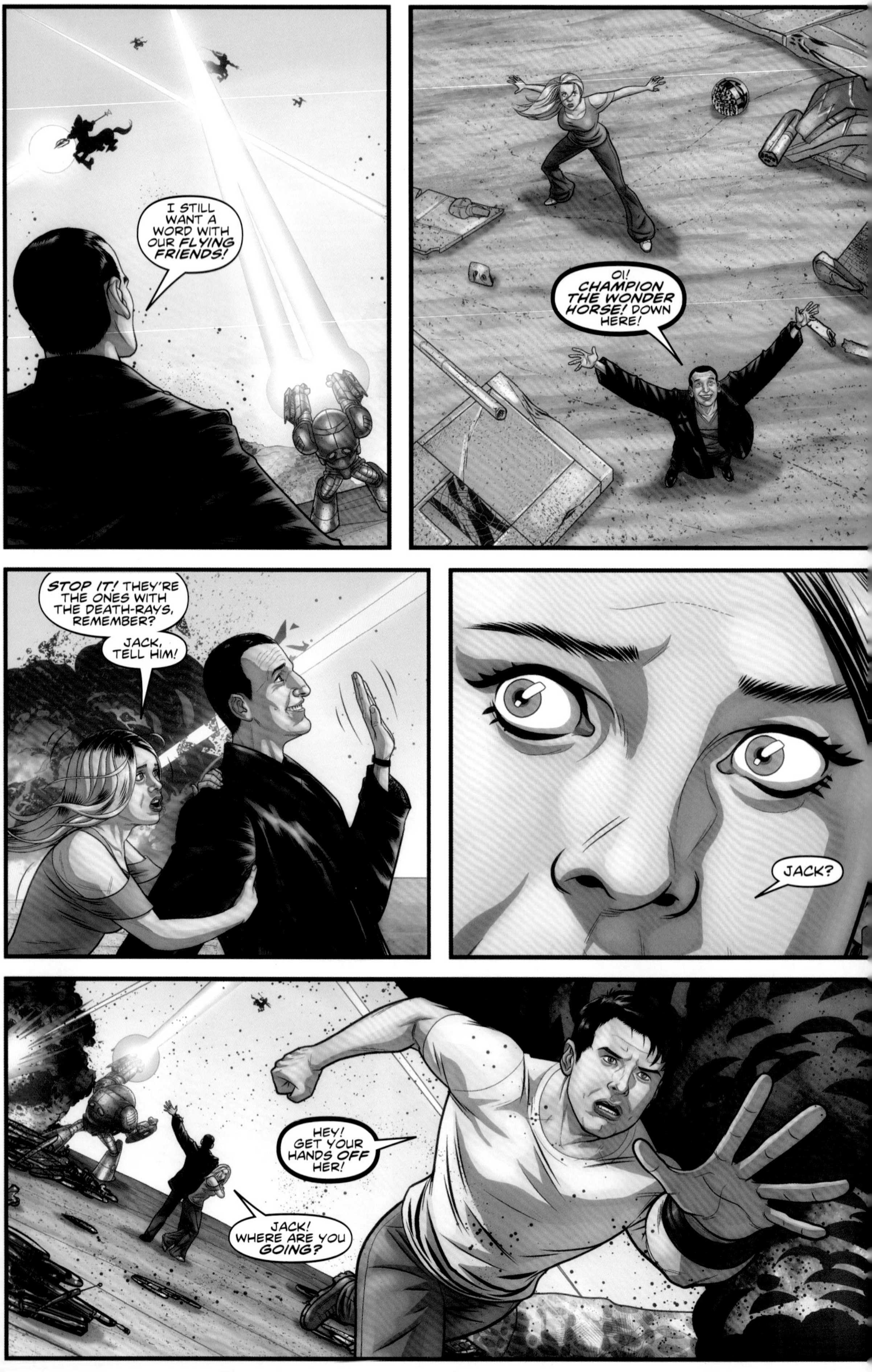
I STILL WANT A WORD WITH OUR FLYING FRIENDS!
OI! CHAMPION THE WONDER HORSE! DOWN HERE!
STOP IT! THEY'RE THE ONES WITH THE DEATH-RAYS, REMEMBER?
JACK, TELL HIM!
JACK?
HEY! GET YOUR HANDS OFF HER!
JACK! WHERE ARE YOU GOING?

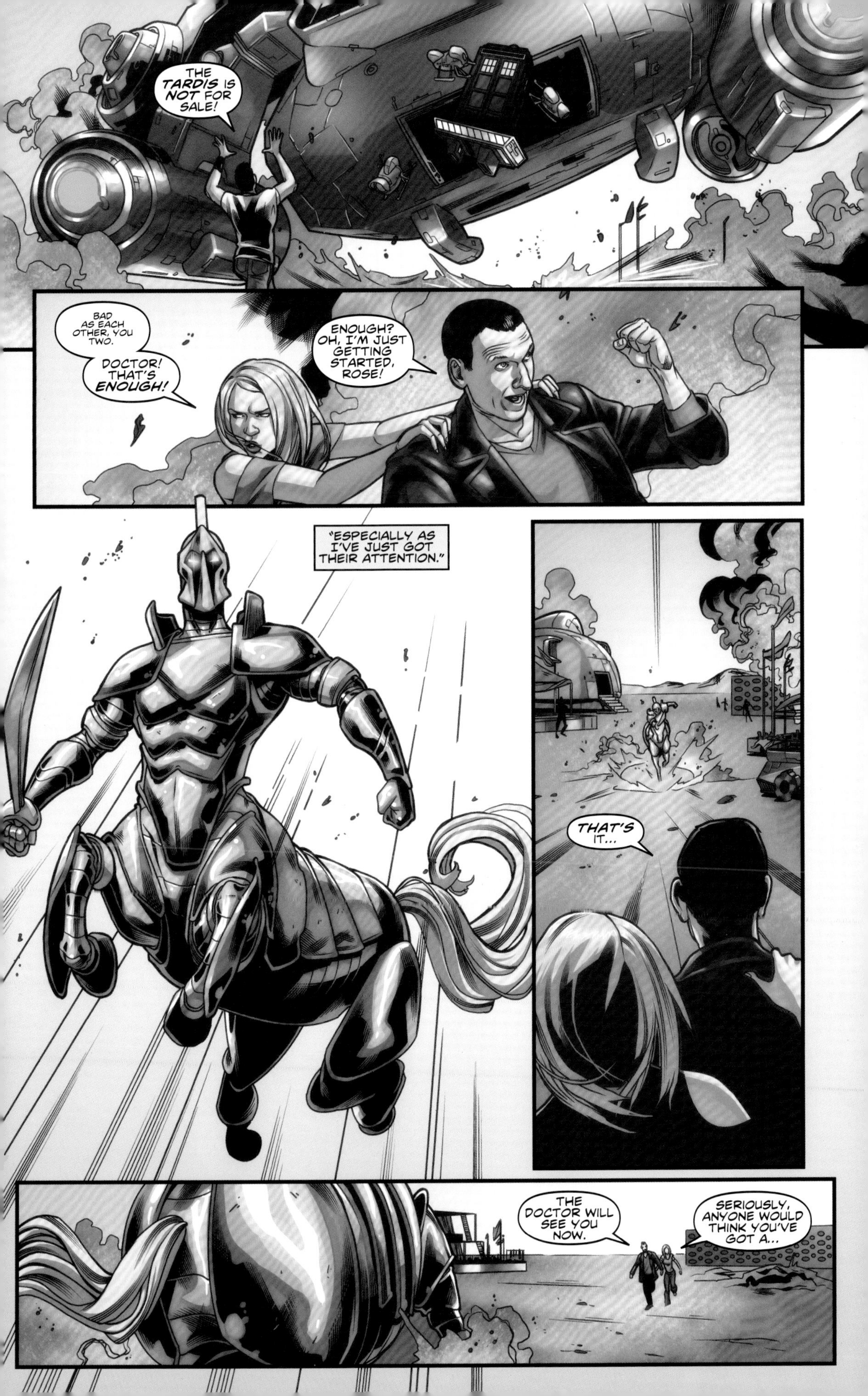
THE TARDIS IS NOT FOR SALE!
BAD AS EACH OTHER, YOU TWO.
DOCTOR! THAT'S ENOUGH!
ENOUGH? OH, I'M JUST GETTING STARTED, ROSE!
"ESPECIALLY AS I'VE JUST GOT THEIR ATTENTION."
THAT'S IT...
THE DOCTOR WILL SEE YOU NOW.
SERIOUSLY, ANYONE WOULD THINK YOU'VE GOT A...

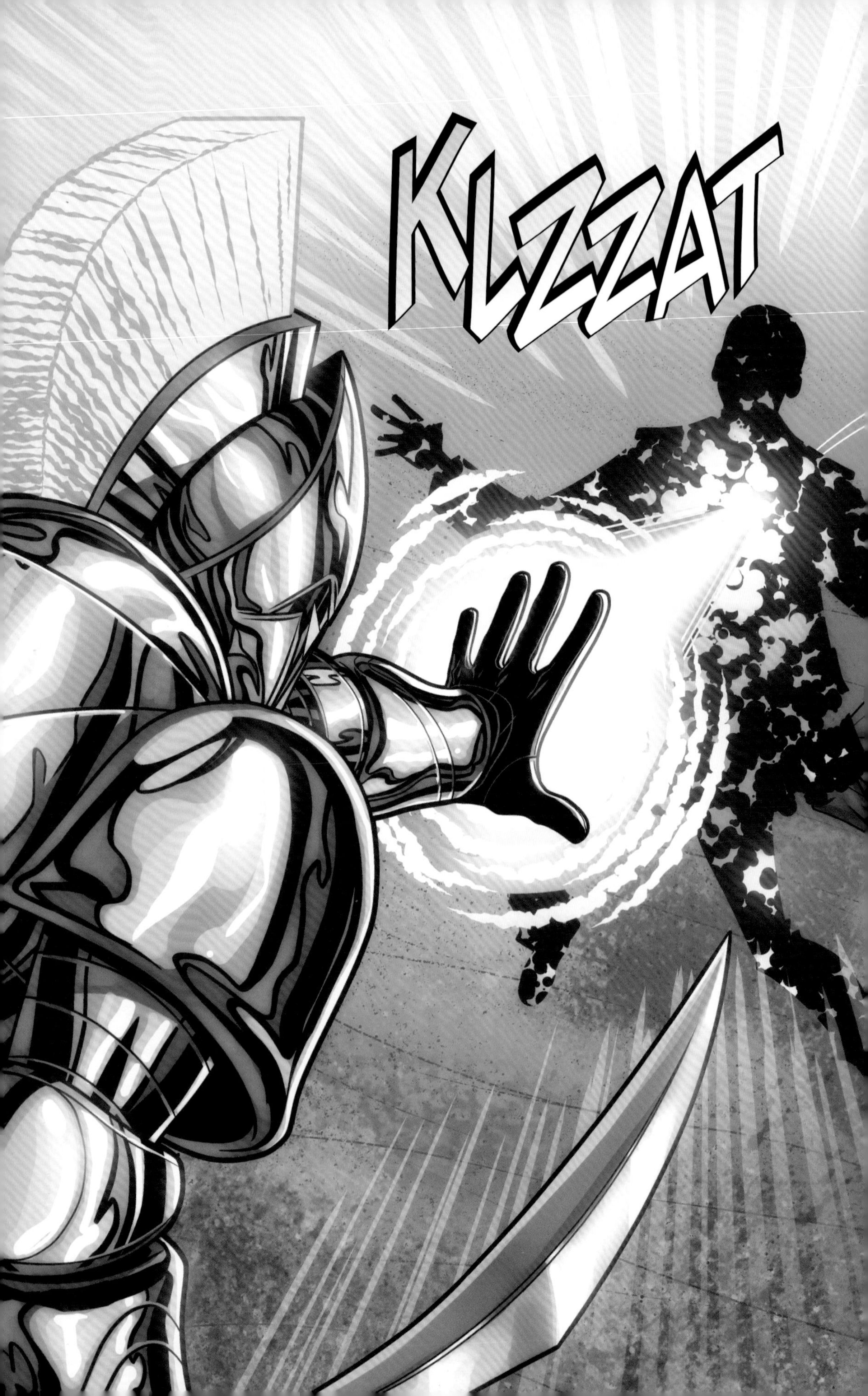
KLZZAT

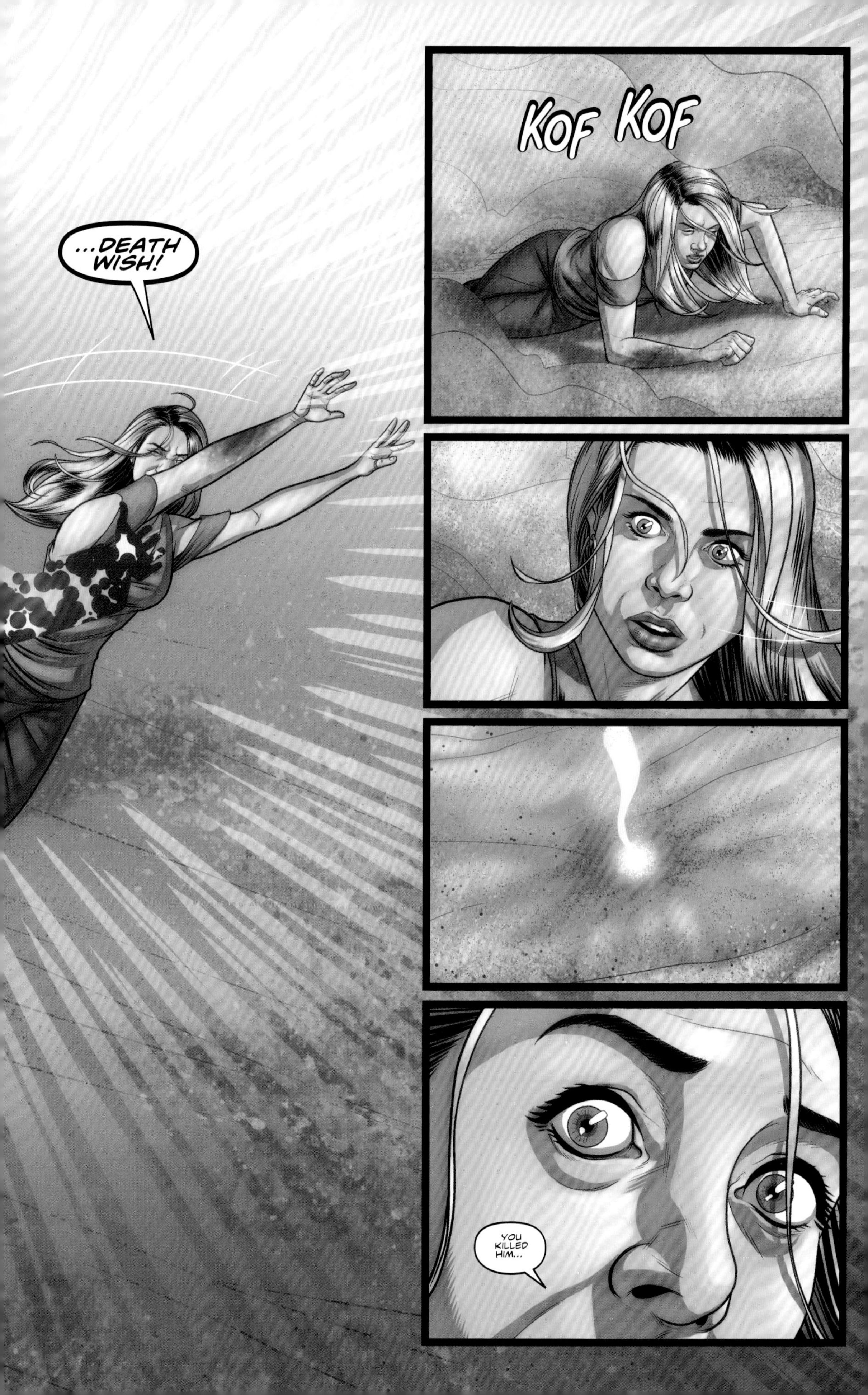
...DEATH WISH!
KOF KOF
YOU KILLED HIM...

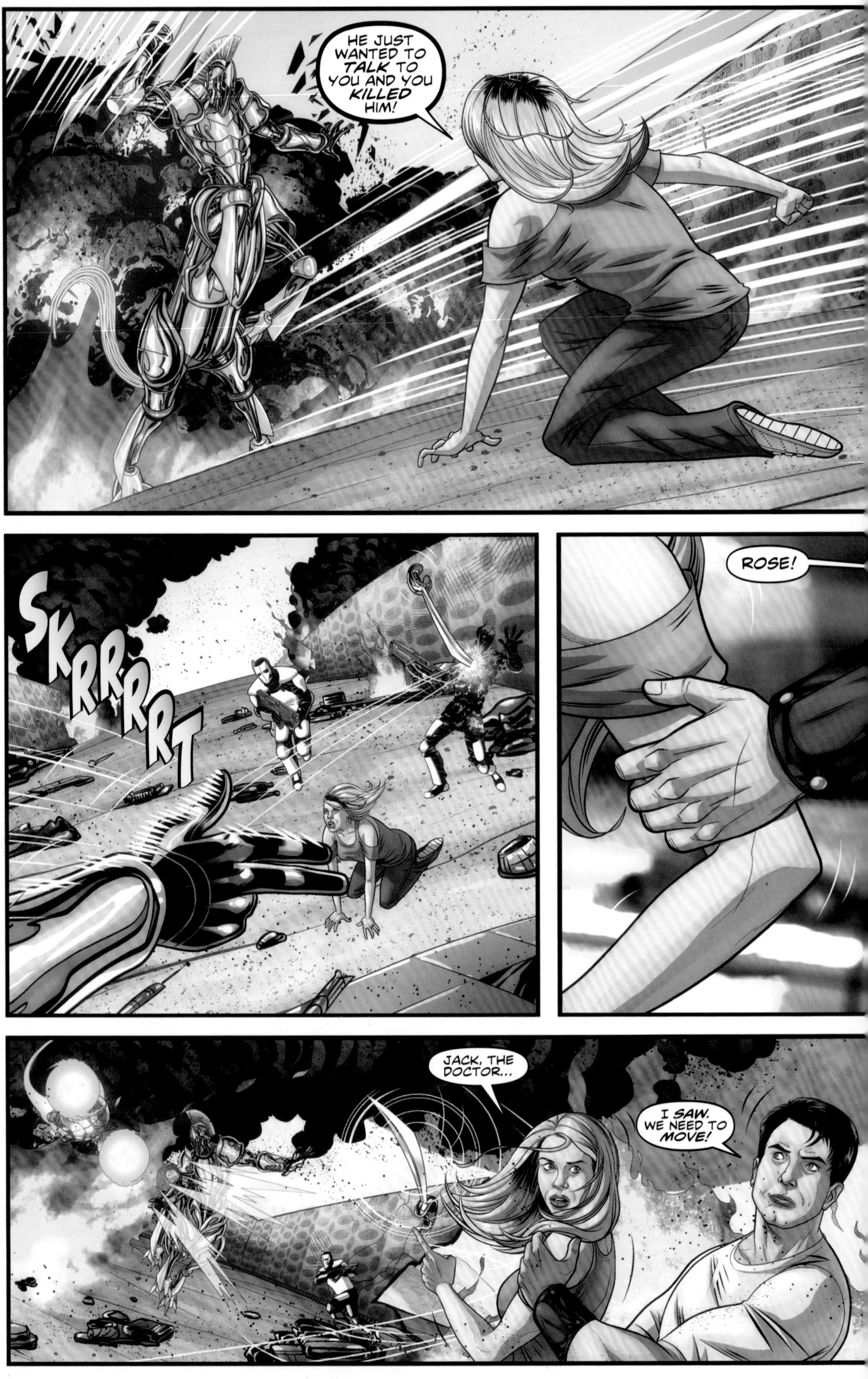
HE JUST WANTED TO TALK TO YOU AND YOU KILLED HIM!
SKRRRRT
ROSE!
JACK, THE DOCTOR...
I SAW. WE NEED TO MOVE!

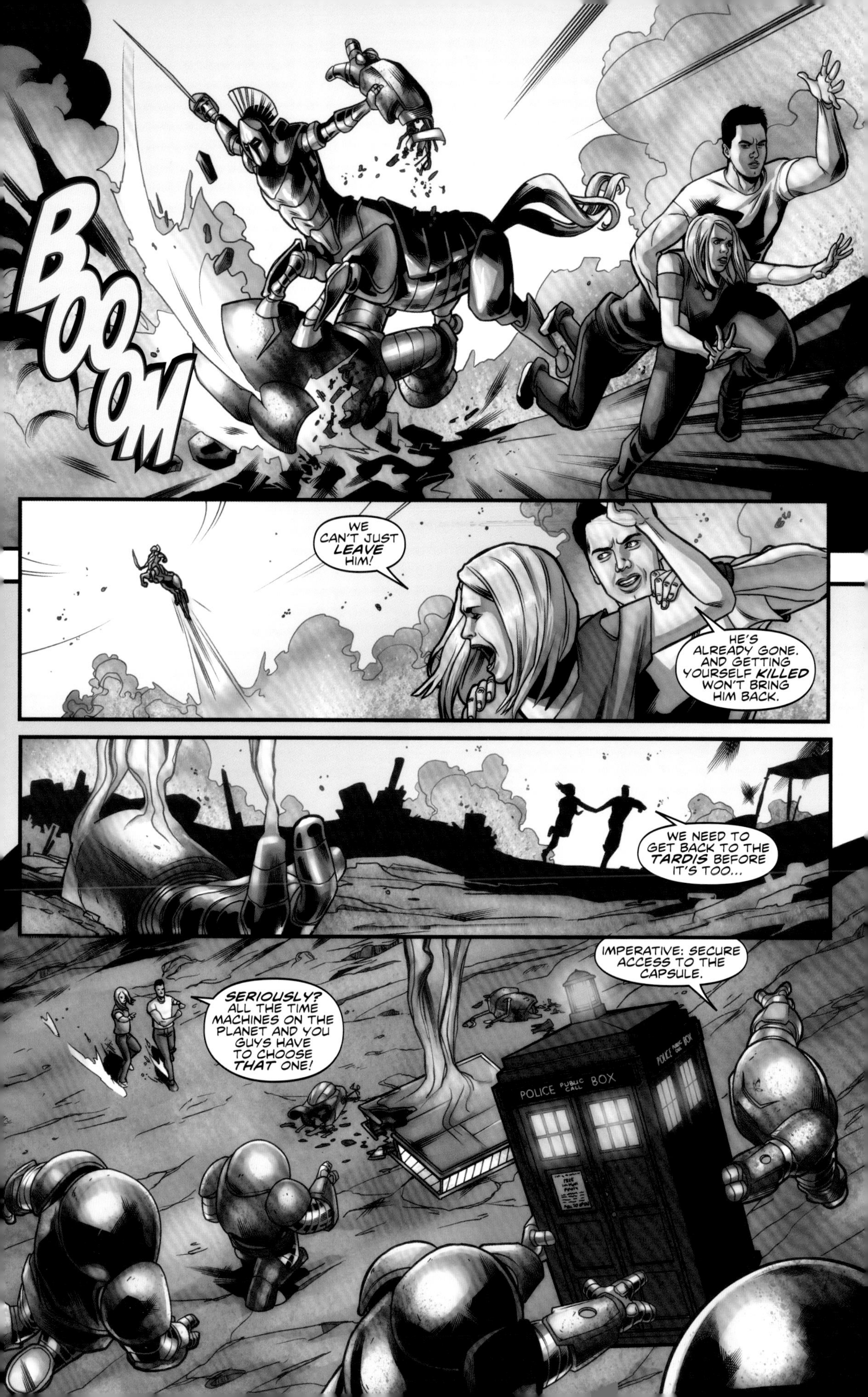
BOOOOM
WE CAN'T JUST LEAVE HIM!
HE'S ALREADY GONE. AND GETTING YOURSELF KILLED WON'T BRING HIM BACK.
WE NEED TO GET BACK TO THE TARDIS BEFORE IT'S TOO...
SERIOUSLY? ALL THE TIME MACHINES ON THE PLANET AND YOU GUYS HAVE TO CHOOSE THAT ONE!
IMPERATIVE: SECURE ACCESS TO THE CAPSULE.
POLICE PUBLIC CALL BOX

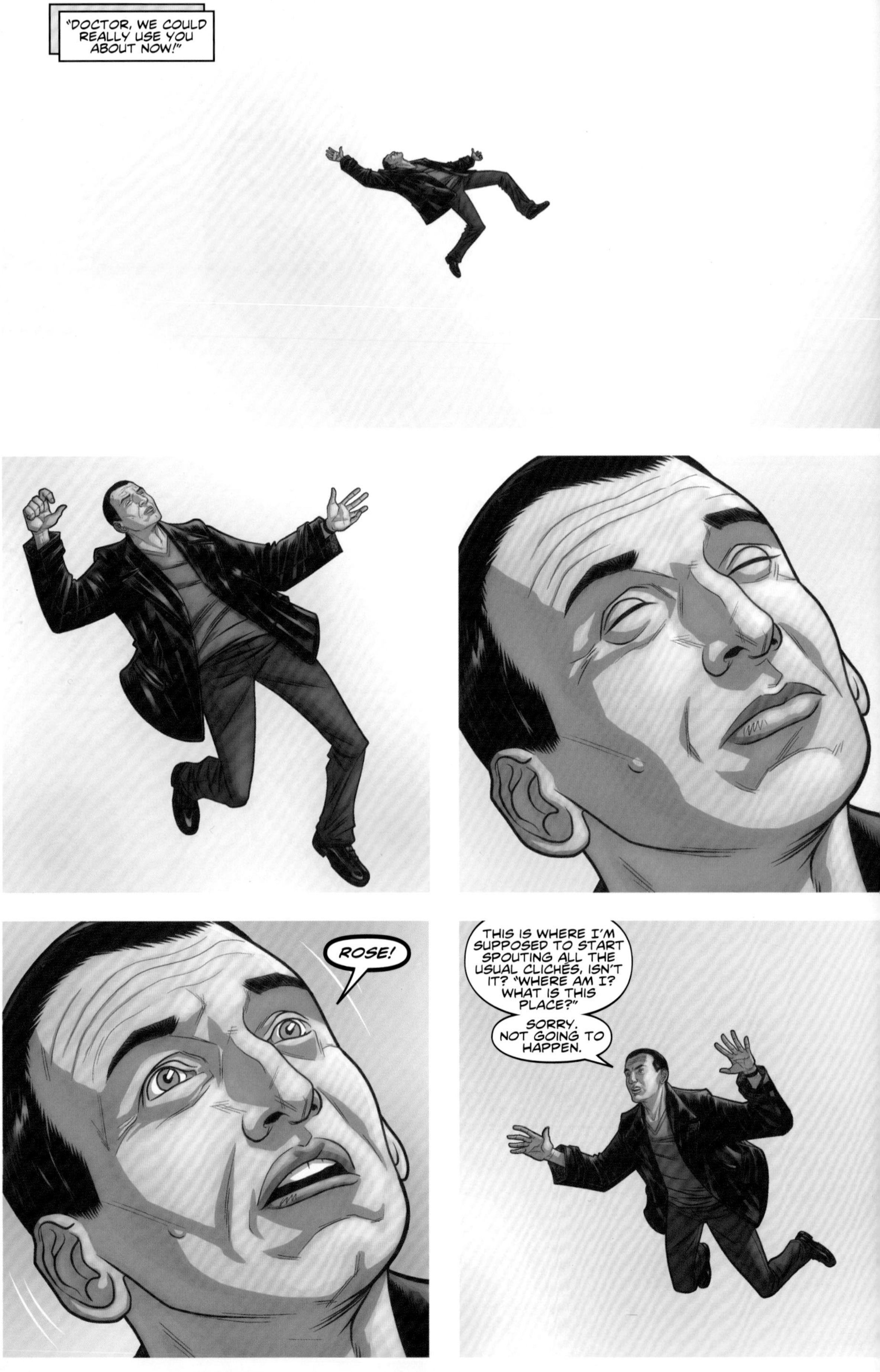
"DOCTOR, WE COULD REALLY USE YOU ABOUT NOW!"
ROSE!
THIS IS WHERE I'M SUPPOSED TO START SPOUTING ALL THE USUAL CLICHÉS, ISN'T IT? "WHERE AM I? WHAT IS THIS PLACE?"
SORRY. NOT GOING TO HAPPEN.

AND YOU MIGHT AS WELL SHOW YOURSELF. TIME-TOT HIDE AND SEEK CHAMPION, ME. FORTY-TWO-YEARS ON THE TROT. NO HIDING PLACE WAS SAFE. USED TO DRIVE THE RANI *NUTS*.

THERE YOU ARE. IT'S *RUDE*, YOU KNOW? DUMPING SOMEONE IN A SUB-DIMENSIONAL VOID. THAT *IS* WHERE WE ARE, ISN'T IT?

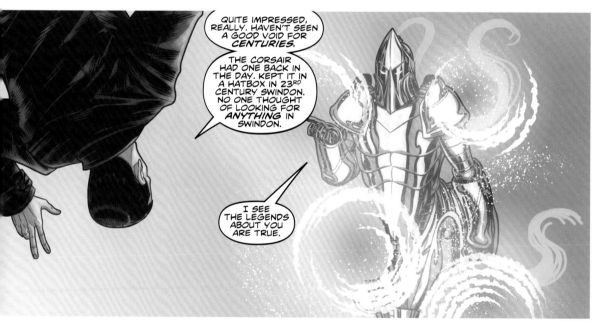

QUITE IMPRESSED, REALLY. HAVEN'T SEEN A GOOD VOID FOR *CENTURIES*.

THE CORSAIR HAD ONE BACK IN THE DAY. KEPT IT IN A HATBOX IN 23RD CENTURY SWINDON. NO ONE THOUGHT OF LOOKING FOR *ANYTHING* IN SWINDON.

I SEE THE LEGENDS ABOUT YOU ARE TRUE.

LEGENDS? GOT TO LOVE A GOOD LEGEND. GO ON THEN -- WHAT DO THEY SAY?

PLEASE DON'T TELL ME THEY MENTION THE EARS.

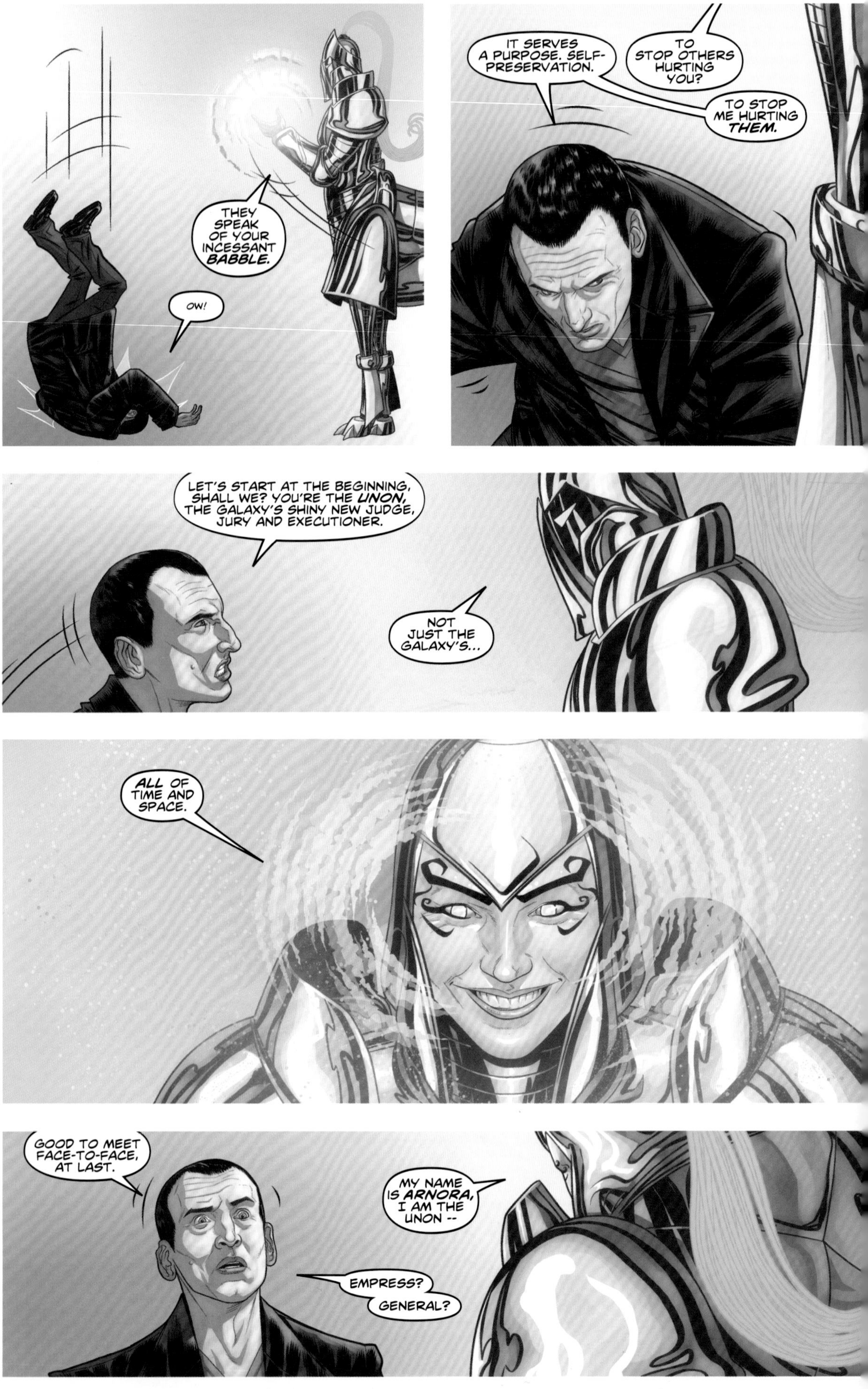
THEY SPEAK OF YOUR INCESSANT BABBLE.
OW!
IT SERVES A PURPOSE. SELF-PRESERVATION.
TO STOP OTHERS HURTING YOU?
TO STOP ME HURTING THEM.
LET'S START AT THE BEGINNING, SHALL WE? YOU'RE THE UNON, THE GALAXY'S SHINY NEW JUDGE, JURY AND EXECUTIONER.
NOT JUST THE GALAXY'S...
ALL OF TIME AND SPACE.
GOOD TO MEET FACE-TO-FACE, AT LAST.
MY NAME IS ARNORA, I AM THE UNON --
EMPRESS?
GENERAL?

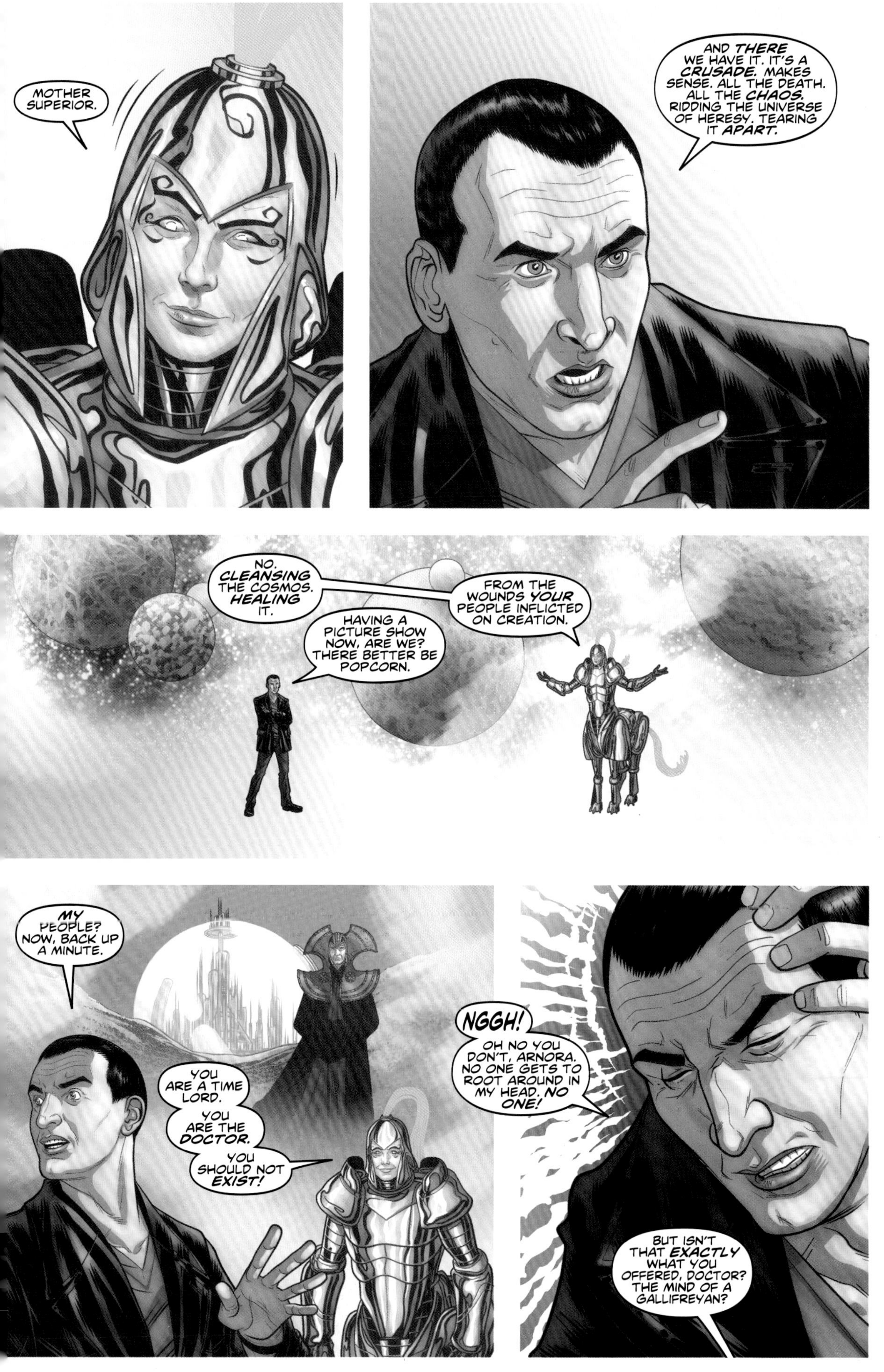
MOTHER SUPERIOR.
AND THERE WE HAVE IT. IT'S A CRUSADE. MAKES SENSE. ALL THE DEATH. ALL THE CHAOS. RIDDING THE UNIVERSE OF HERESY. TEARING IT APART.
NO. CLEANSING THE COSMOS. HEALING IT.
FROM THE WOUNDS YOUR PEOPLE INFLICTED ON CREATION.
HAVING A PICTURE SHOW NOW, ARE WE? THERE BETTER BE POPCORN.
MY PEOPLE? NOW, BACK UP A MINUTE.
YOU ARE A TIME LORD.
YOU ARE THE DOCTOR.
YOU SHOULD NOT EXIST!
NGGH!
OH NO YOU DON'T, ARNORA. NO ONE GETS TO ROOT AROUND IN MY HEAD. NO ONE!
BUT ISN'T THAT EXACTLY WHAT YOU OFFERED, DOCTOR? THE MIND OF A GALLIFREYAN?

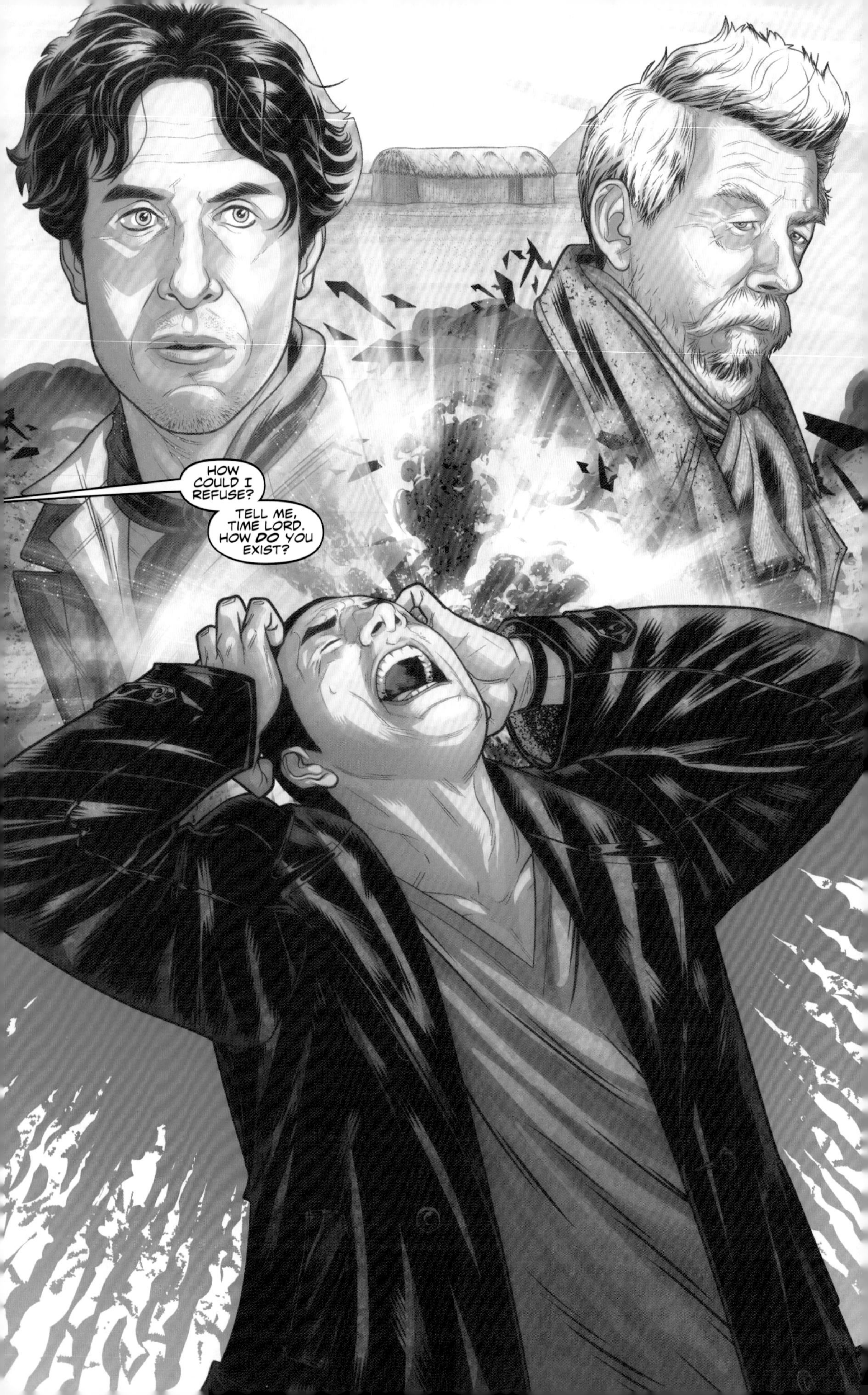
HOW COULD I REFUSE?
TELL ME, TIME LORD. HOW DO YOU EXIST?

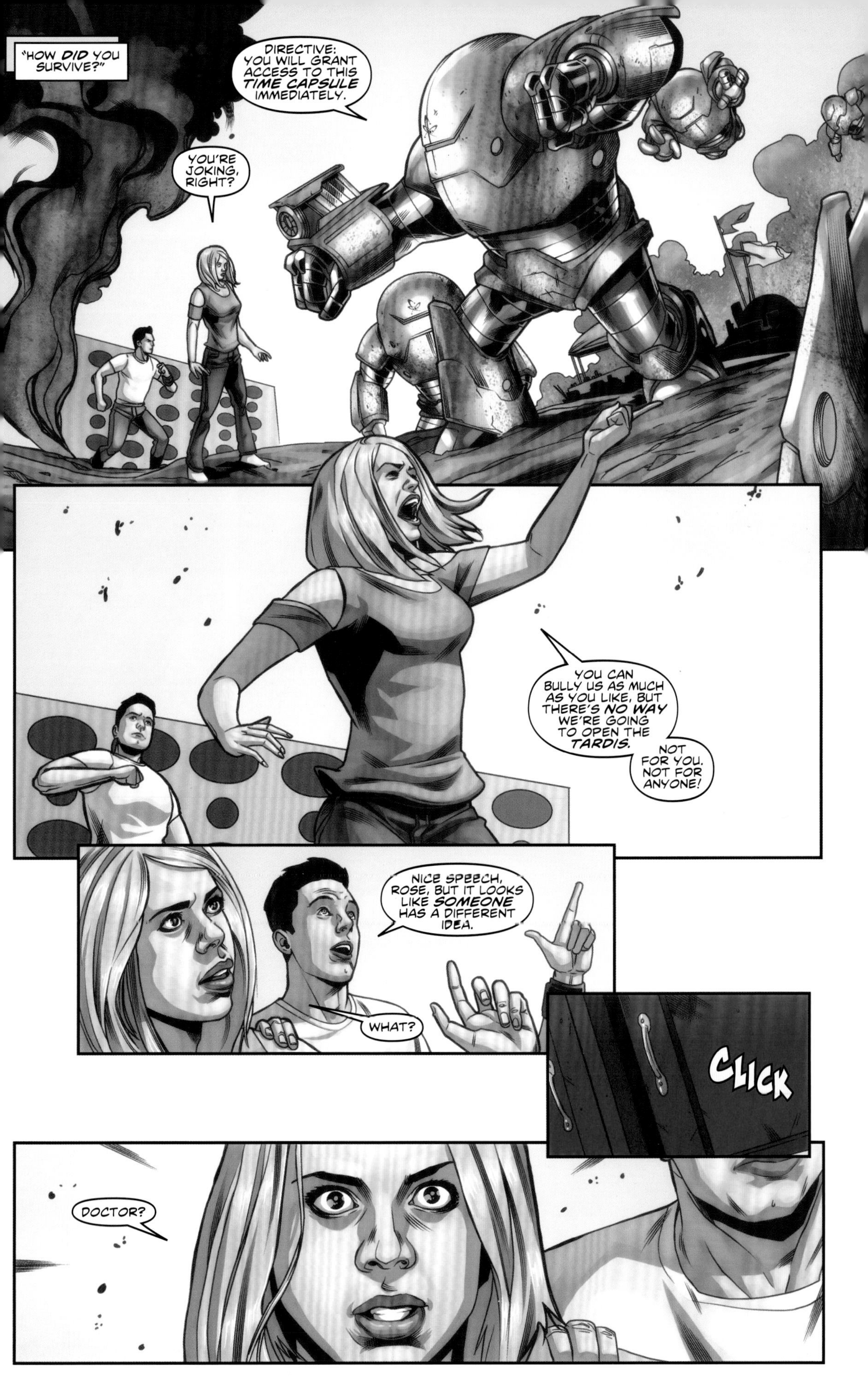
"HOW *DID* YOU SURVIVE?"
DIRECTIVE: YOU WILL GRANT ACCESS TO THIS *TIME CAPSULE* IMMEDIATELY.
YOU'RE JOKING, RIGHT?
YOU CAN BULLY US AS MUCH AS YOU LIKE, BUT THERE'S *NO WAY* WE'RE GOING TO OPEN THE *TARDIS.*
NOT FOR YOU. NOT FOR ANYONE!
NICE SPEECH, ROSE, BUT IT LOOKS LIKE *SOMEONE* HAS A DIFFERENT IDEA.
WHAT?
CLICK
DOCTOR?

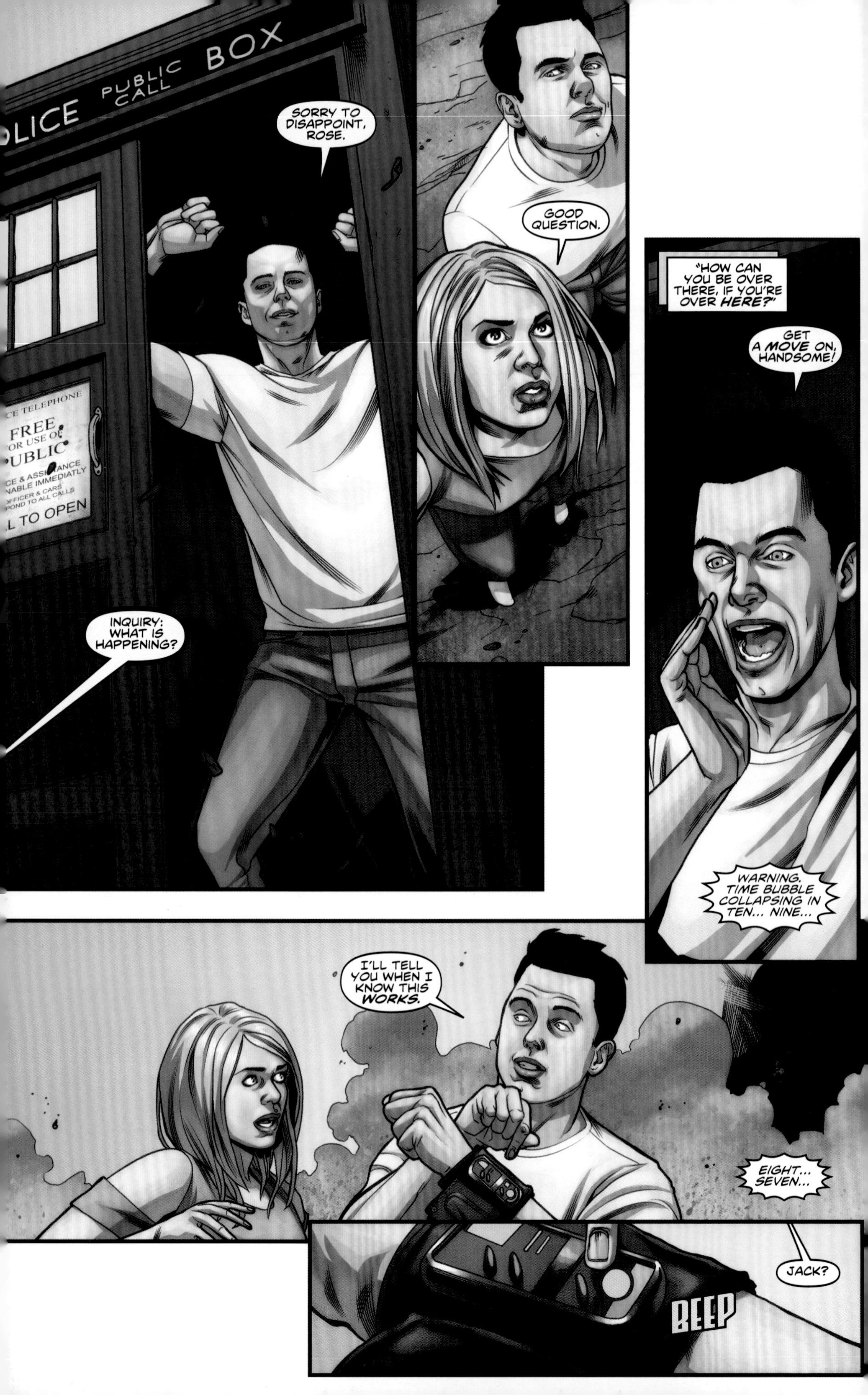
POLICE PUBLIC CALL BOX
SORRY TO DISAPPOINT, ROSE.
GOOD QUESTION.
"HOW CAN YOU BE OVER THERE, IF YOU'RE OVER HERE?"
GET A MOVE ON, HANDSOME!
INQUIRY: WHAT IS HAPPENING?
WARNING. TIME BUBBLE COLLAPSING IN TEN... NINE...
I'LL TELL YOU WHEN I KNOW THIS WORKS.
EIGHT... SEVEN...
JACK?
BEEP

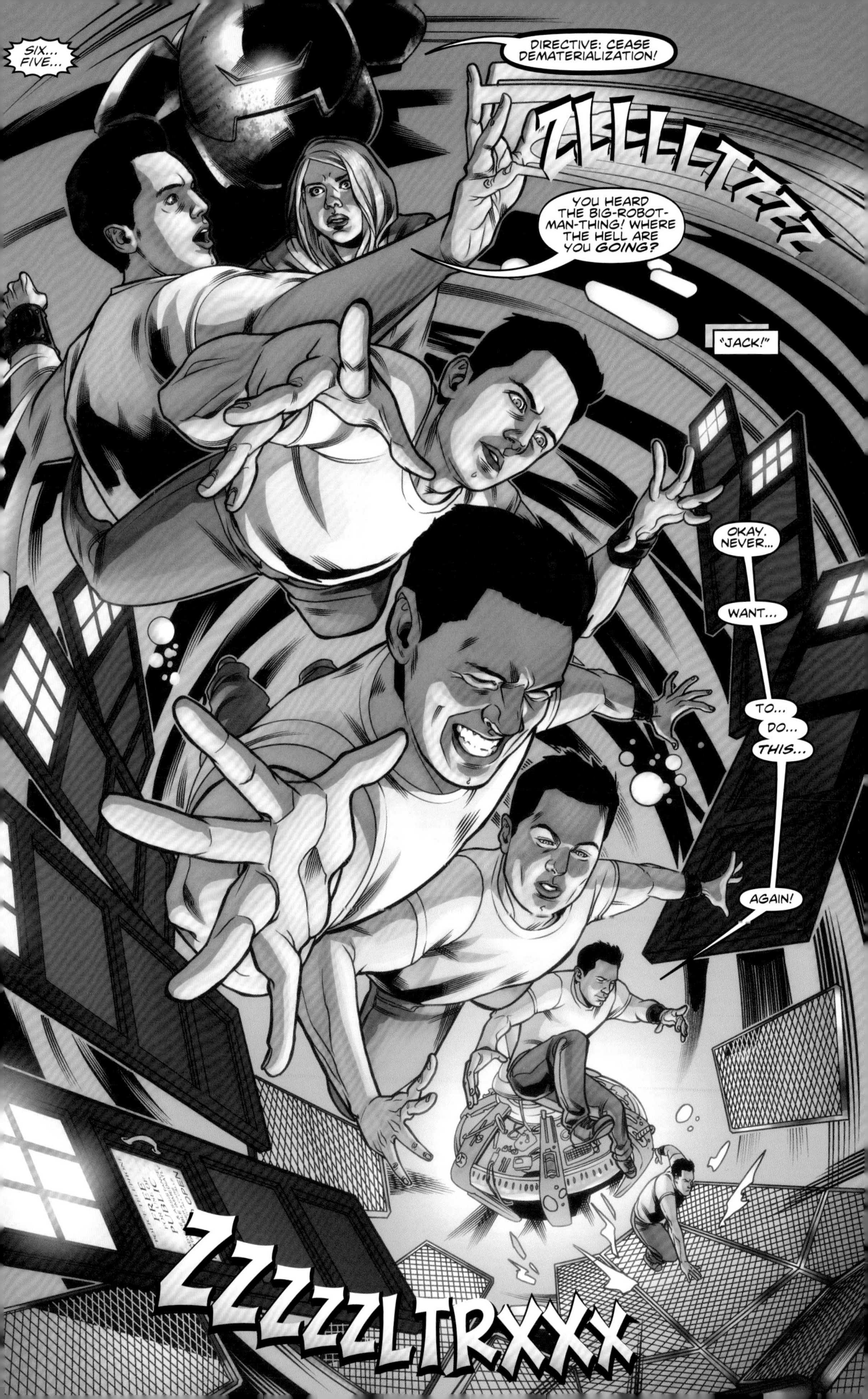
SIX... FIVE...
DIRECTIVE: CEASE DEMATERIALIZATION!
ZLLLLTZZZ
YOU HEARD THE BIG-ROBOT-MAN-THING! WHERE THE HELL ARE YOU GOING?
"JACK!"
OKAY. NEVER...
WANT...
TO...
DO...
THIS...
AGAIN!
ZZZZZZLTRXXX

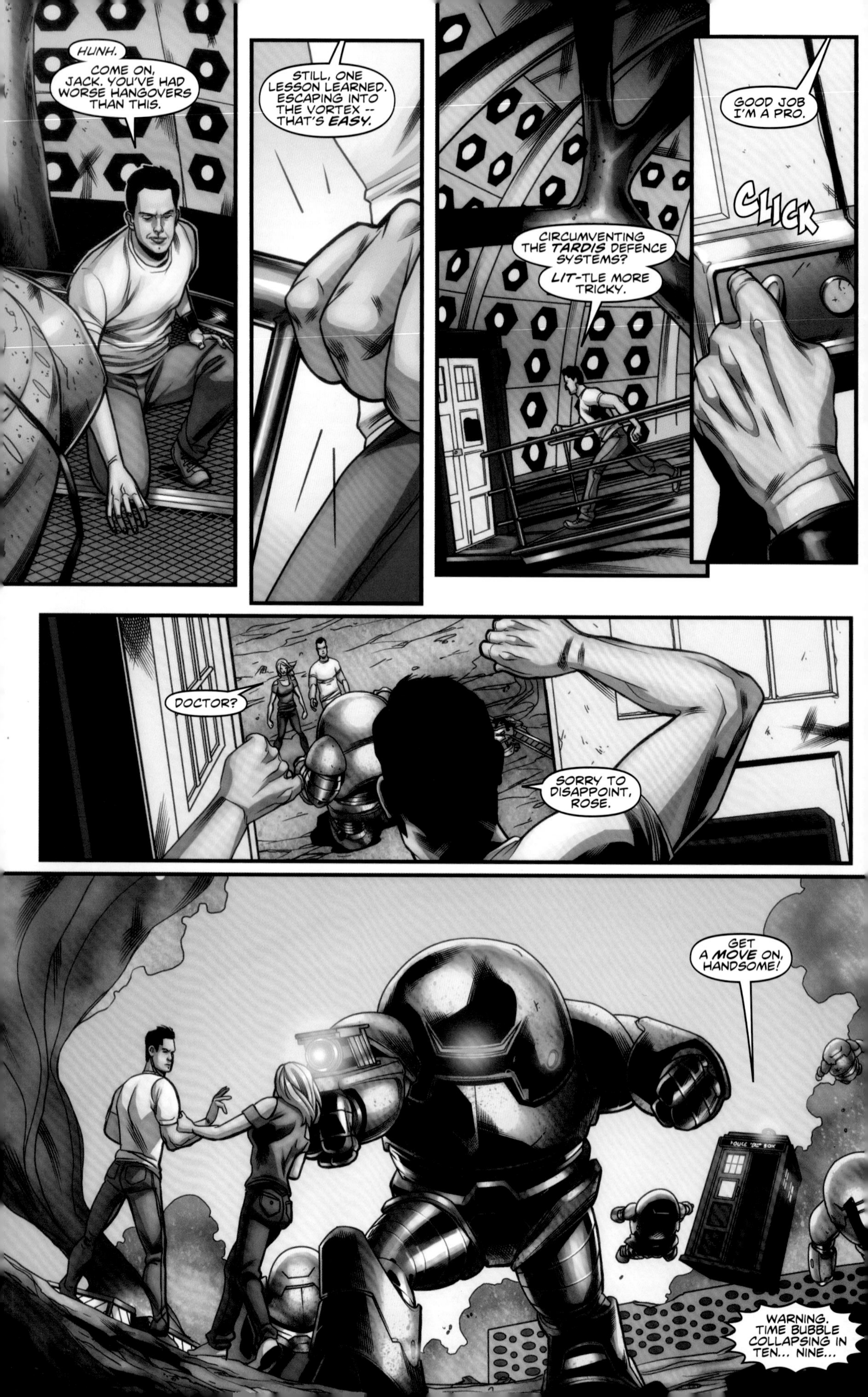
HUNH.
COME ON, JACK. YOU'VE HAD WORSE HANGOVERS THAN THIS.
STILL, ONE LESSON LEARNED. ESCAPING INTO THE VORTEX -- THAT'S EASY.
CIRCUMVENTING THE TARDIS DEFENCE SYSTEMS?
LIT-TLE MORE TRICKY.
GOOD JOB I'M A PRO.
CLICK
DOCTOR?
SORRY TO DISAPPOINT, ROSE.
GET A MOVE ON, HANDSOME!
WARNING. TIME BUBBLE COLLAPSING IN TEN... NINE...

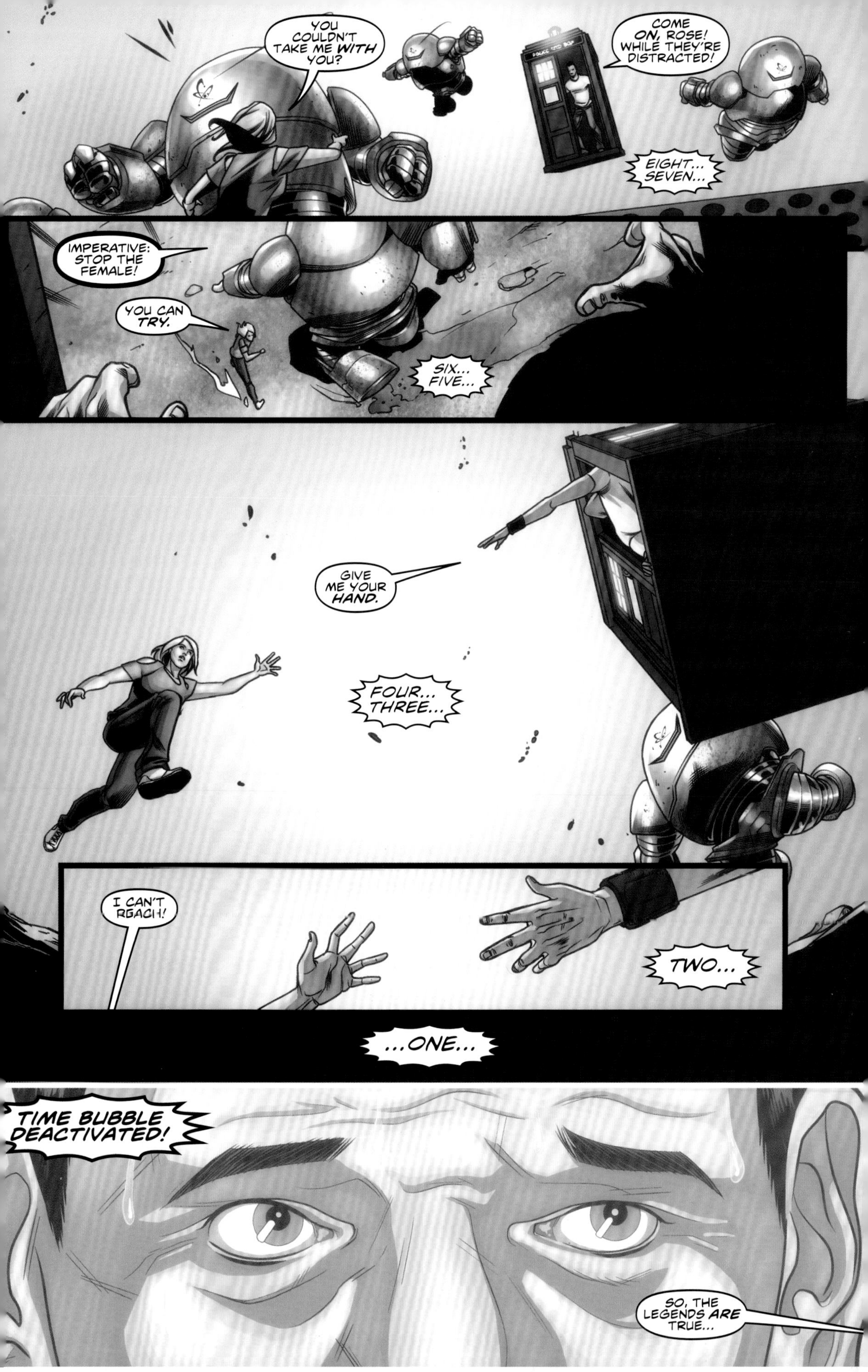
YOU COULDN'T TAKE ME WITH YOU?
COME ON, ROSE! WHILE THEY'RE DISTRACTED!
EIGHT... SEVEN...
IMPERATIVE: STOP THE FEMALE!
YOU CAN TRY.
SIX... FIVE...
GIVE ME YOUR HAND.
FOUR... THREE...
I CAN'T REACH!
TWO...
...ONE...
TIME BUBBLE DEACTIVATED!
SO, THE LEGENDS ARE TRUE...

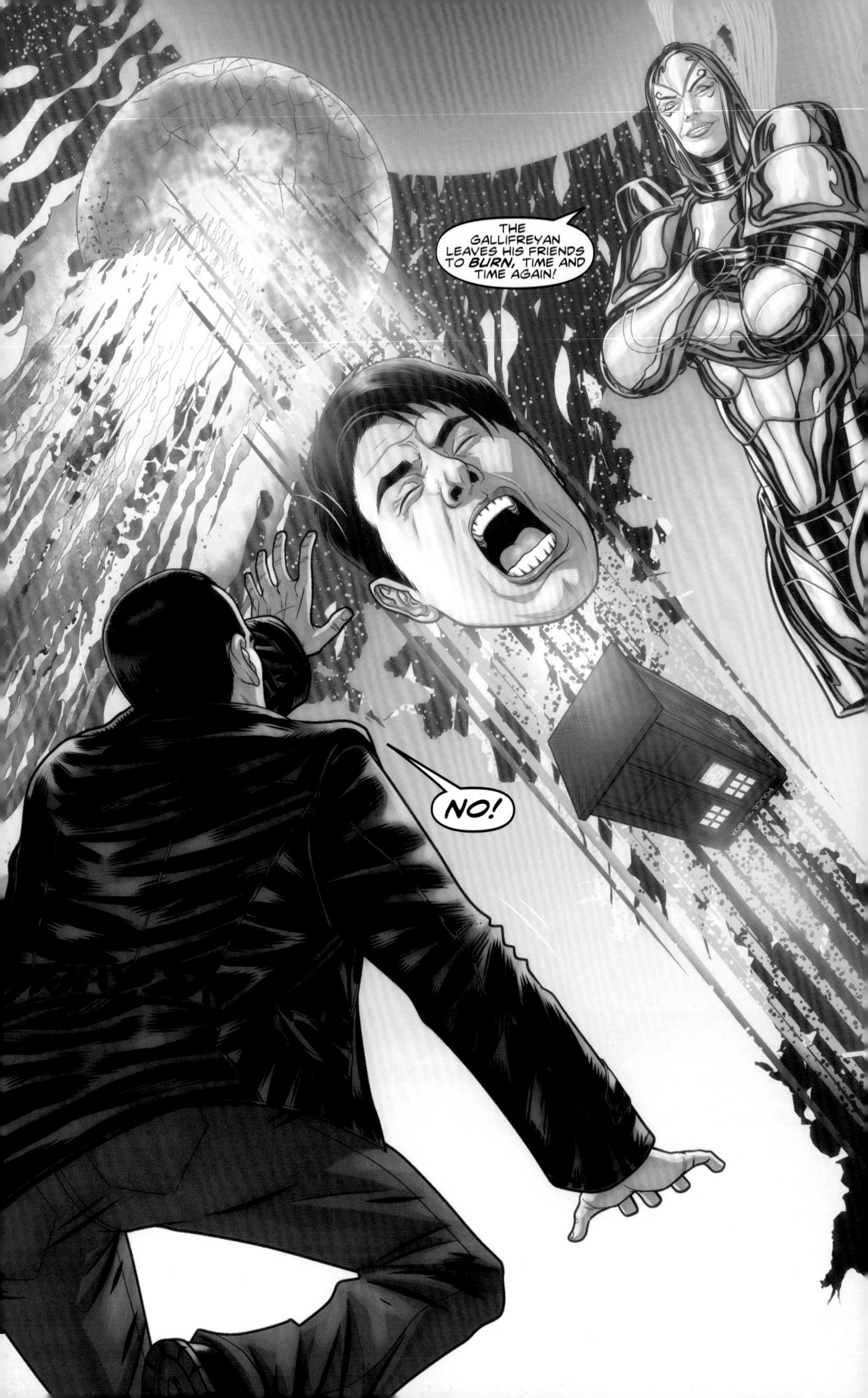
THE GALLIFREYAN LEAVES HIS FRIENDS TO BURN, TIME AND TIME AGAIN!
NO!
POLICE BOX

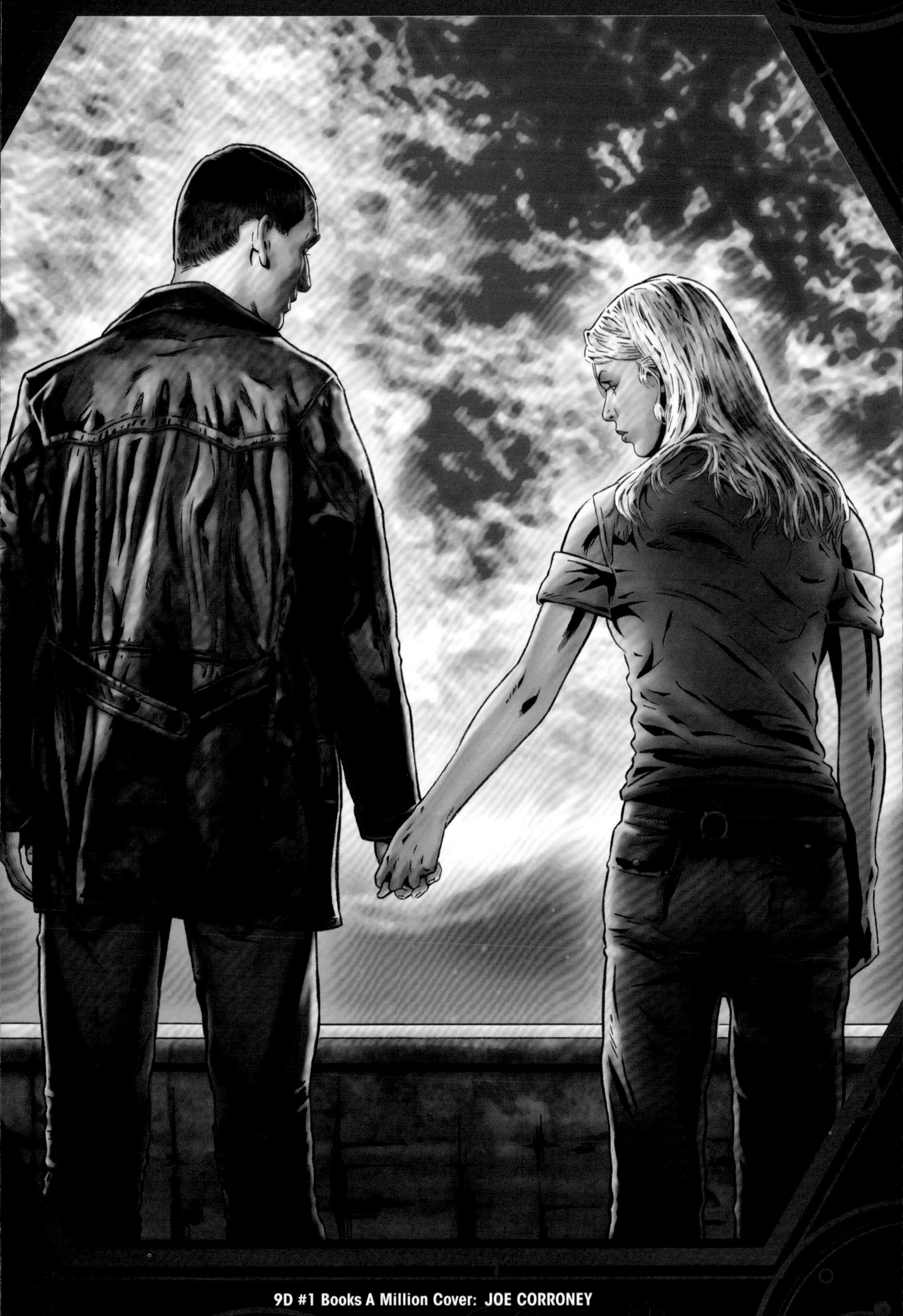

9D #1 Books A Million Cover: JOE CORRONEY

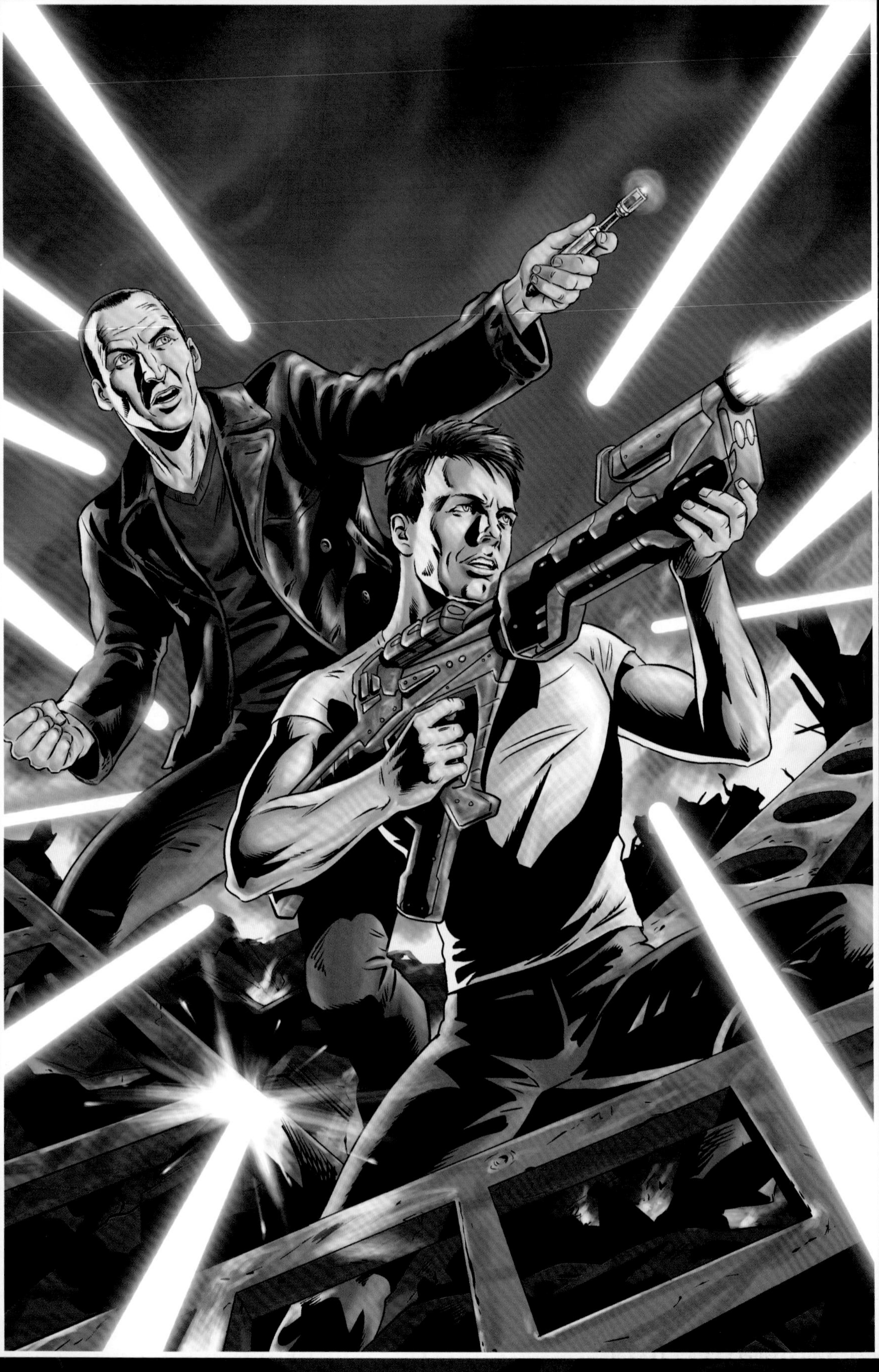

9D #4 Cover A: LEE SULLIVAN

I'VE BEEN IN TIGHT SCRAPES BEFORE.

GIVE ME YOUR HAND.

HEISTS. CONS. JEALOUS HUSBANDS. JEALOUS *WIVES*, COME TO THINK OF IT.

I CAN'T REACH!

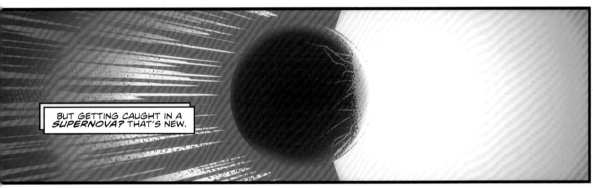

BUT GETTING CAUGHT IN A *SUPERNOVA?* THAT'S NEW.

ONE THING I KNOW, THE HEAT OF AN EXPLODING SUN WILL BE *NOTHING* COMPARED TO THE DOCTOR, WHEN HE FINDS OUT I LEFT ROSE BEHIND.

IGNORING THE FACT THAT THE POOR GUY'S ALREADY *DEAD*, OF COURSE.

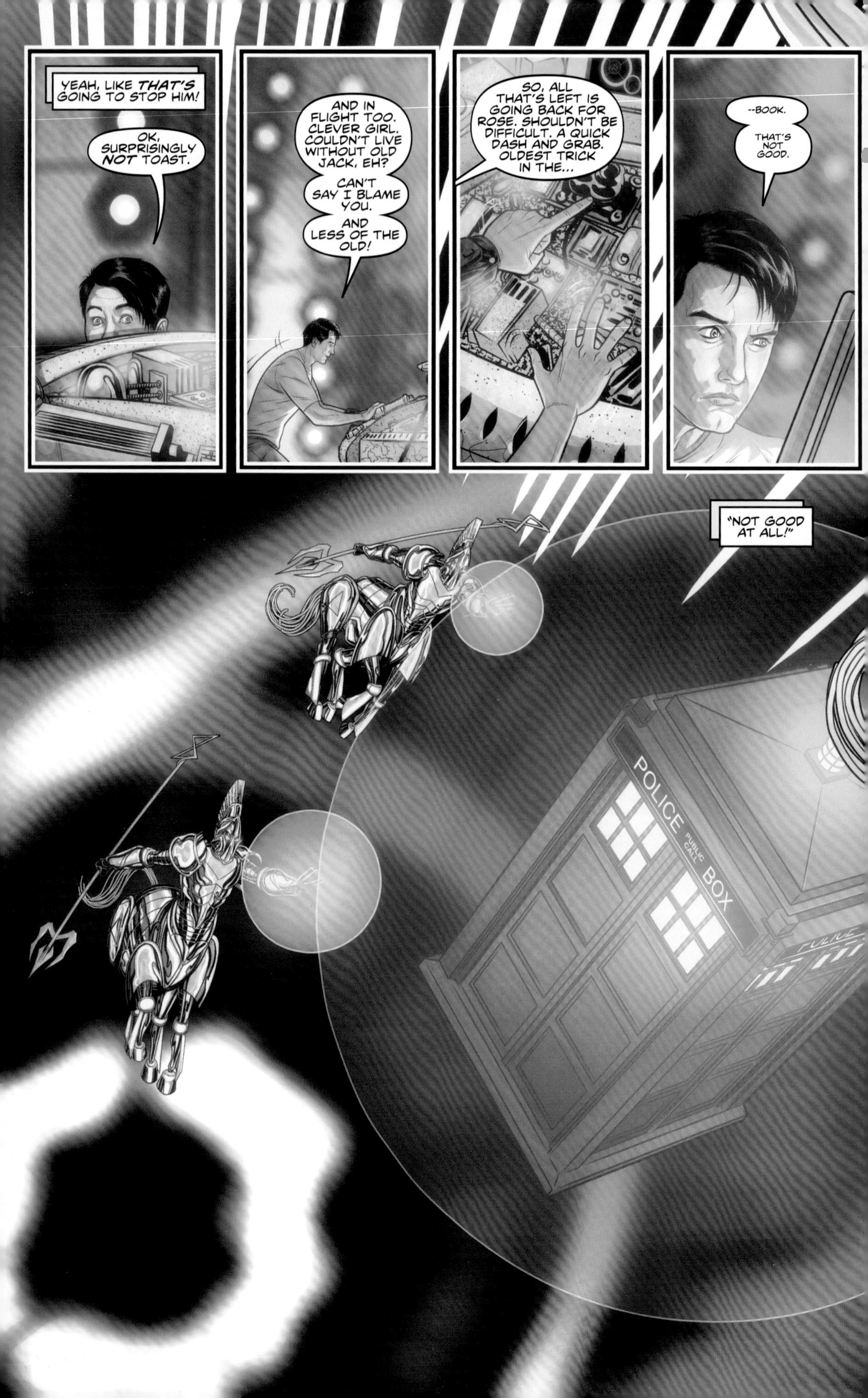
YEAH, LIKE THAT'S GOING TO STOP HIM!
OK, SURPRISINGLY NOT TOAST.
AND IN FLIGHT TOO. CLEVER GIRL. COULDN'T LIVE WITHOUT OLD JACK, EH?
CAN'T SAY I BLAME YOU.
AND LESS OF THE OLD!
SO, ALL THAT'S LEFT IS GOING BACK FOR ROSE. SHOULDN'T BE DIFFICULT. A QUICK DASH AND GRAB. OLDEST TRICK IN THE...
--BOOK.
THAT'S NOT GOOD.
"NOT GOOD AT ALL!"
POLICE PUBLIC CALL BOX

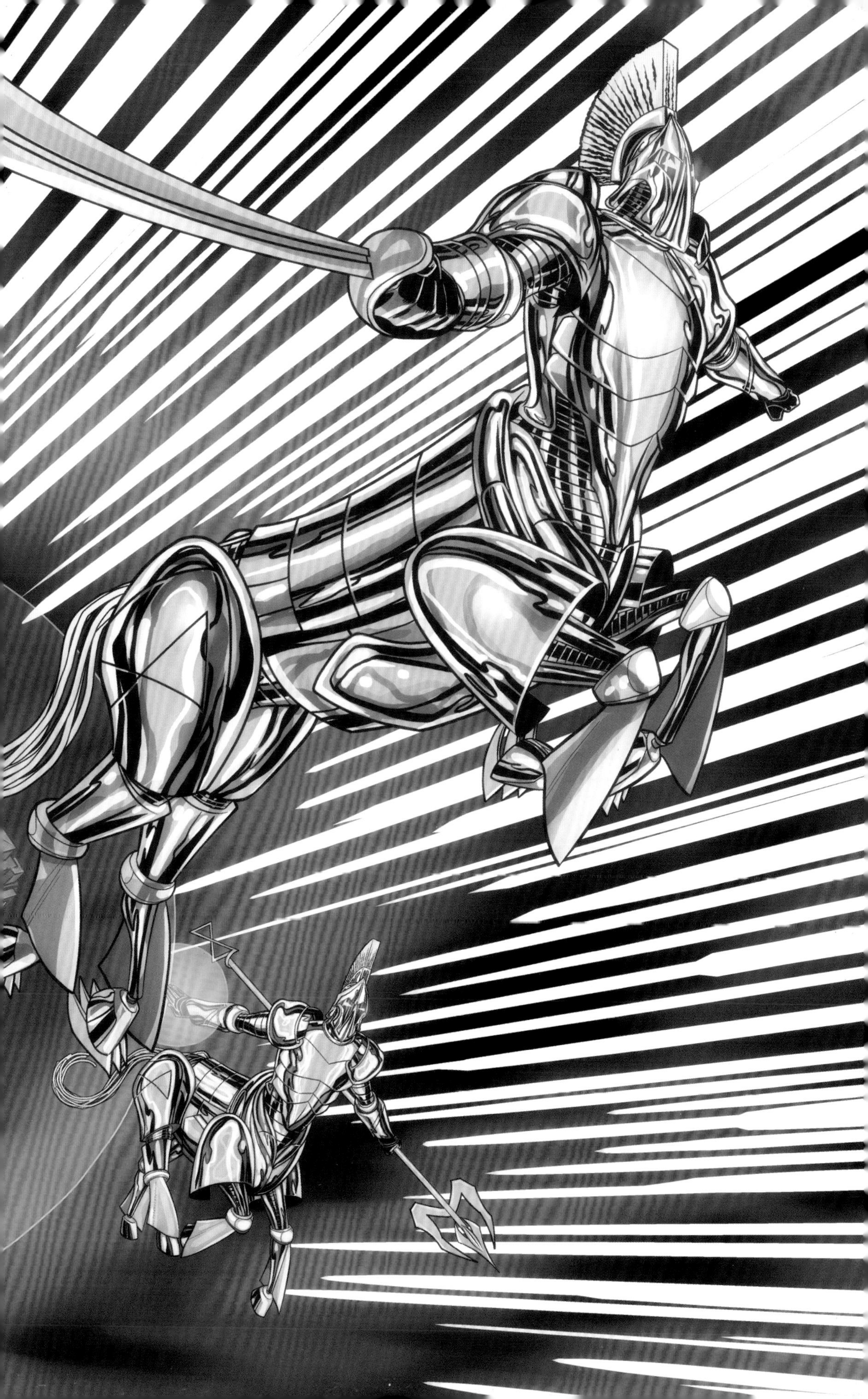

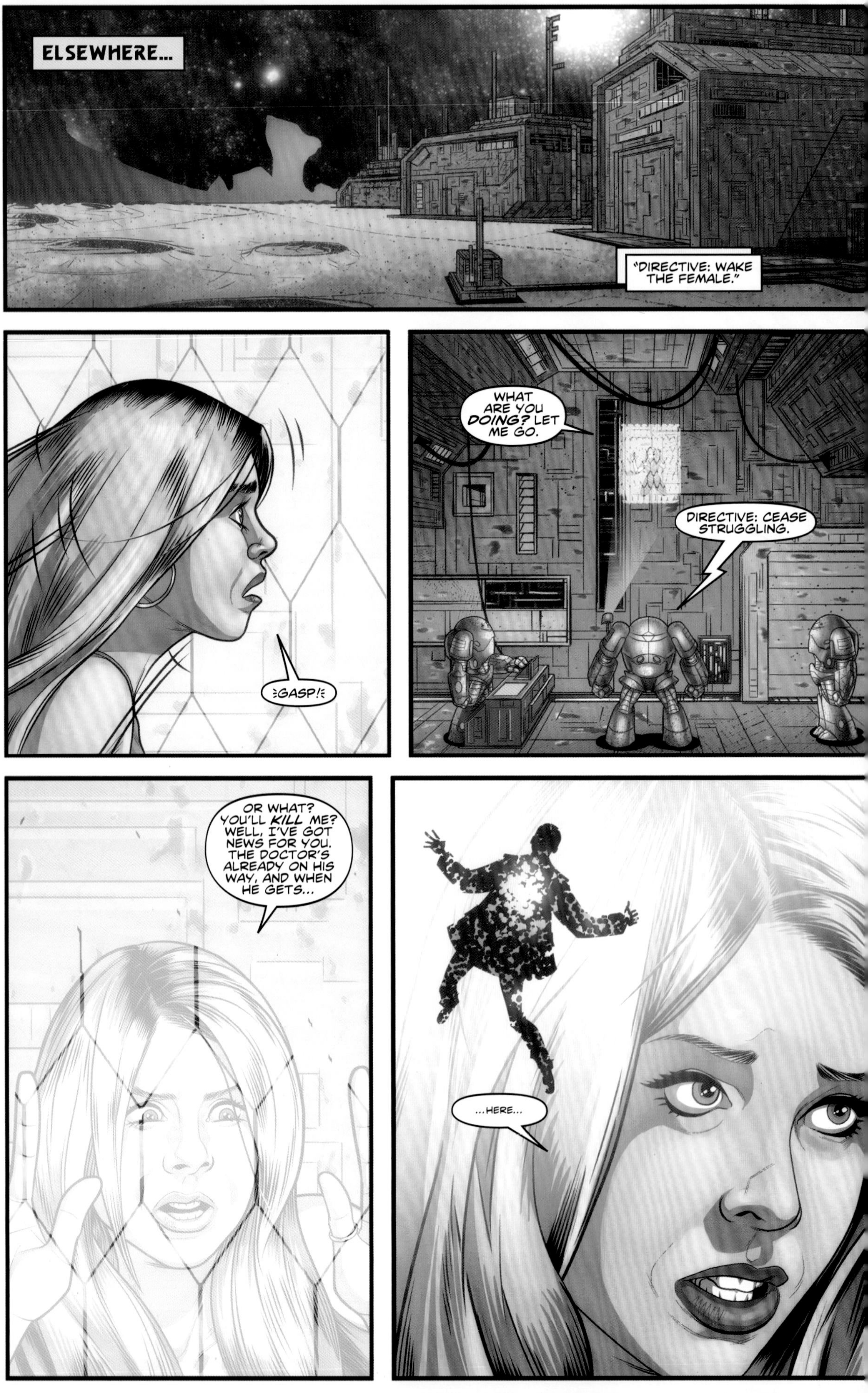
ELSEWHERE...
"DIRECTIVE: WAKE THE FEMALE."
GASP!
WHAT ARE YOU DOING? LET ME GO.
DIRECTIVE: CEASE STRUGGLING.
OR WHAT? YOU'LL KILL ME? WELL, I'VE GOT NEWS FOR YOU. THE DOCTOR'S ALREADY ON HIS WAY, AND WHEN HE GETS...
...HERE...

OBSERVATION: YOUR ASSOCIATE IS DEAD. KILLED BY THE UNON.

DON'T SAY THAT.

INFORMATION: IT IS A MATTER OF FACT.

EXTERNAL SHIELDS: 100%

DON'T SAY THAT!

DIRECTIVE: YOU WILL JOIN THE FIGHT AGAINST THE UNON. YOU WILL *SERVE* THE LECT.

AND WHAT IF I DON'T? YOU'LL TORTURE ME? THAT'S WHAT'S COMING *NEXT,* ISN'T IT? I'M GETTING THE HANG OF ALL THIS NOW. KNOW THE DRILL.

WHAT *IS* IT WITH YOU ALIENS ANYWAY? HIDING BEHIND YOUR ARMOR AND DISGUISES?

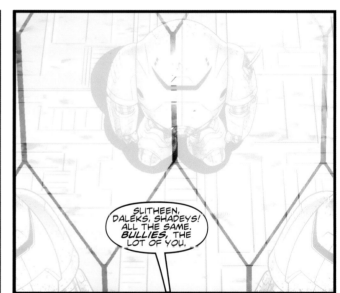

SLITHEEN, DALEKS, SHADEYS! ALL THE SAME. *BULLIES,* THE LOT OF YOU.

COWARDS.

SO, WHAT ARE YOU WAITING FOR? IT'S NOT LIKE YOU CAN SCARE ME ANY MORE THAN I ALREADY AM.

CLARIFICATION: YOU THINK YOU KNOW TORTURE?

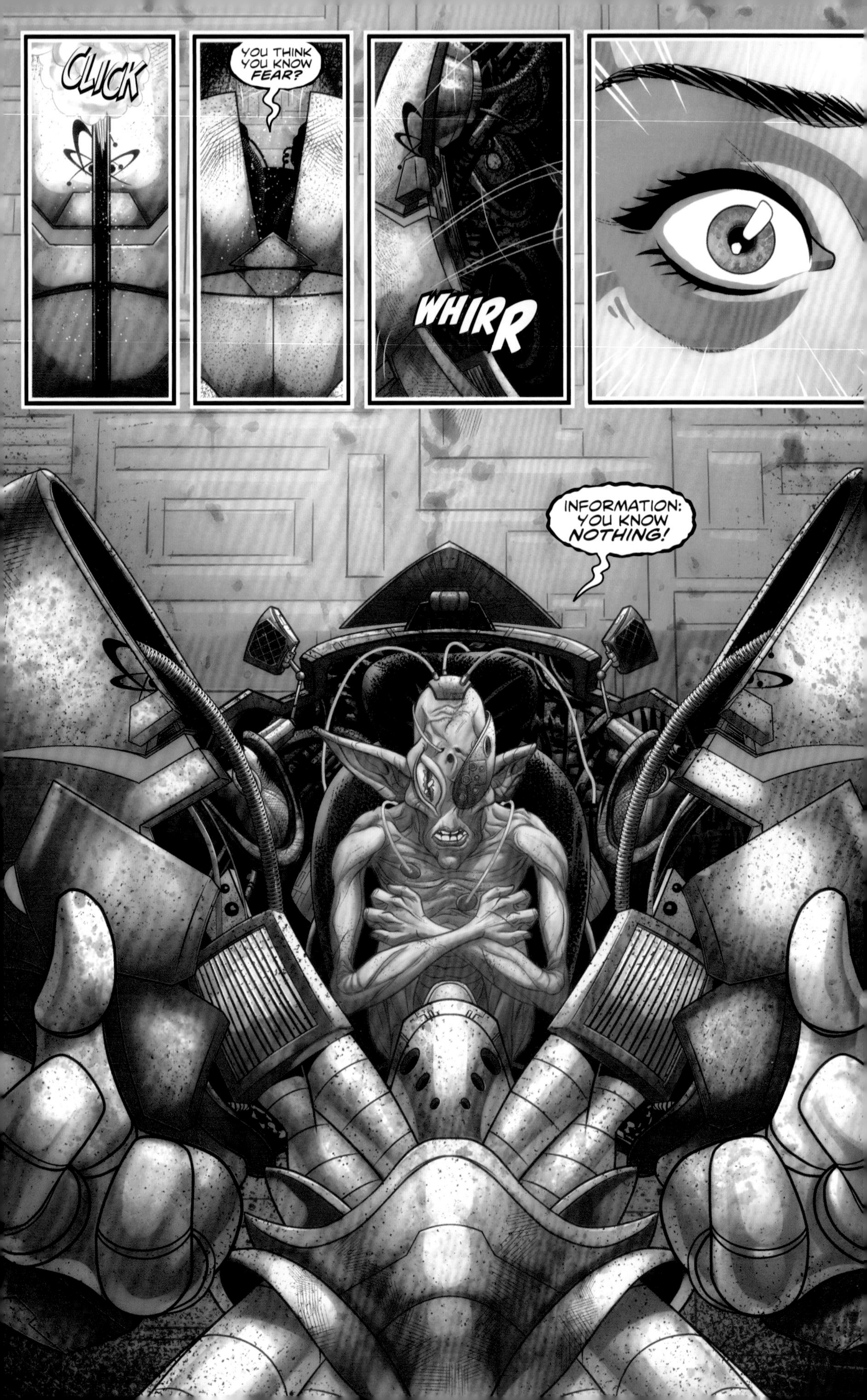
CLICK
YOU THINK YOU KNOW FEAR?
WHIRR
INFORMATION: YOU KNOW NOTHING!

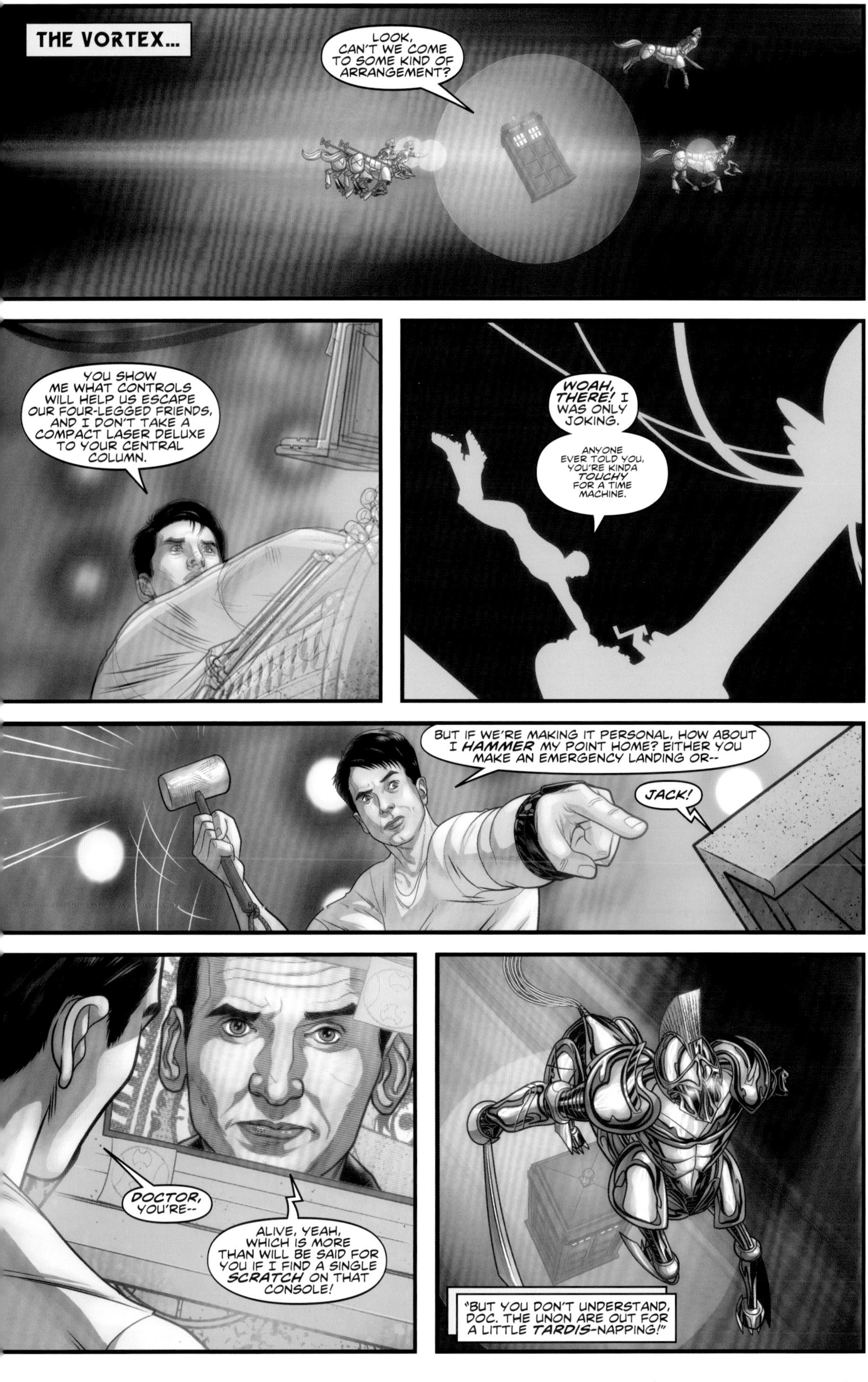
THE VORTEX...
LOOK, CAN'T WE COME TO SOME KIND OF ARRANGEMENT?
YOU SHOW ME WHAT CONTROLS WILL HELP US ESCAPE OUR FOUR-LEGGED FRIENDS, AND I DON'T TAKE A COMPACT LASER DELUXE TO YOUR CENTRAL COLUMN.
WOAH, THERE! I WAS ONLY JOKING.
ANYONE EVER TOLD YOU, YOU'RE KINDA TOUCHY FOR A TIME MACHINE.
BUT IF WE'RE MAKING IT PERSONAL, HOW ABOUT I HAMMER MY POINT HOME? EITHER YOU MAKE AN EMERGENCY LANDING OR--
JACK!
DOCTOR, YOU'RE--
ALIVE, YEAH, WHICH IS MORE THAN WILL BE SAID FOR YOU IF I FIND A SINGLE SCRATCH ON THAT CONSOLE!
"BUT YOU DON'T UNDERSTAND, DOC. THE UNON ARE OUT FOR A LITTLE TARDIS-NAPPING!"

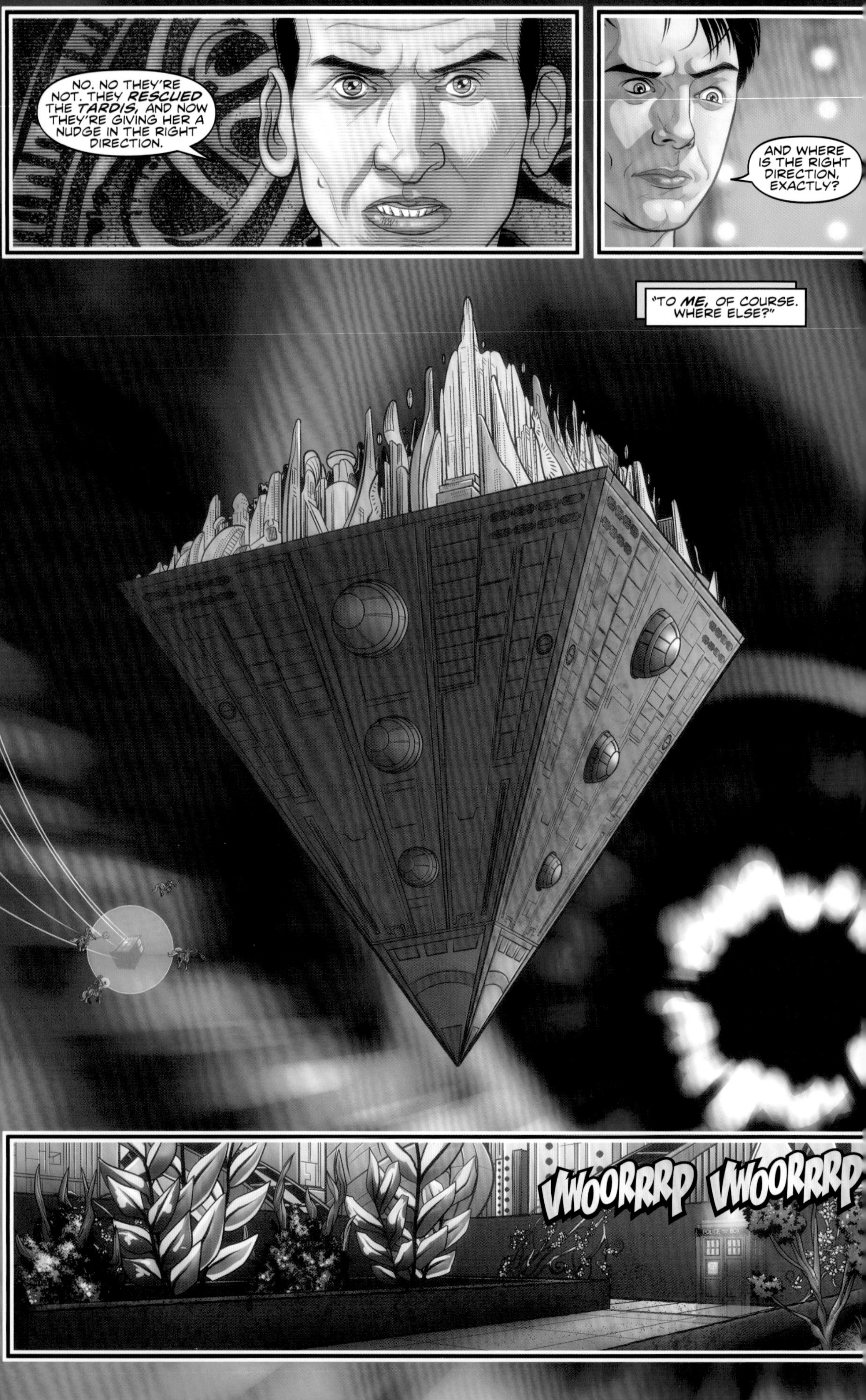
NO. NO THEY'RE NOT. THEY RESCUED THE TARDIS, AND NOW THEY'RE GIVING HER A NUDGE IN THE RIGHT DIRECTION.
AND WHERE IS THE RIGHT DIRECTION, EXACTLY?
"TO ME, OF COURSE. WHERE ELSE?"
VWOORRRP VWOORRRP
POLICE BOX

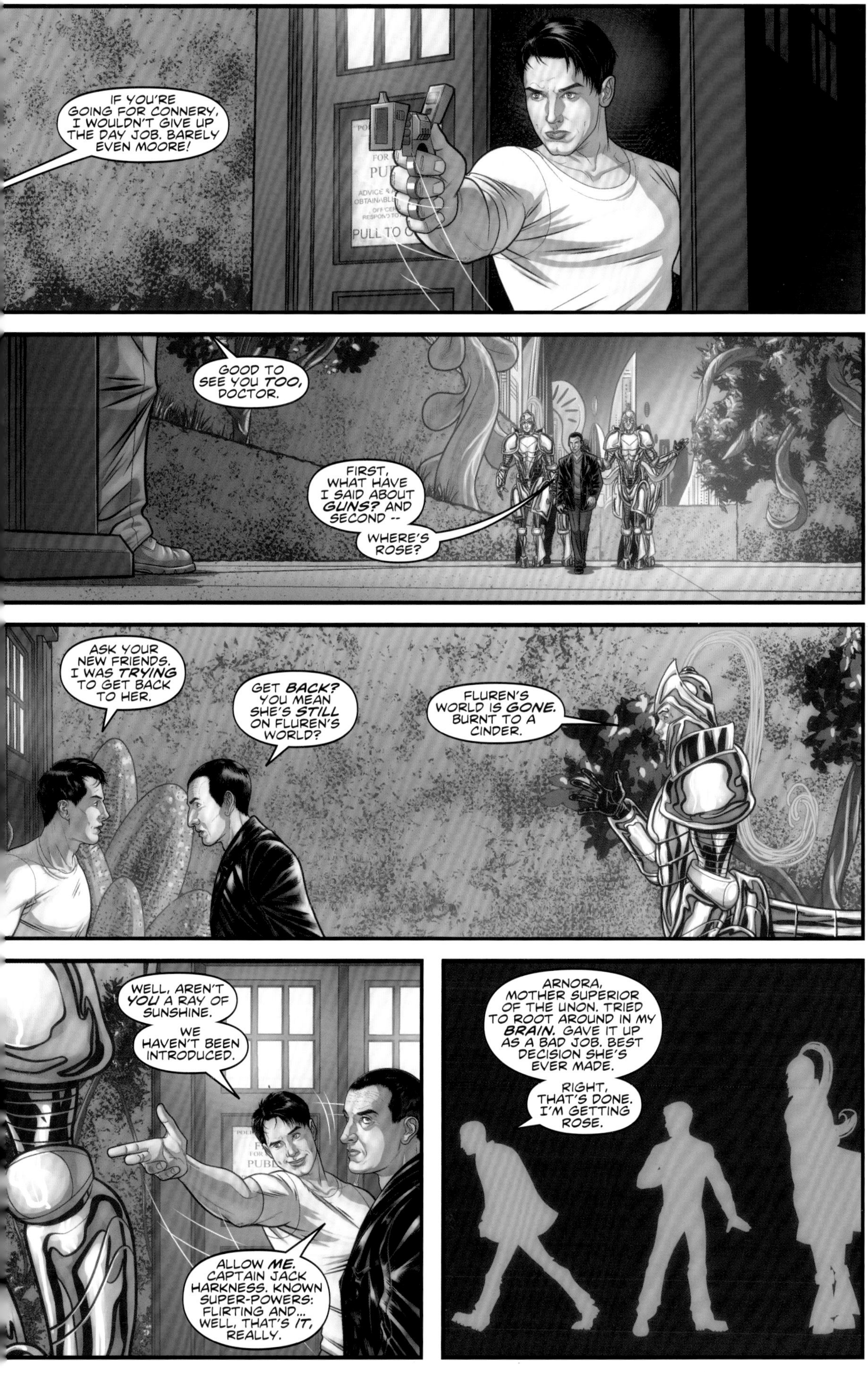

IF YOU'RE GOING FOR CONNERY, I WOULDN'T GIVE UP THE DAY JOB. BARELY EVEN MOORE!
GOOD TO SEE YOU TOO, DOCTOR.
FIRST, WHAT HAVE I SAID ABOUT GUNS? AND SECOND --
WHERE'S ROSE?
ASK YOUR NEW FRIENDS. I WAS TRYING TO GET BACK TO HER.
GET BACK? YOU MEAN SHE'S STILL ON FLUREN'S WORLD?
FLUREN'S WORLD IS GONE. BURNT TO A CINDER.
WELL, AREN'T YOU A RAY OF SUNSHINE.
WE HAVEN'T BEEN INTRODUCED.
ALLOW ME. CAPTAIN JACK HARKNESS. KNOWN SUPER-POWERS: FLIRTING AND... WELL, THAT'S IT, REALLY.
ARNORA, MOTHER SUPERIOR OF THE UNON. TRIED TO ROOT AROUND IN MY BRAIN. GAVE IT UP AS A BAD JOB. BEST DECISION SHE'S EVER MADE.
RIGHT, THAT'S DONE. I'M GETTING ROSE.

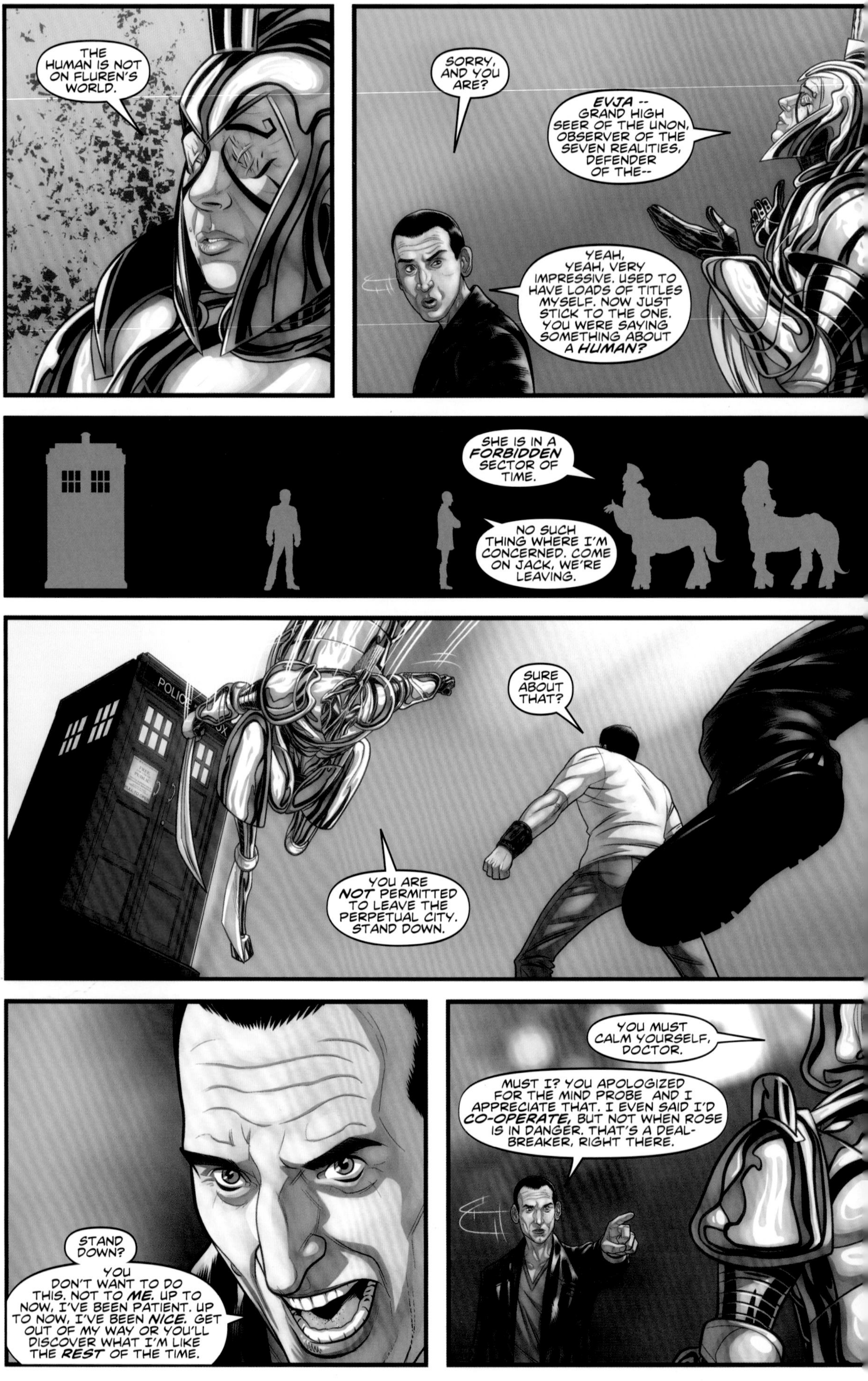
THE HUMAN IS NOT ON FLUREN'S WORLD.
SORRY, AND YOU ARE?
EVJA -- GRAND HIGH SEER OF THE UNON, OBSERVER OF THE SEVEN REALITIES, DEFENDER OF THE--
YEAH, YEAH, VERY IMPRESSIVE. USED TO HAVE LOADS OF TITLES MYSELF. NOW JUST STICK TO THE ONE. YOU WERE SAYING SOMETHING ABOUT A HUMAN?
SHE IS IN A FORBIDDEN SECTOR OF TIME.
NO SUCH THING WHERE I'M CONCERNED. COME ON JACK, WE'RE LEAVING.
POLICE BOX
SURE ABOUT THAT?
YOU ARE NOT PERMITTED TO LEAVE THE PERPETUAL CITY. STAND DOWN.
STAND DOWN?
YOU DON'T WANT TO DO THIS. NOT TO ME. UP TO NOW, I'VE BEEN PATIENT. UP TO NOW, I'VE BEEN NICE. GET OUT OF MY WAY OR YOU'LL DISCOVER WHAT I'M LIKE THE REST OF THE TIME.
YOU MUST CALM YOURSELF, DOCTOR.
MUST I? YOU APOLOGIZED FOR THE MIND PROBE AND I APPRECIATE THAT. I EVEN SAID I'D CO-OPERATE, BUT NOT WHEN ROSE IS IN DANGER. THAT'S A DEAL-BREAKER, RIGHT THERE.

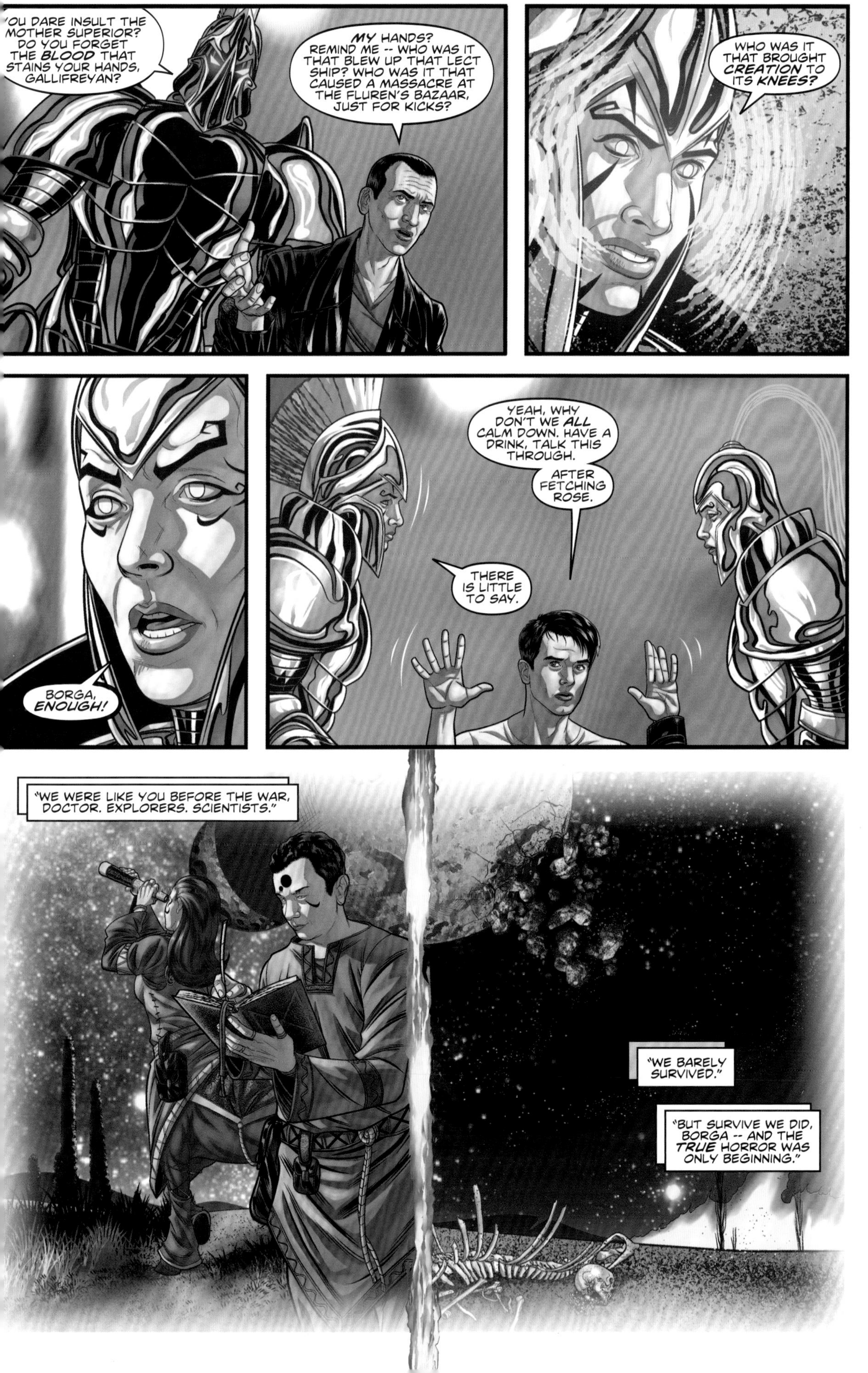
YOU DARE INSULT THE MOTHER SUPERIOR? DO YOU FORGET THE BLOOD THAT STAINS YOUR HANDS, GALLIFREYAN?
MY HANDS? REMIND ME -- WHO WAS IT THAT BLEW UP THAT LECT SHIP? WHO WAS IT THAT CAUSED A MASSACRE AT THE FLUREN'S BAZAAR, JUST FOR KICKS?
WHO WAS IT THAT BROUGHT CREATION TO ITS KNEES?
BORGA, ENOUGH!
YEAH, WHY DON'T WE ALL CALM DOWN. HAVE A DRINK, TALK THIS THROUGH.
AFTER FETCHING ROSE.
THERE IS LITTLE TO SAY.
"WE WERE LIKE YOU BEFORE THE WAR, DOCTOR. EXPLORERS. SCIENTISTS."
"WE BARELY SURVIVED."
"BUT SURVIVE WE DID, BORGA -- AND THE TRUE HORROR WAS ONLY BEGINNING."

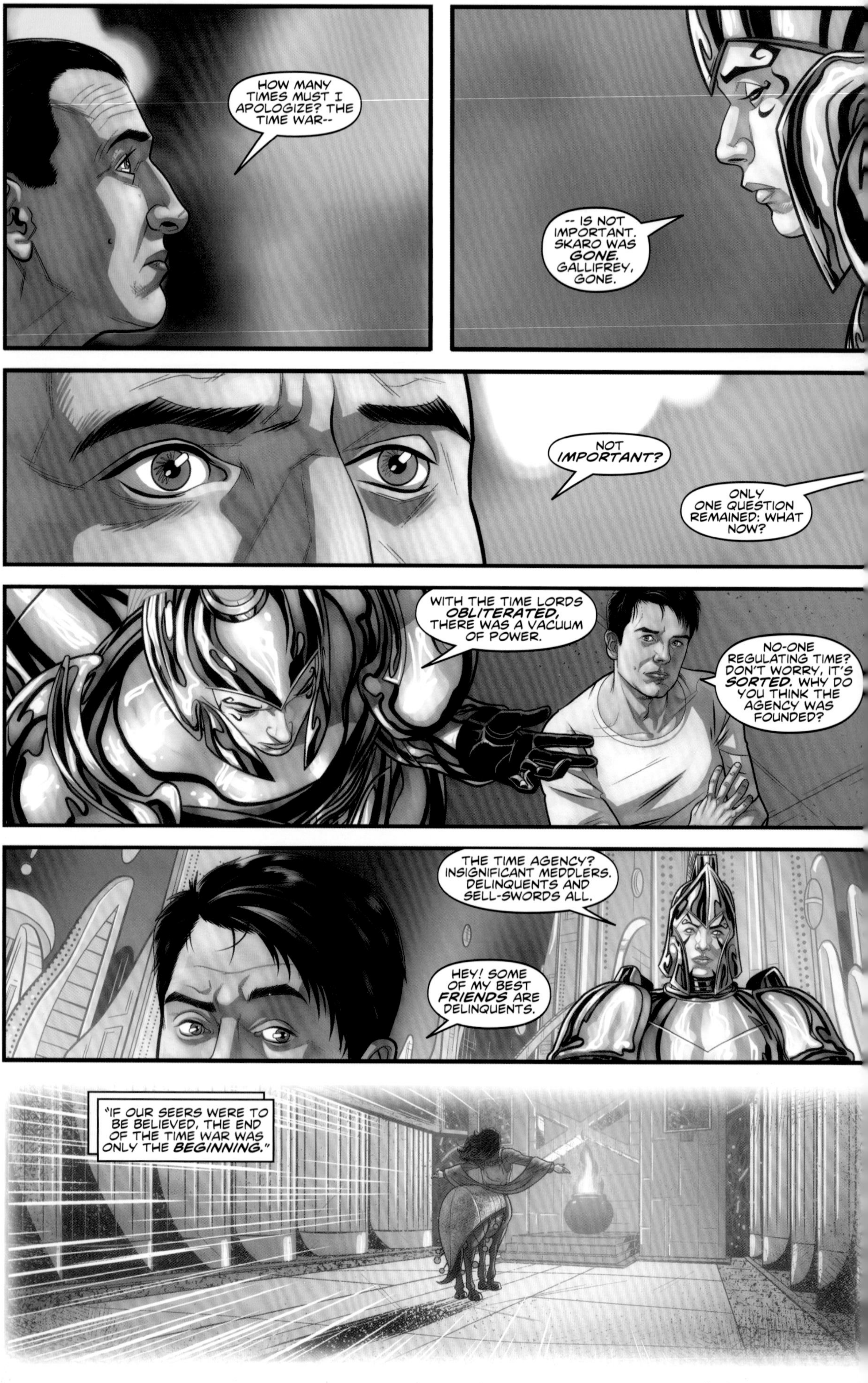
HOW MANY TIMES MUST I APOLOGIZE? THE TIME WAR--
-- IS NOT IMPORTANT. SKARO WAS GONE. GALLIFREY, GONE.
NOT IMPORTANT?
ONLY ONE QUESTION REMAINED: WHAT NOW?
WITH THE TIME LORDS OBLITERATED, THERE WAS A VACUUM OF POWER.
NO-ONE REGULATING TIME? DON'T WORRY, IT'S SORTED. WHY DO YOU THINK THE AGENCY WAS FOUNDED?
THE TIME AGENCY? INSIGNIFICANT MEDDLERS. DELINQUENTS AND SELL-SWORDS ALL.
HEY! SOME OF MY BEST FRIENDS ARE DELINQUENTS.
"IF OUR SEERS WERE TO BE BELIEVED, THE END OF THE TIME WAR WAS ONLY THE BEGINNING."

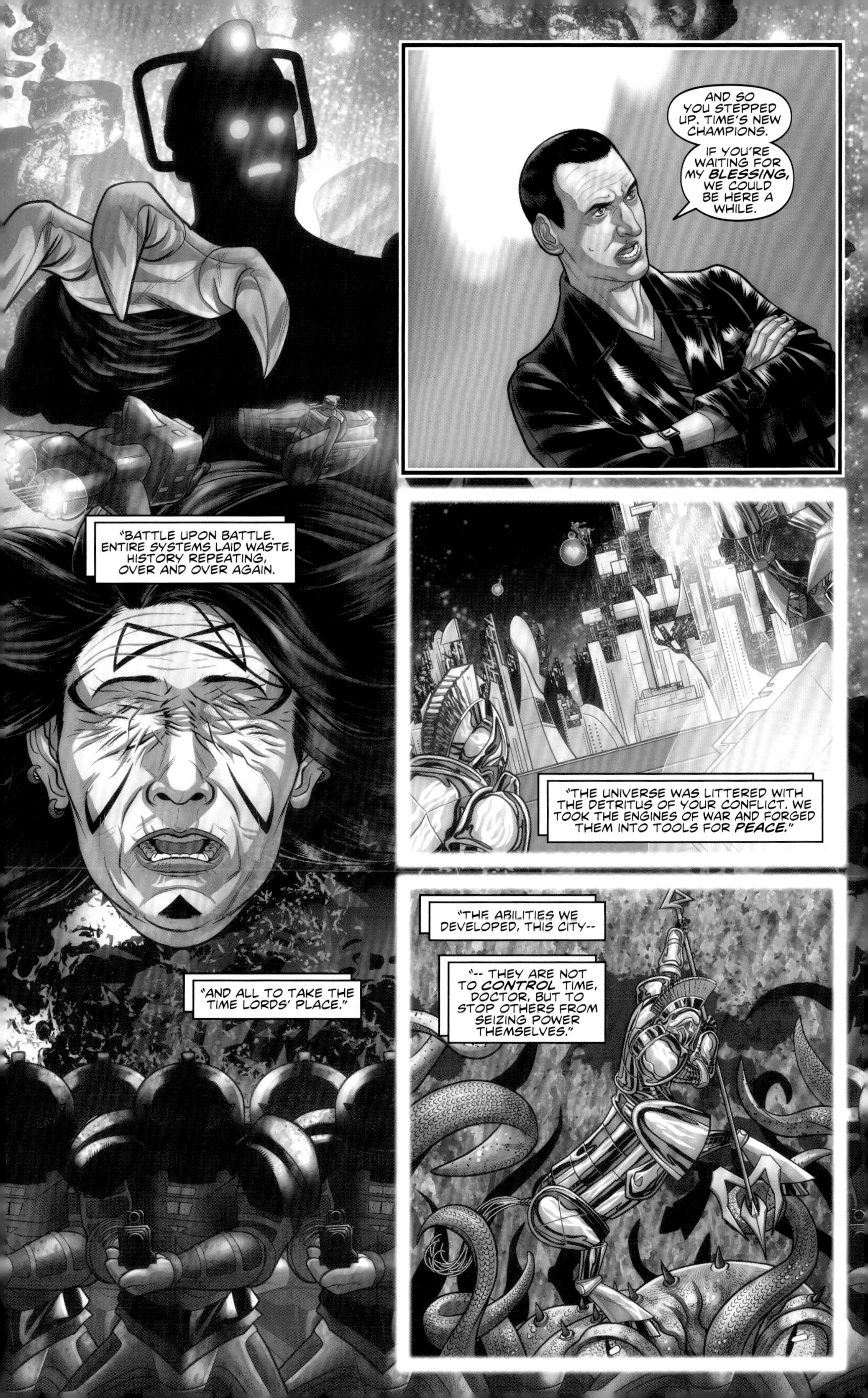
AND SO YOU STEPPED UP. TIME'S NEW CHAMPIONS.
IF YOU'RE WAITING FOR MY BLESSING, WE COULD BE HERE A WHILE.
"BATTLE UPON BATTLE. ENTIRE SYSTEMS LAID WASTE. HISTORY REPEATING, OVER AND OVER AGAIN.
"THE UNIVERSE WAS LITTERED WITH THE DETRITUS OF YOUR CONFLICT. WE TOOK THE ENGINES OF WAR AND FORGED THEM INTO TOOLS FOR PEACE."
"AND ALL TO TAKE THE TIME LORDS' PLACE."
"THE ABILITIES WE DEVELOPED, THIS CITY--
"-- THEY ARE NOT TO CONTROL TIME, DOCTOR, BUT TO STOP OTHERS FROM SEIZING POWER THEMSELVES."

OTHERS LIKE THE LECT?

IT WOULD EXPLAIN THE TIME DISTORTIONS ON THEIR SHIP.

THE LECT ARE *SCUM!*

THAT'S AN *UGLY* WORD, BORGA. I'M NOT KEEN ON UGLY WORDS. UGLY *DEEDS* USUALLY COME NEXT.

WE DO NOT *FIGHT* YOU, DOCTOR. YOU ARE A *GOOD MAN.*

IS THAT RIGHT?

I SAW INSIDE YOUR MIND, DOCTOR. I SAW THE *SACRIFICE* YOU MADE. HOW IT ALL BUT BROKE YOU -- BUT THE UNIVERSE IS IN DESPERATE NEED OF GOOD MEN.

AND SO ARE WE.

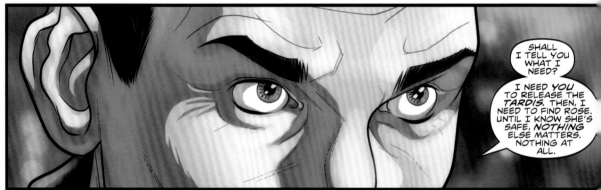

SHALL I TELL YOU WHAT I NEED?

I NEED *YOU* TO RELEASE THE *TARDIS.* THEN, I NEED TO FIND ROSE. UNTIL I KNOW SHE'S SAFE, *NOTHING* ELSE MATTERS. NOTHING AT ALL.

NOT EVEN TIME ITSELF?

...WHAT IS THIS?

A FRACTURE IN TIME. THE TIME WAR HAS LEFT *FISSURES* RUNNING THROUGH THE VERY FABRIC OF THE UNIVERSE. CHRONAL FAULT LINES.

THE PLANET IS *TRAXIS*, A CLASS-9 WORLD WITH A POPULATION OF 7.2 BILLION.

AND IT IS BEING TORN *APART*. A FAULT LINE HAS OPENED, THE PAST, PRESENT AND THE FUTURE CRASHING TOGETHER.

AND IF IT IS LEFT UNCHECKED...

THE FISSURE WILL SPREAD OUT FROM TRAXIS.

ACROSS THE ENTIRE SECTOR. TIME WILL UNRAVEL--

-- LEAVING A *NIGHTMARE* IN ITS WAKE.

A TEMPORAL STORM THAT WILL RAGE FOR MILLENNIA, MAYBE UNTIL THE END OF DAYS.

FORTUNATELY, WE HAVE A SOLUTION.

VZZZT

HANG ON --

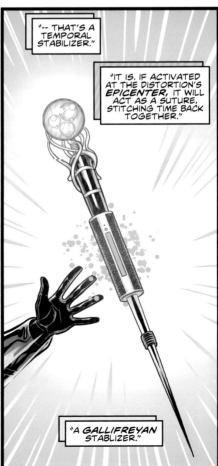

"-- THAT'S A TEMPORAL STABILIZER."

"IT IS. IF ACTIVATED AT THE DISTORTION'S *EPICENTER*, IT WILL ACT AS A SUTURE, STITCHING TIME BACK TOGETHER."

"A *GALLIFREYAN* STABILIZER."

THEN WHO BETTER THAN A TIME LORD TO OPERATE IT?

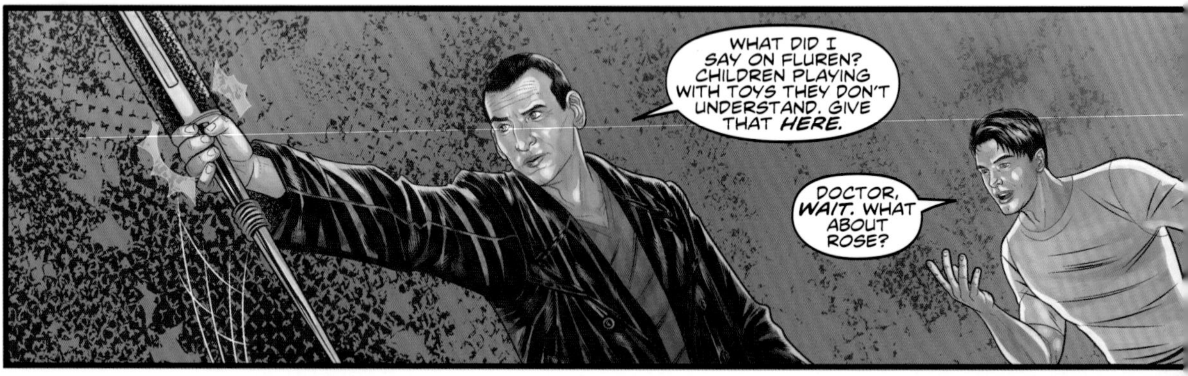
WHAT DID I SAY ON FLUREN? CHILDREN PLAYING WITH TOYS THEY DON'T UNDERSTAND. GIVE THAT HERE.
DOCTOR, WAIT. WHAT ABOUT ROSE?
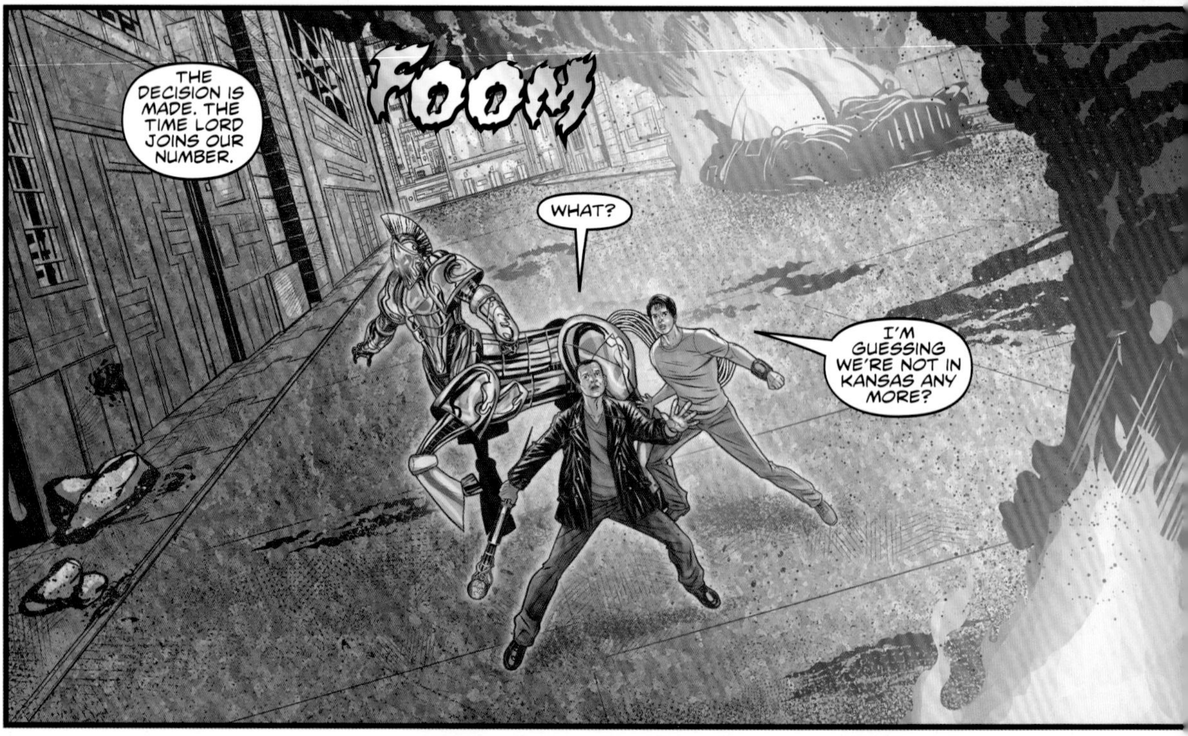
FOOM
THE DECISION IS MADE. THE TIME LORD JOINS OUR NUMBER.
WHAT?
I'M GUESSING WE'RE NOT IN KANSAS ANY MORE?
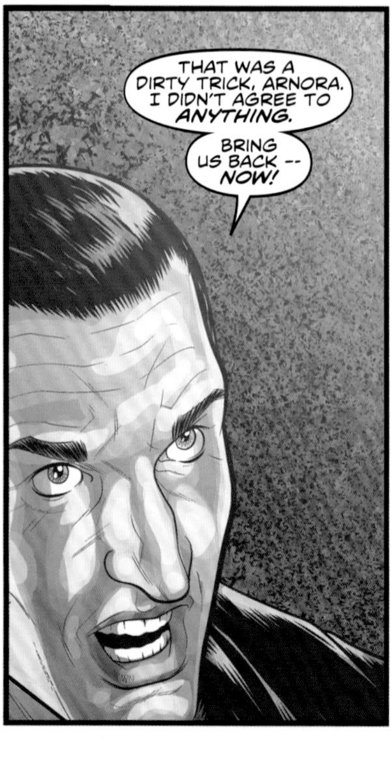
THAT WAS A DIRTY TRICK, ARNORA. I DIDN'T AGREE TO ANYTHING.
BRING US BACK -- NOW!
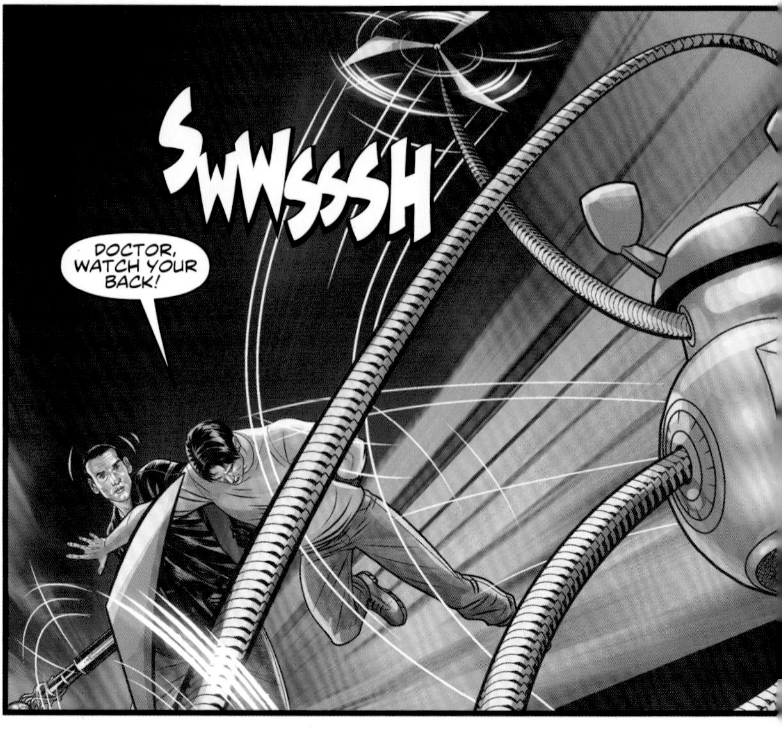
SWWSSSH
DOCTOR, WATCH YOUR BACK!

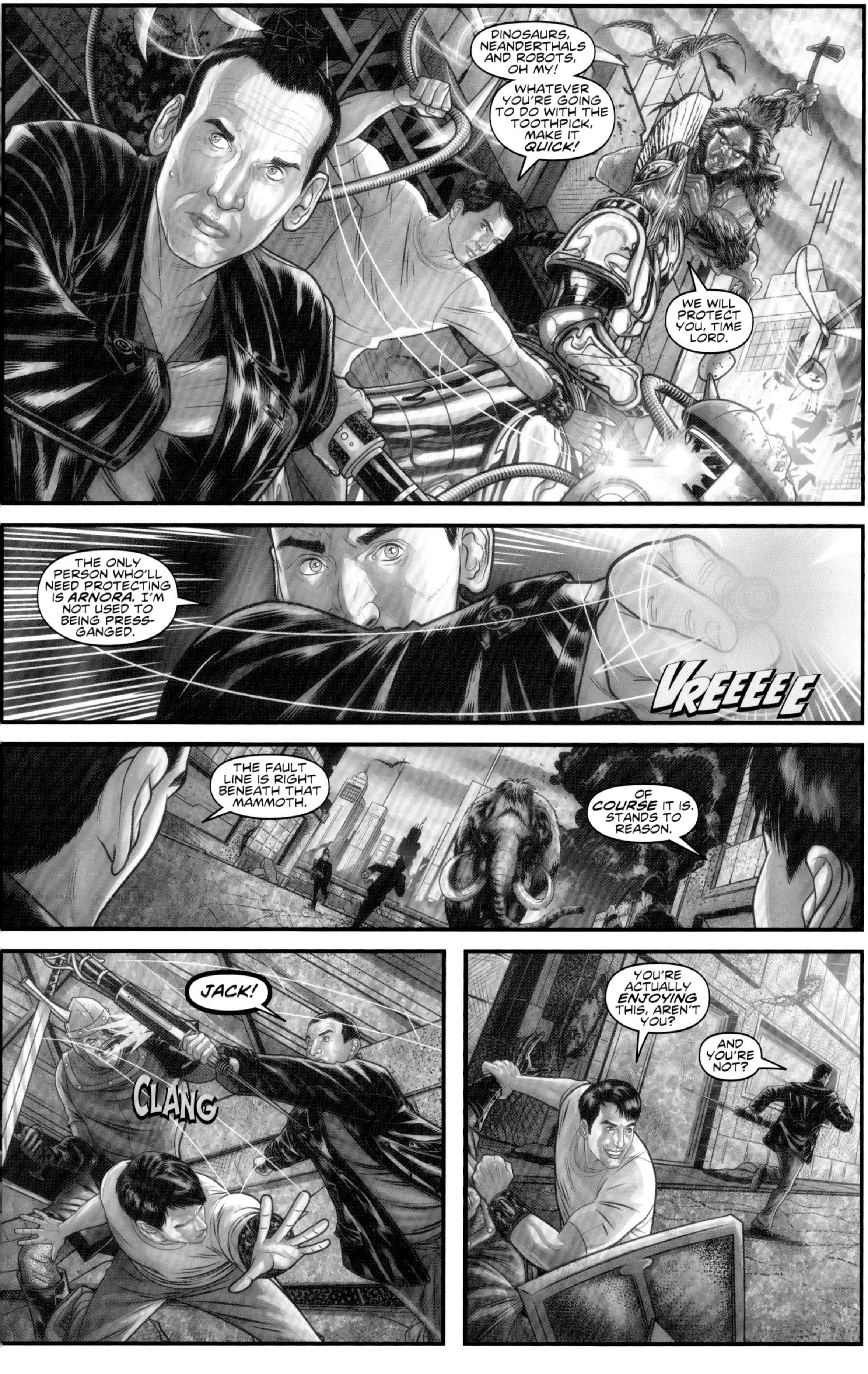
DINOSAURS, NEANDERTHALS AND ROBOTS, OH MY!
WHATEVER YOU'RE GOING TO DO WITH THE TOOTHPICK, MAKE IT QUICK!
WE WILL PROTECT YOU, TIME LORD.
THE ONLY PERSON WHO'LL NEED PROTECTING IS ARNORA. I'M NOT USED TO BEING PRESS-GANGED.
VREEEEEE
THE FAULT LINE IS RIGHT BENEATH THAT MAMMOTH.
OF COURSE IT IS. STANDS TO REASON.
JACK!
CLANG
YOU'RE ACTUALLY ENJOYING THIS, AREN'T YOU?
AND YOU'RE NOT?

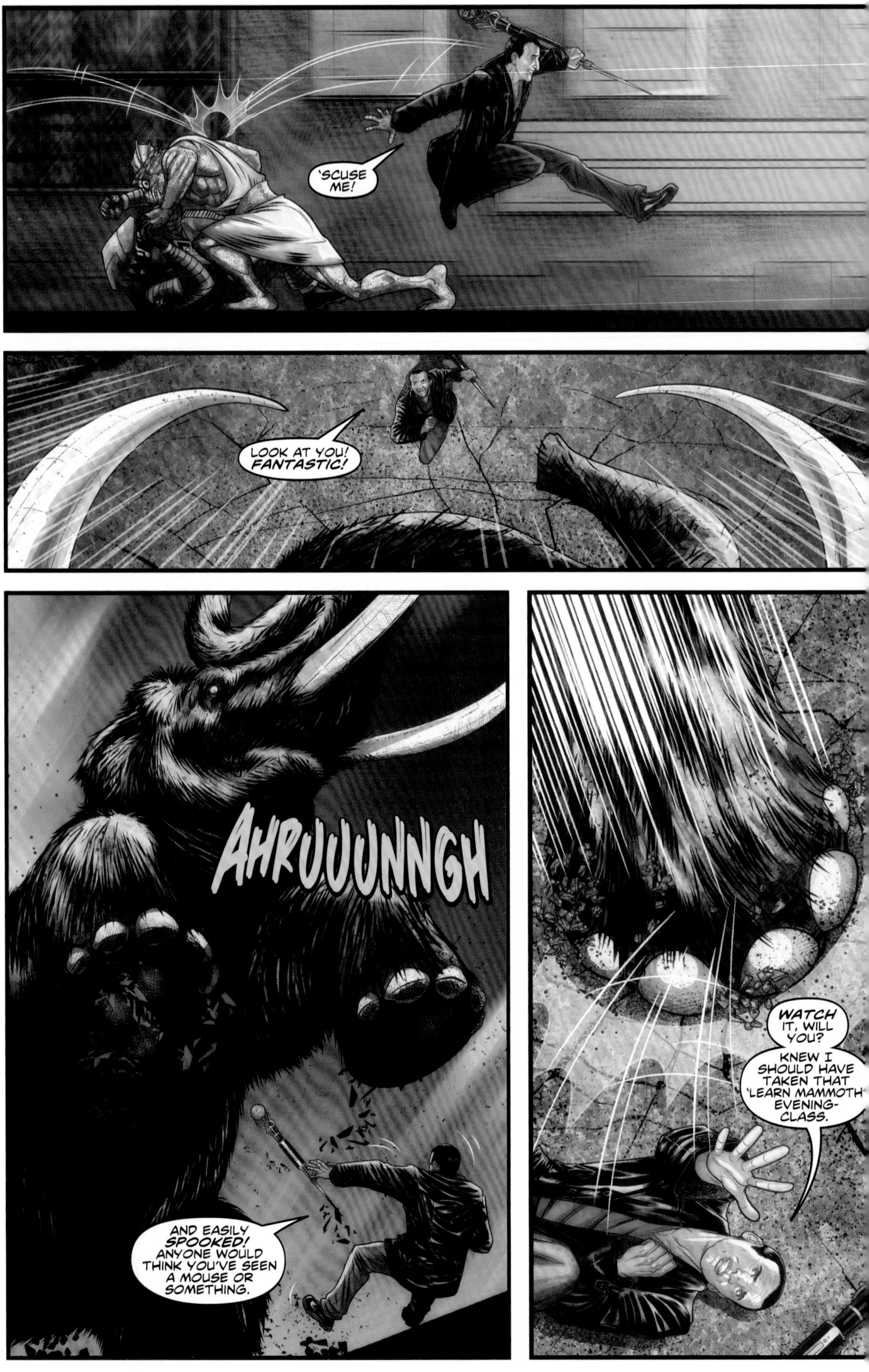
'SCUSE ME!
LOOK AT YOU! FANTASTIC!
AHRUUUNNGH
AND EASILY SPOOKED! ANYONE WOULD THINK YOU'VE SEEN A MOUSE OR SOMETHING.
WATCH IT, WILL YOU?
KNEW I SHOULD HAVE TAKEN THAT 'LEARN MAMMOTH' EVENING-CLASS.

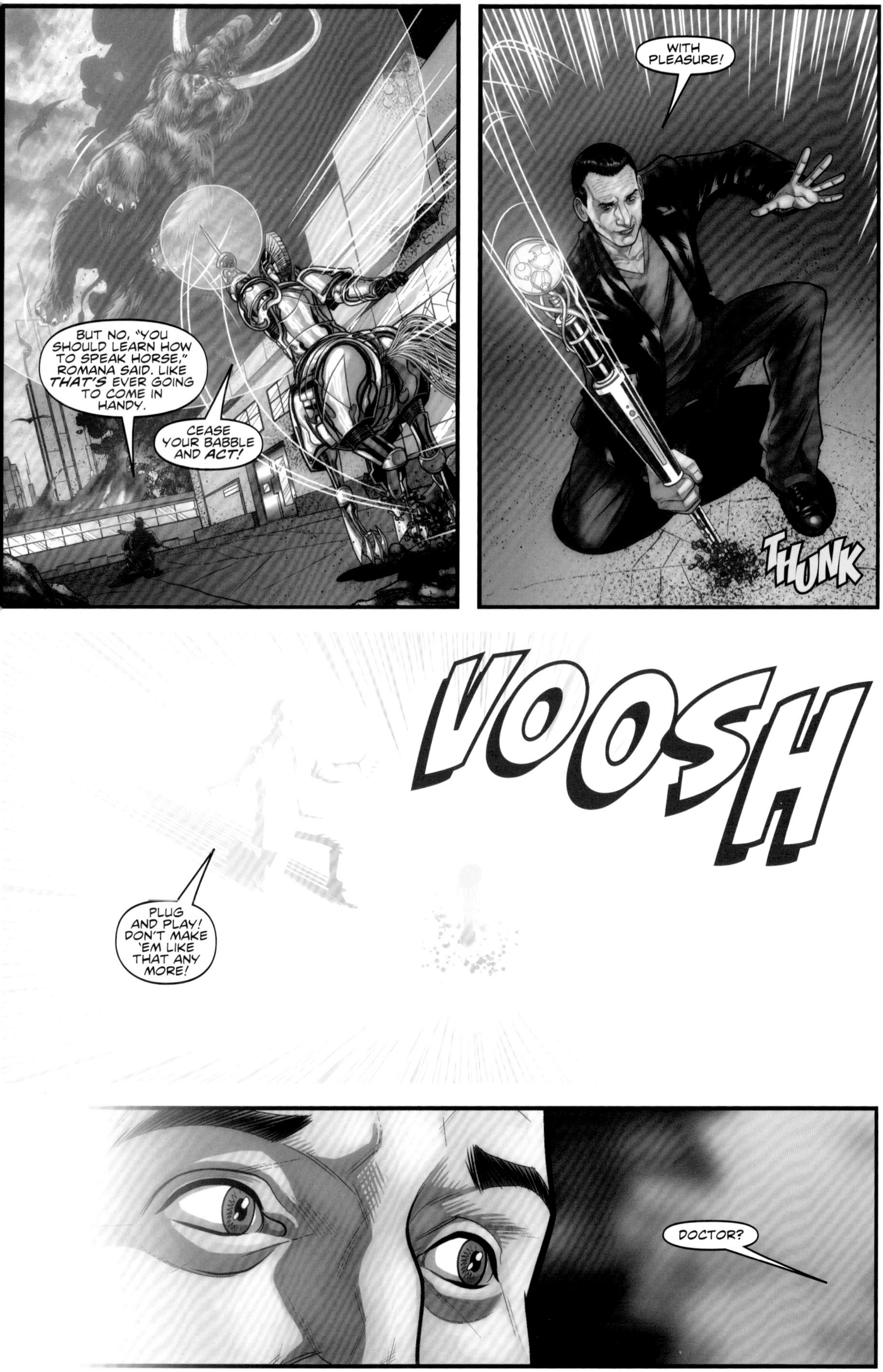
BUT NO, "YOU SHOULD LEARN HOW TO SPEAK HORSE," ROMANA SAID. LIKE *THAT'S* EVER GOING TO COME IN HANDY.
CEASE YOUR BABBLE AND *ACT!*
WITH PLEASURE!
THUNK
VOOSH
PLUG AND PLAY! DON'T MAKE 'EM LIKE THAT ANY MORE!
DOCTOR?

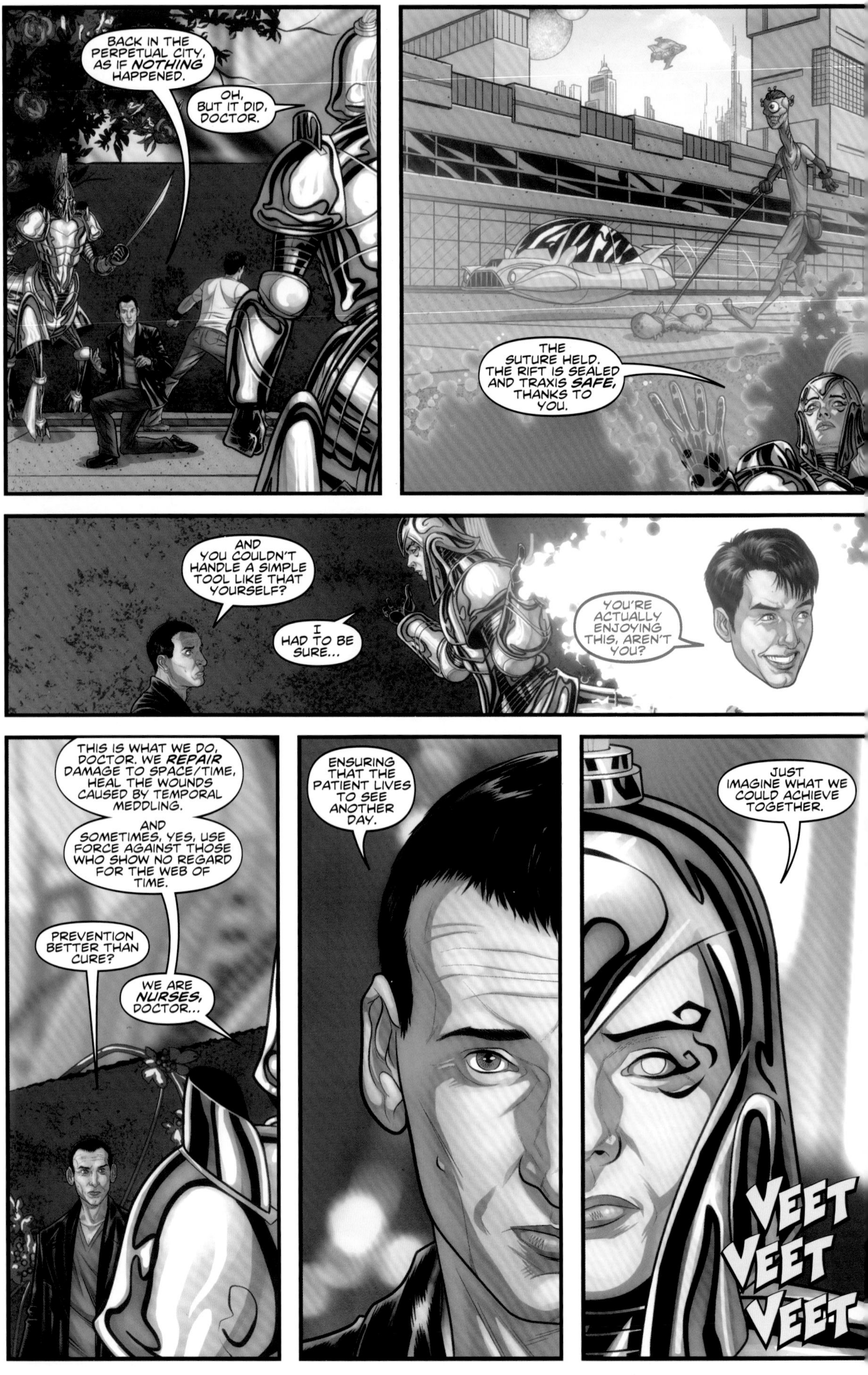
BACK IN THE PERPETUAL CITY, AS IF NOTHING HAPPENED.
OH, BUT IT DID, DOCTOR.
THE SUTURE HELD. THE RIFT IS SEALED AND TRAXIS SAFE, THANKS TO YOU.
AND YOU COULDN'T HANDLE A SIMPLE TOOL LIKE THAT YOURSELF?
I HAD TO BE SURE...
YOU'RE ACTUALLY ENJOYING THIS, AREN'T YOU?
THIS IS WHAT WE DO, DOCTOR. WE REPAIR DAMAGE TO SPACE/TIME, HEAL THE WOUNDS CAUSED BY TEMPORAL MEDDLING.
AND SOMETIMES, YES, USE FORCE AGAINST THOSE WHO SHOW NO REGARD FOR THE WEB OF TIME.
PREVENTION BETTER THAN CURE?
WE ARE NURSES, DOCTOR...
ENSURING THAT THE PATIENT LIVES TO SEE ANOTHER DAY.
JUST IMAGINE WHAT WE COULD ACHIEVE TOGETHER.
VEET VEET VEET

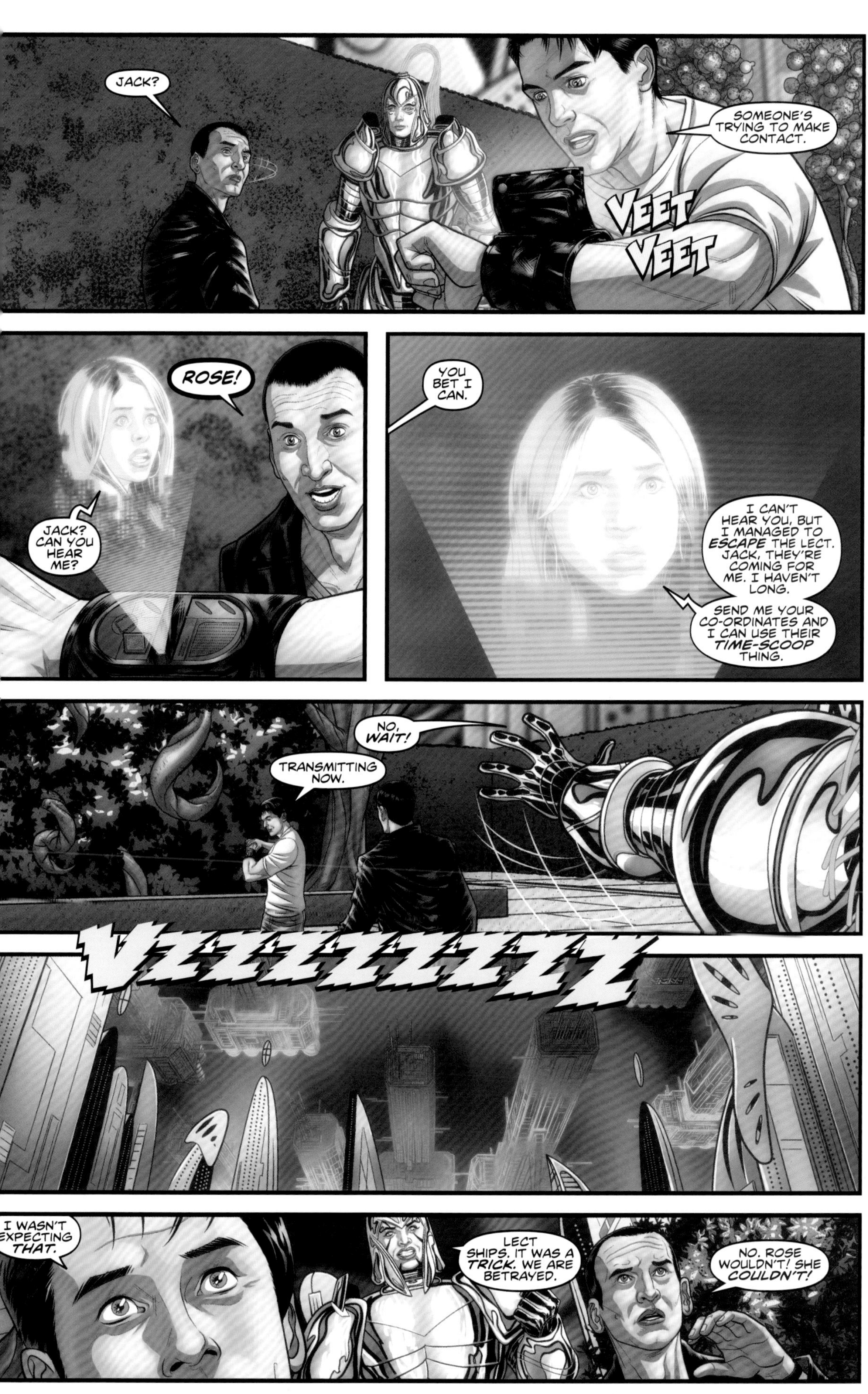
JACK?
SOMEONE'S TRYING TO MAKE CONTACT.
VEET VEET
ROSE!
JACK? CAN YOU HEAR ME?
YOU BET I CAN.
I CAN'T HEAR YOU, BUT I MANAGED TO ESCAPE THE LECT. JACK, THEY'RE COMING FOR ME. I HAVEN'T LONG.
SEND ME YOUR CO-ORDINATES AND I CAN USE THEIR TIME-SCOOP THING.
TRANSMITTING NOW.
NO, WAIT!
VZZZZZZZZ
I WASN'T EXPECTING THAT.
LECT SHIPS. IT WAS A TRICK. WE ARE BETRAYED.
NO. ROSE WOULDN'T! SHE COULDN'T!

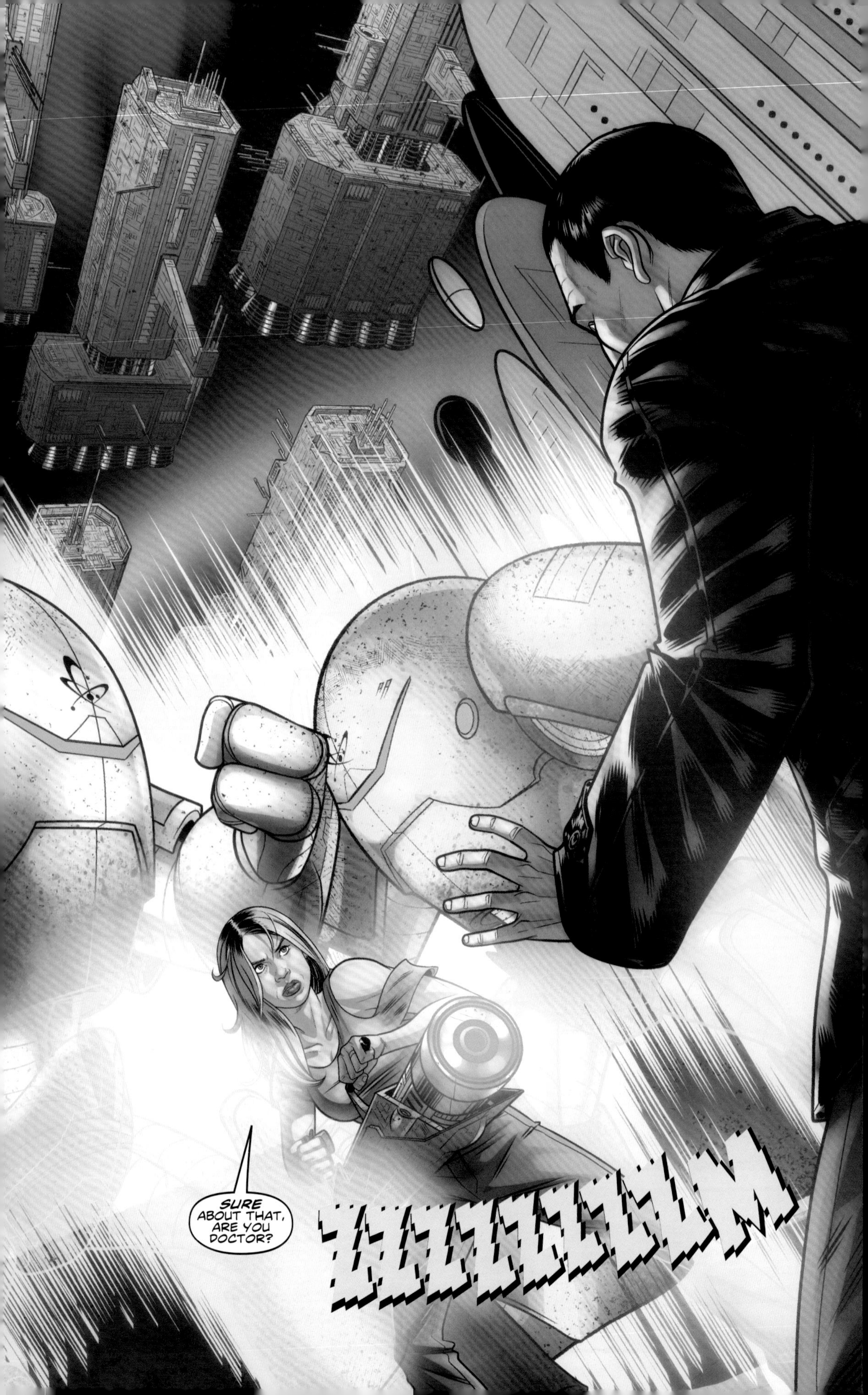
SURE ABOUT THAT, ARE YOU DOCTOR?
ZZZZZOOM

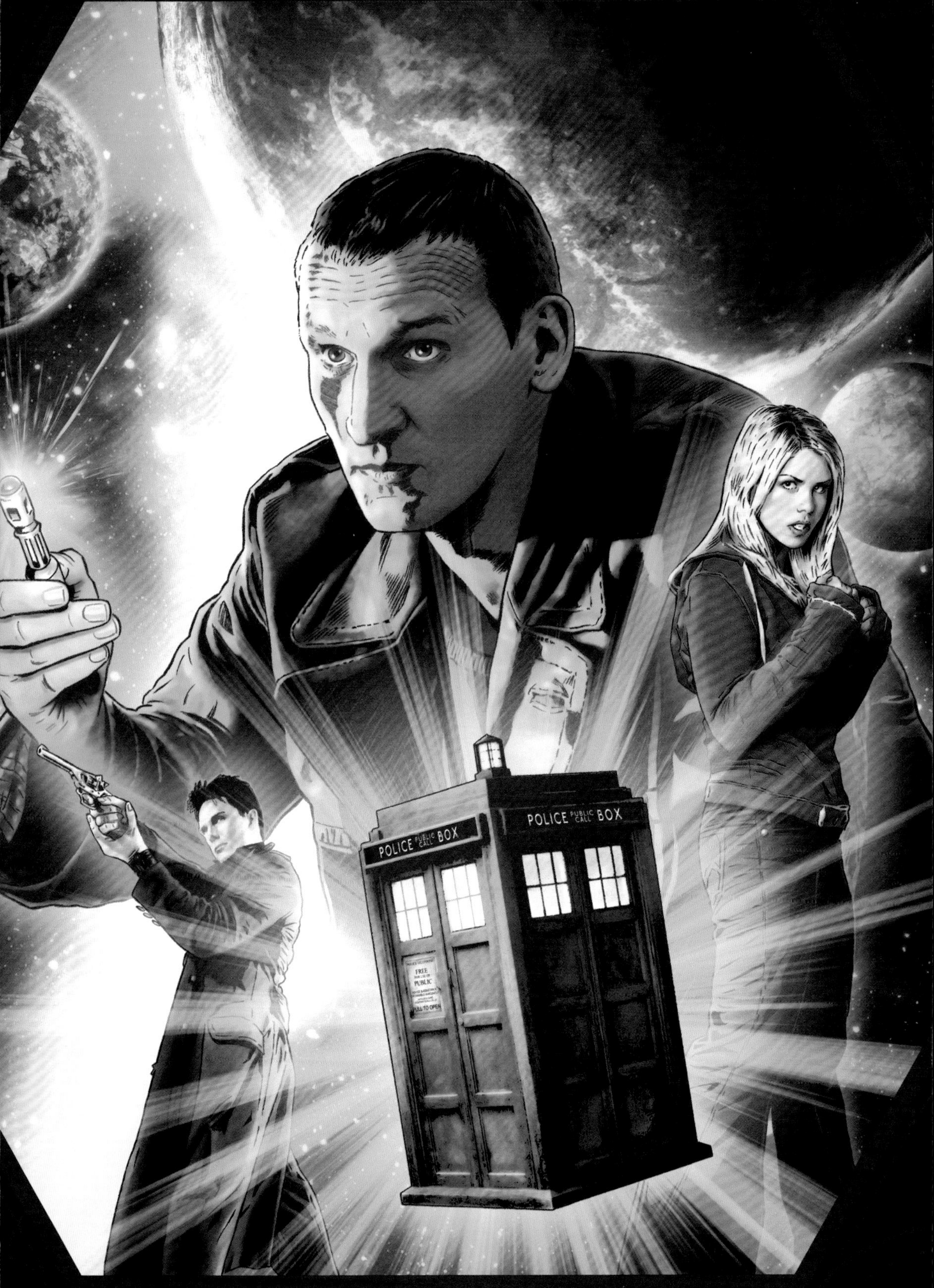
POLICE PUBLIC CALL BOX
POLICE PUBLIC CALL BOX

9D #5 Cover C: JOE CORRONEY

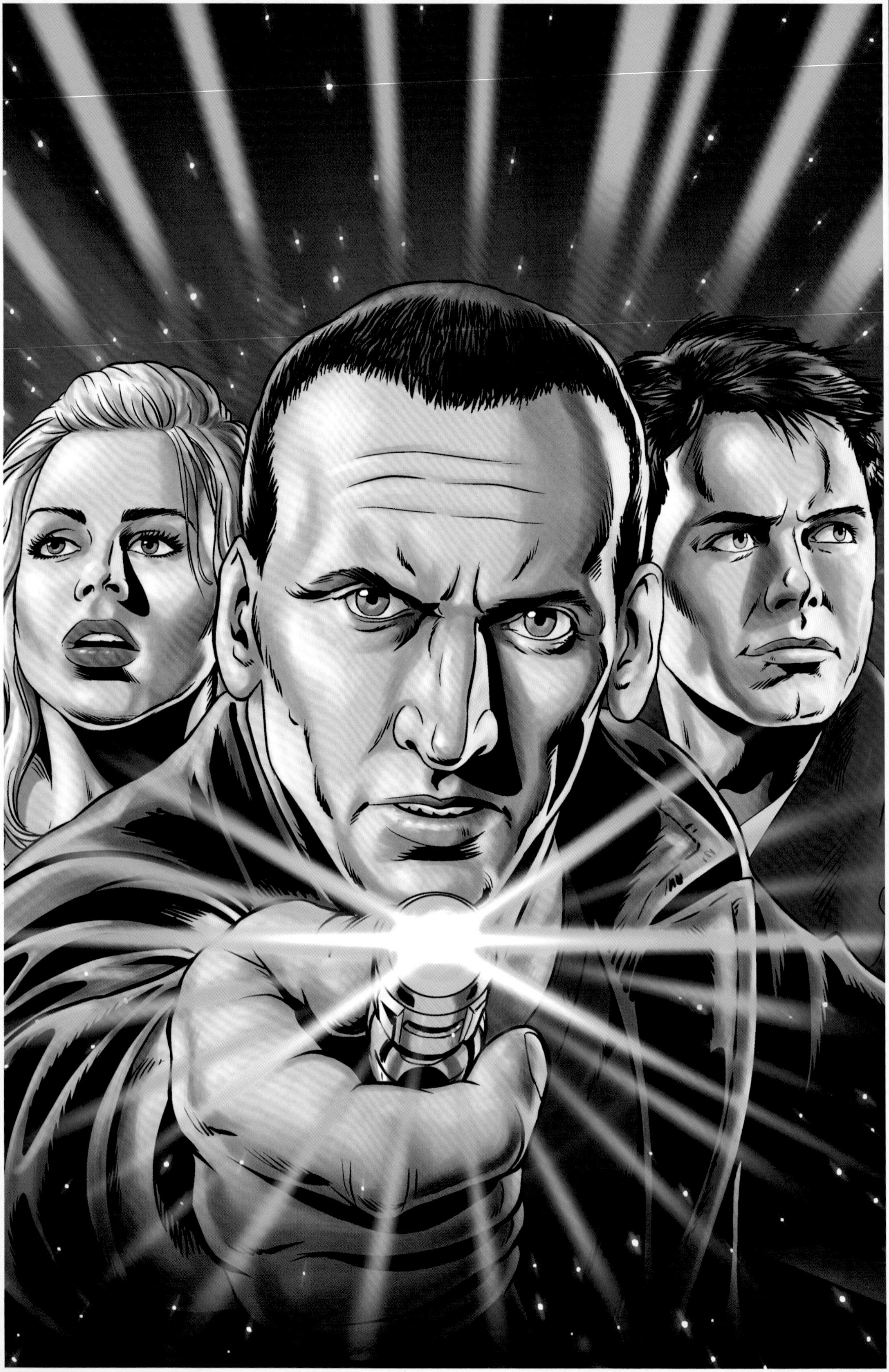

9D #5 Cover A: LEE SULLIVAN

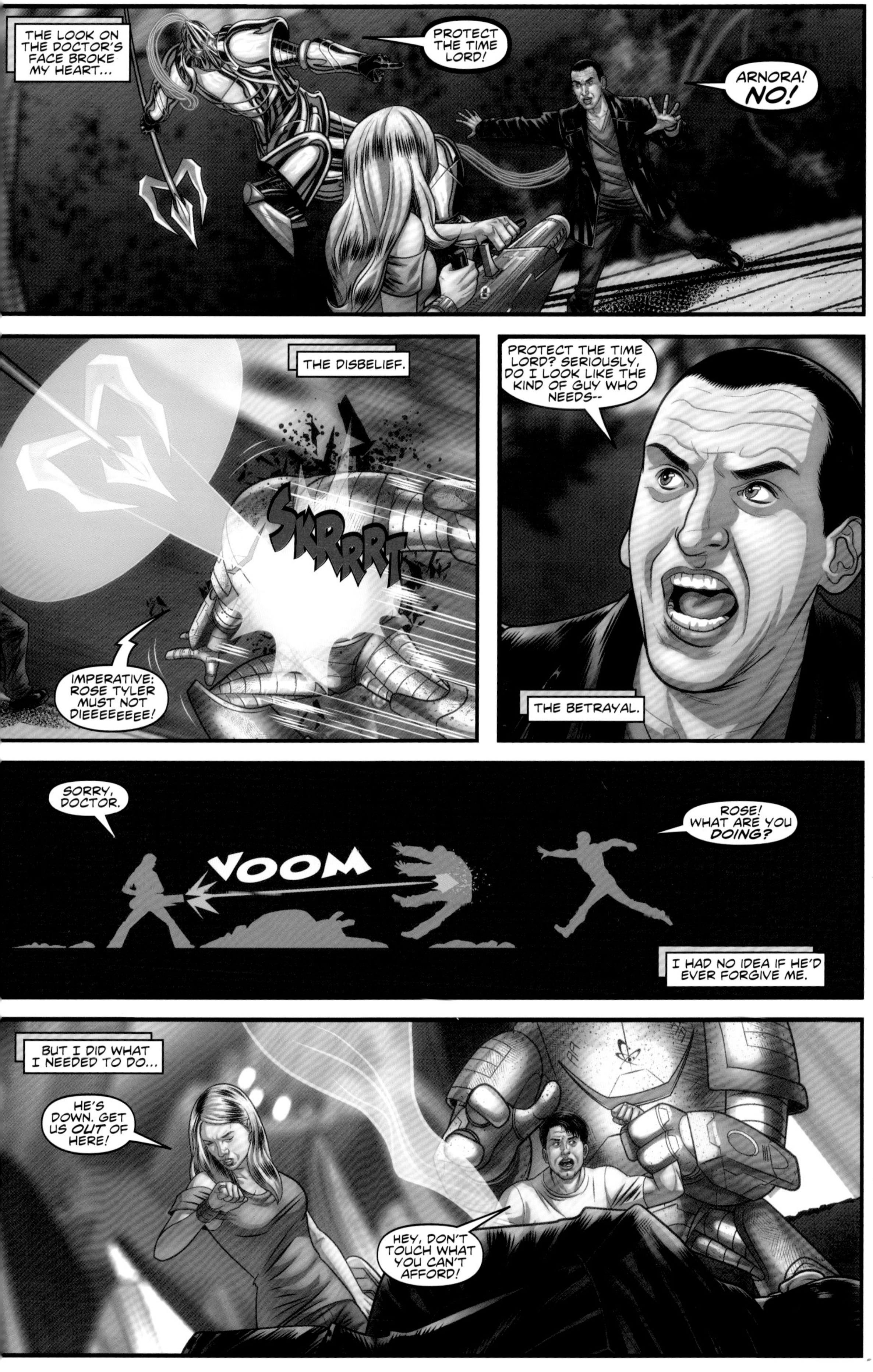
THE LOOK ON THE DOCTOR'S FACE BROKE MY HEART...
PROTECT THE TIME LORD!
ARNORA! NO!
THE DISBELIEF.
SKRRRT
IMPERATIVE: ROSE TYLER MUST NOT DIEEEEEEEE!
PROTECT THE TIME LORD? SERIOUSLY, DO I LOOK LIKE THE KIND OF GUY WHO NEEDS--
THE BETRAYAL.
SORRY, DOCTOR.
VOOM
ROSE! WHAT ARE YOU DOING?
I HAD NO IDEA IF HE'D EVER FORGIVE ME.
BUT I DID WHAT I NEEDED TO DO...
HE'S DOWN. GET US OUT OF HERE!
HEY, DON'T TOUCH WHAT YOU CAN'T AFFORD!

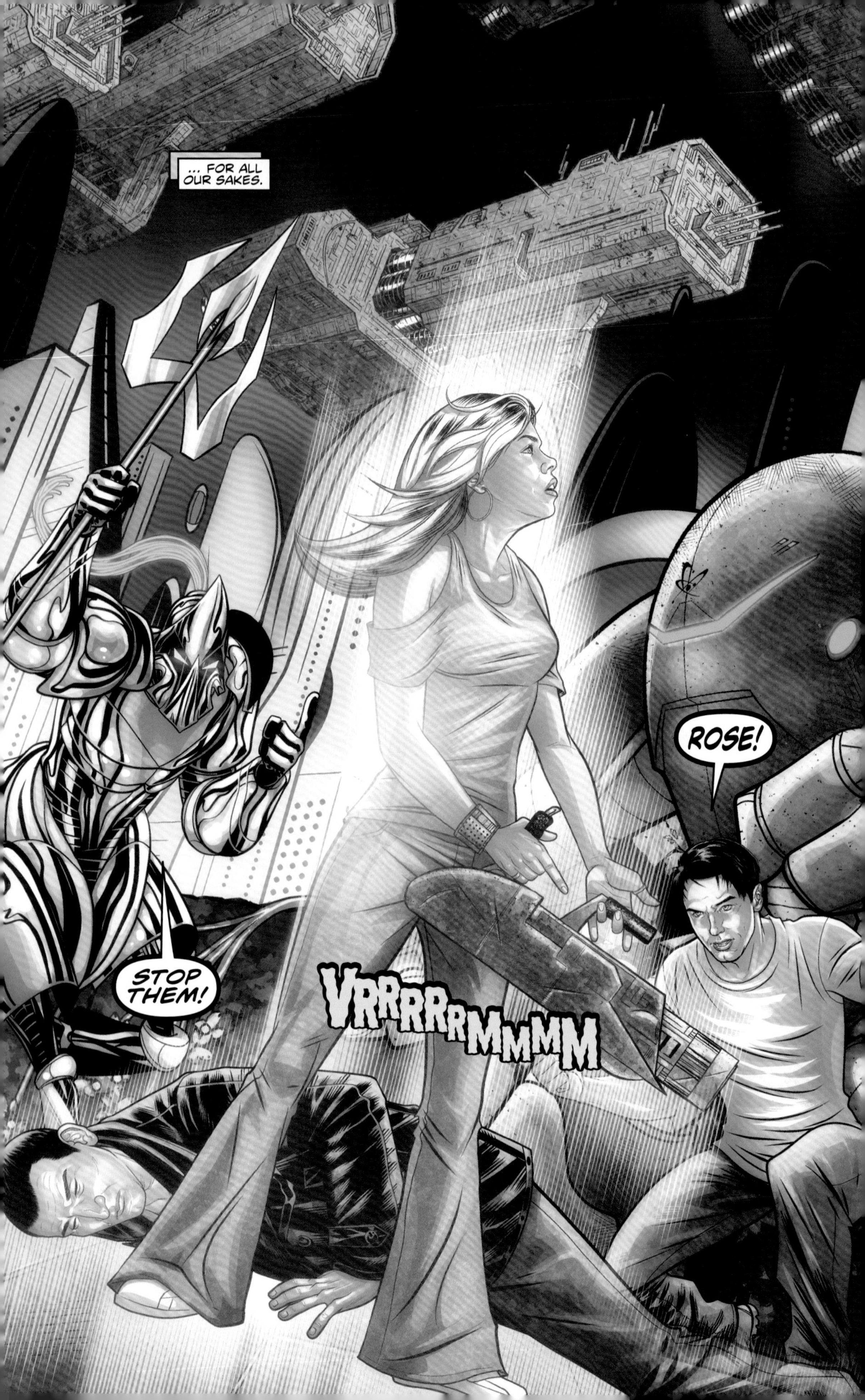
... FOR ALL OUR SAKES.
STOP THEM!
VRRRRRRMMMMM
ROSE!

RELEASE THE HUMAN!

KREEEE

WOAH! WATCH WHERE YOU'RE *SWINGING* THAT THING!

MOTHER SUPERIOR. LECT ARE MATERIALIZING ACROSS THE CITY. MORE THAN EVER BEFORE.

THIS IS YOUR FRIENDS' DOING!

HEY, DON'T BLAME ME. I JUST *MET* THEM.

SHHHHHK

"ALTHOUGH, THIS DOESN'T SEEM LIKE ROSE'S STYLE AT *ALL!*"

THOSE LECT MUST--

SKRRRRT

NNNNGH!

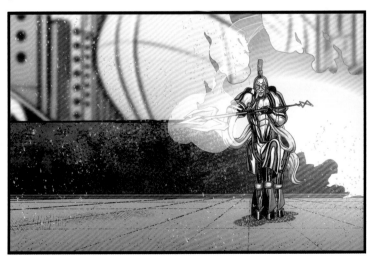

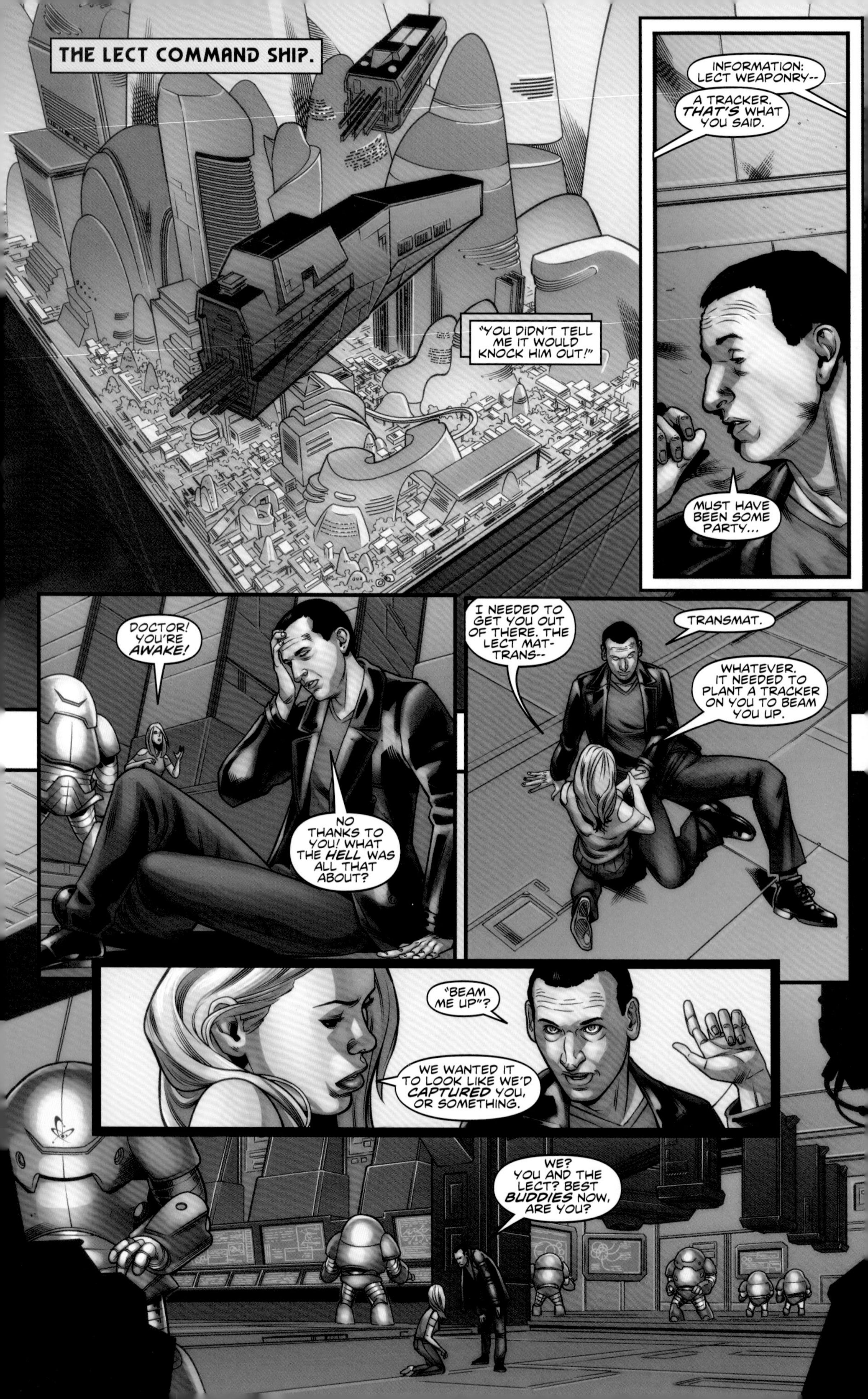
THE LECT COMMAND SHIP.
"YOU DIDN'T TELL ME IT WOULD KNOCK HIM OUT!"
INFORMATION: LECT WEAPONRY--
A TRACKER. THAT'S WHAT YOU SAID.
MUST HAVE BEEN SOME PARTY...
DOCTOR! YOU'RE AWAKE!
NO THANKS TO YOU! WHAT THE HELL WAS ALL THAT ABOUT?
I NEEDED TO GET YOU OUT OF THERE. THE LECT MAT-TRANS--
TRANSMAT.
WHATEVER. IT NEEDED TO PLANT A TRACKER ON YOU TO BEAM YOU UP.
"BEAM ME UP"?
WE WANTED IT TO LOOK LIKE WE'D CAPTURED YOU, OR SOMETHING.
WE? YOU AND THE LECT? BEST BUDDIES NOW, ARE YOU?

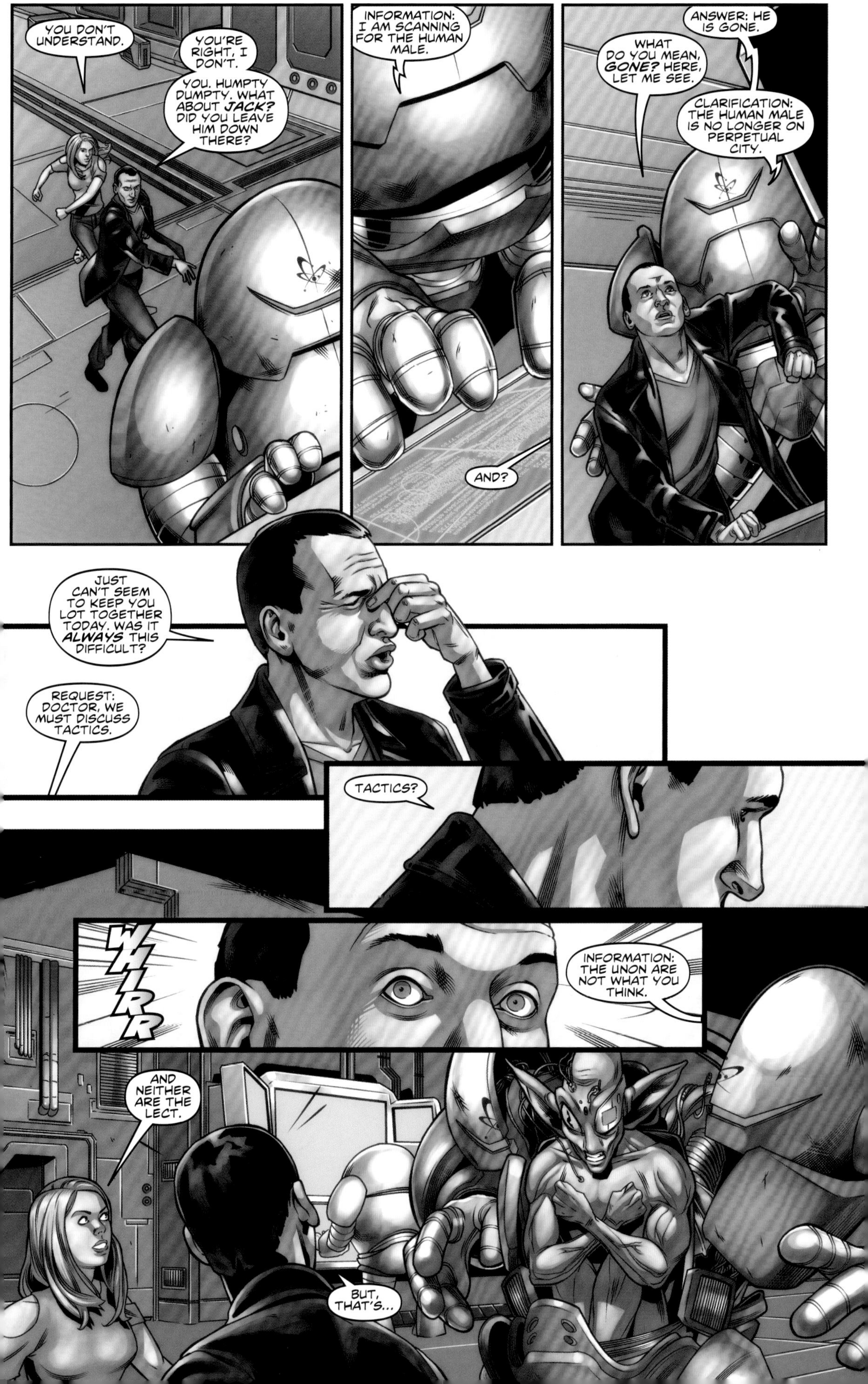
YOU DON'T UNDERSTAND.
YOU'RE RIGHT, I DON'T.
YOU. HUMPTY DUMPTY. WHAT ABOUT JACK? DID YOU LEAVE HIM DOWN THERE?
INFORMATION: I AM SCANNING FOR THE HUMAN MALE.
AND?
ANSWER: HE IS GONE.
WHAT DO YOU MEAN, GONE? HERE, LET ME SEE.
CLARIFICATION: THE HUMAN MALE IS NO LONGER ON PERPETUAL CITY.
JUST CAN'T SEEM TO KEEP YOU LOT TOGETHER TODAY. WAS IT ALWAYS THIS DIFFICULT?
REQUEST: DOCTOR, WE MUST DISCUSS TACTICS.
TACTICS?
WHIRR
INFORMATION: THE UNON ARE NOT WHAT YOU THINK.
AND NEITHER ARE THE LECT.
BUT, THAT'S...

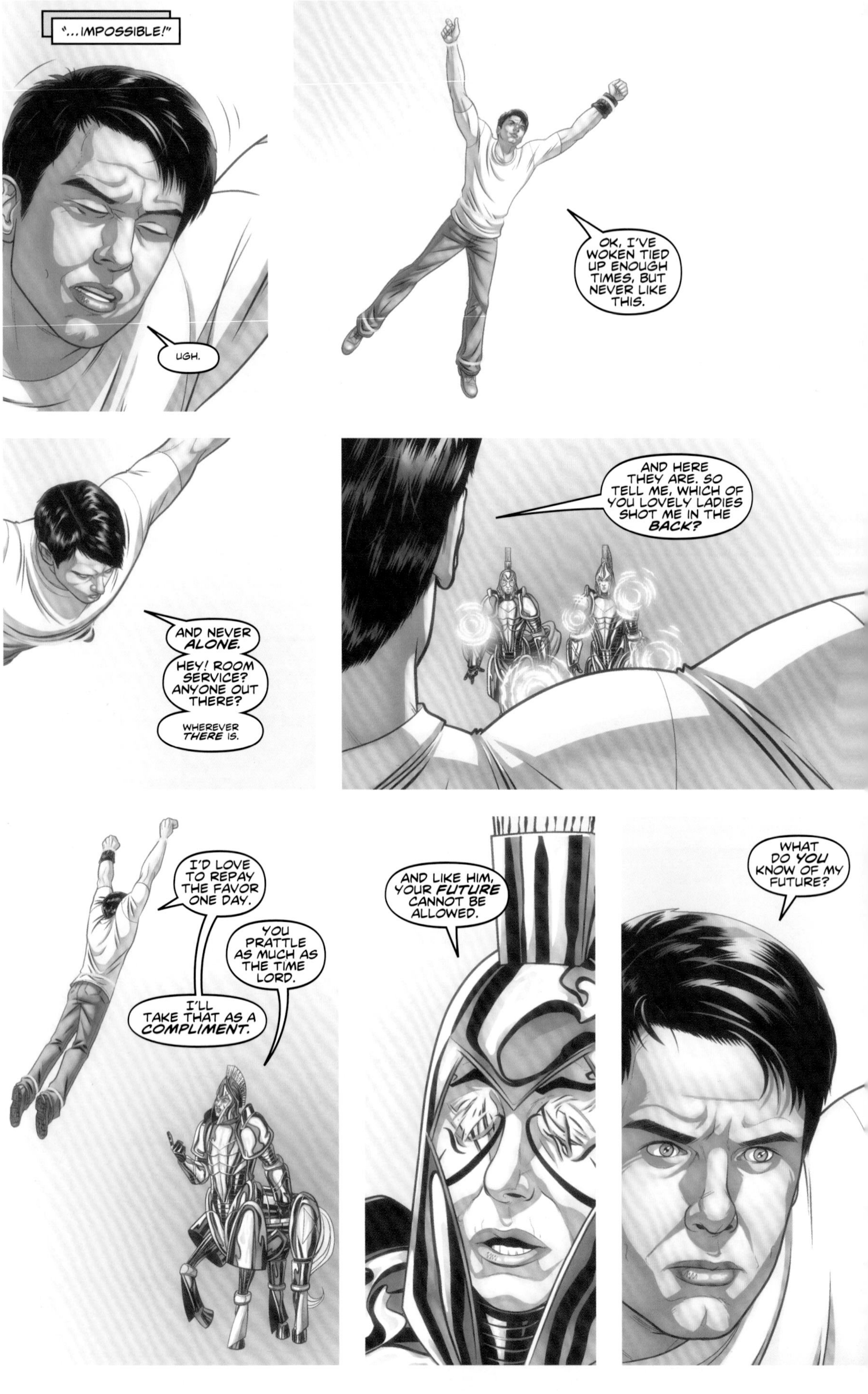
"...IMPOSSIBLE!"
UGH.
OK, I'VE WOKEN TIED UP ENOUGH TIMES, BUT NEVER LIKE THIS.
AND NEVER ALONE.
HEY! ROOM SERVICE? ANYONE OUT THERE?
WHEREVER THERE IS.
AND HERE THEY ARE. SO TELL ME, WHICH OF YOU LOVELY LADIES SHOT ME IN THE BACK?
I'D LOVE TO REPAY THE FAVOR ONE DAY.
YOU PRATTLE AS MUCH AS THE TIME LORD.
I'LL TAKE THAT AS A COMPLIMENT.
AND LIKE HIM, YOUR FUTURE CANNOT BE ALLOWED.
WHAT DO YOU KNOW OF MY FUTURE?

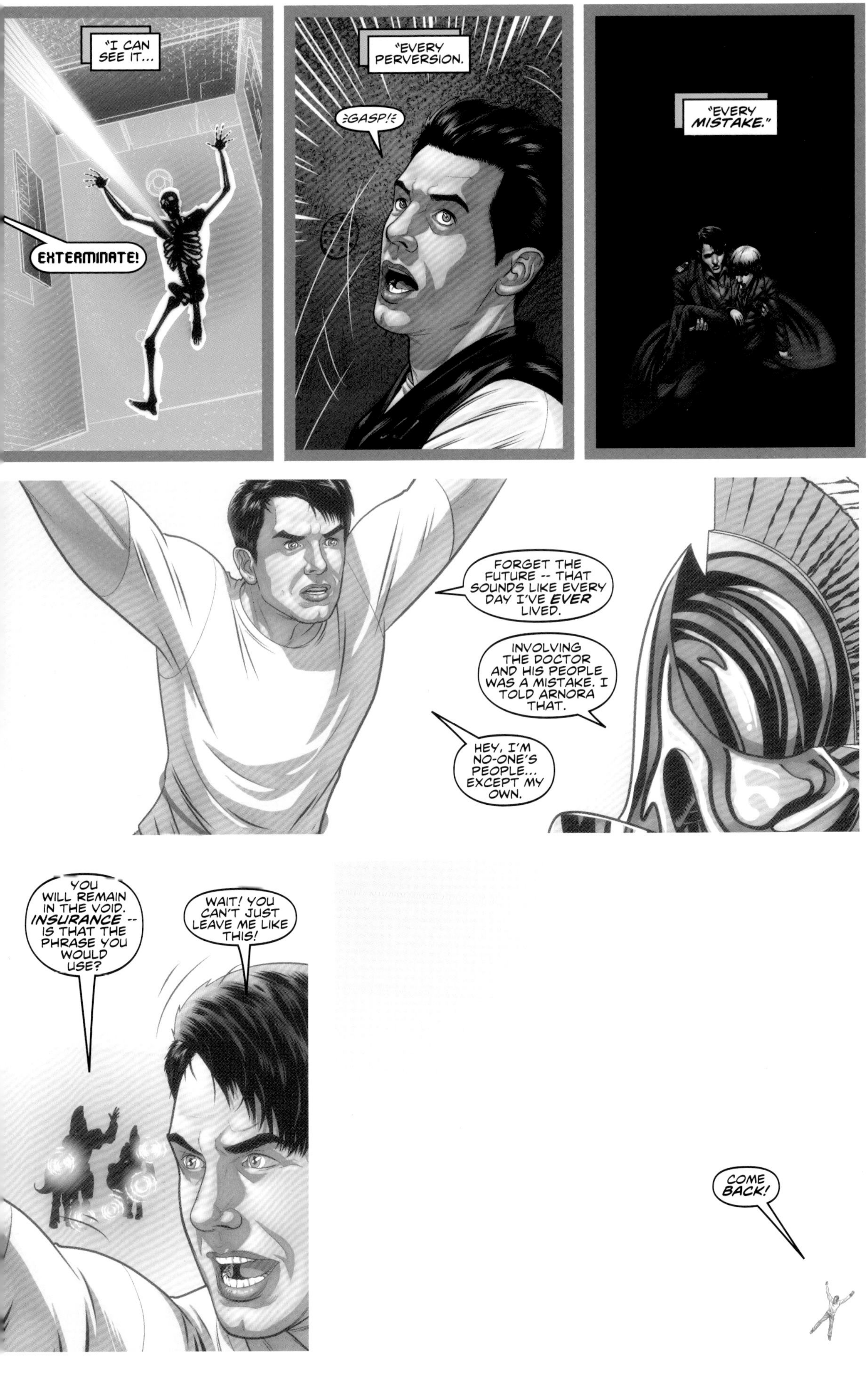

"I CAN SEE IT...
EXTERMINATE!
"EVERY PERVERSION.
GASP!
"EVERY MISTAKE."
FORGET THE FUTURE -- THAT SOUNDS LIKE EVERY DAY I'VE EVER LIVED.
INVOLVING THE DOCTOR AND HIS PEOPLE WAS A MISTAKE. I TOLD ARNORA THAT.
HEY, I'M NO-ONE'S PEOPLE... EXCEPT MY OWN.
YOU WILL REMAIN IN THE VOID. INSURANCE -- IS THAT THE PHRASE YOU WOULD USE?
WAIT! YOU CAN'T JUST LEAVE ME LIKE THIS!
COME BACK!

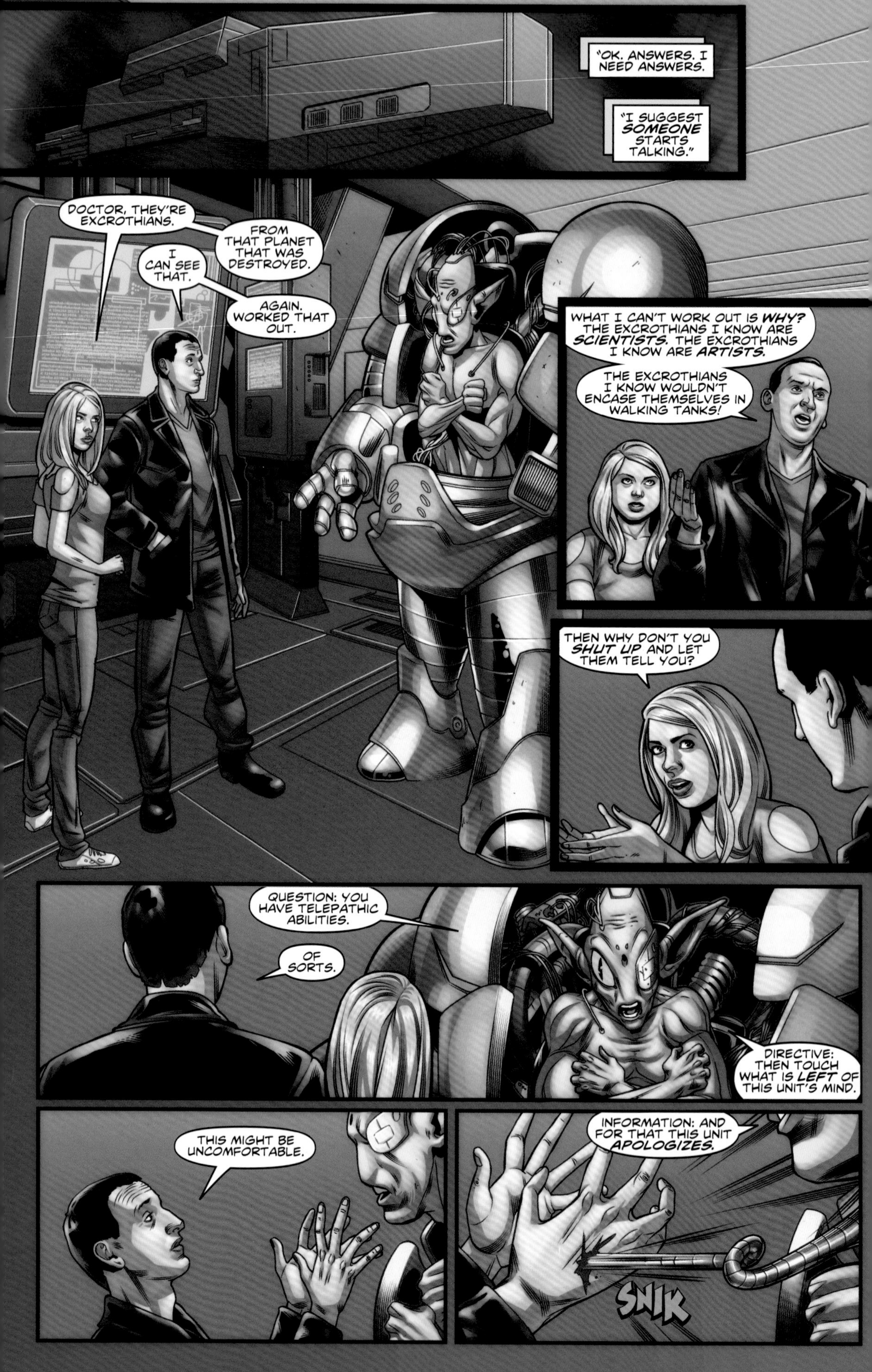
"OK. ANSWERS. I NEED ANSWERS.
"I SUGGEST SOMEONE STARTS TALKING."
DOCTOR, THEY'RE EXCROTHIANS.
FROM THAT PLANET THAT WAS DESTROYED.
I CAN SEE THAT.
AGAIN. WORKED THAT OUT.
WHAT I CAN'T WORK OUT IS WHY? THE EXCROTHIANS I KNOW ARE SCIENTISTS. THE EXCROTHIANS I KNOW ARE ARTISTS.
THE EXCROTHIANS I KNOW WOULDN'T ENCASE THEMSELVES IN WALKING TANKS!
THEN WHY DON'T YOU SHUT UP AND LET THEM TELL YOU?
QUESTION: YOU HAVE TELEPATHIC ABILITIES.
OF SORTS.
DIRECTIVE: THEN TOUCH WHAT IS LEFT OF THIS UNIT'S MIND.
THIS MIGHT BE UNCOMFORTABLE.
INFORMATION: AND FOR THAT THIS UNIT APOLOGIZES.
SNIK

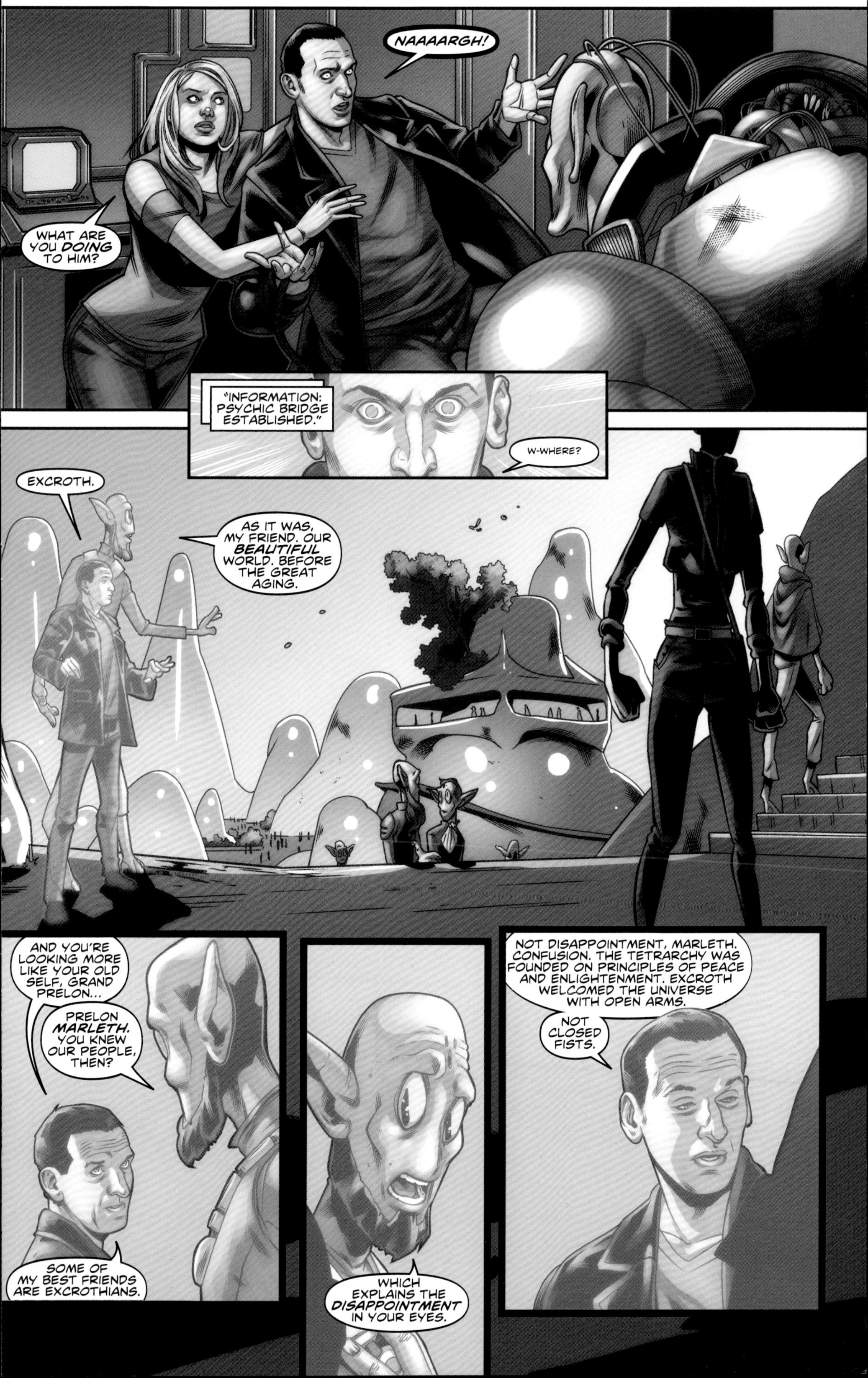
NAAAARGH!
WHAT ARE YOU DOING TO HIM?
"INFORMATION: PSYCHIC BRIDGE ESTABLISHED."
W-WHERE?
EXCROTH.
AS IT WAS, MY FRIEND. OUR BEAUTIFUL WORLD. BEFORE THE GREAT AGING.
AND YOU'RE LOOKING MORE LIKE YOUR OLD SELF, GRAND PRELON...
PRELON MARLETH. YOU KNEW OUR PEOPLE, THEN?
SOME OF MY BEST FRIENDS ARE EXCROTHIANS.
WHICH EXPLAINS THE DISAPPOINTMENT IN YOUR EYES.
NOT DISAPPOINTMENT, MARLETH. CONFUSION. THE TETRARCHY WAS FOUNDED ON PRINCIPLES OF PEACE AND ENLIGHTENMENT. EXCROTH WELCOMED THE UNIVERSE WITH OPEN ARMS.
NOT CLOSED FISTS.

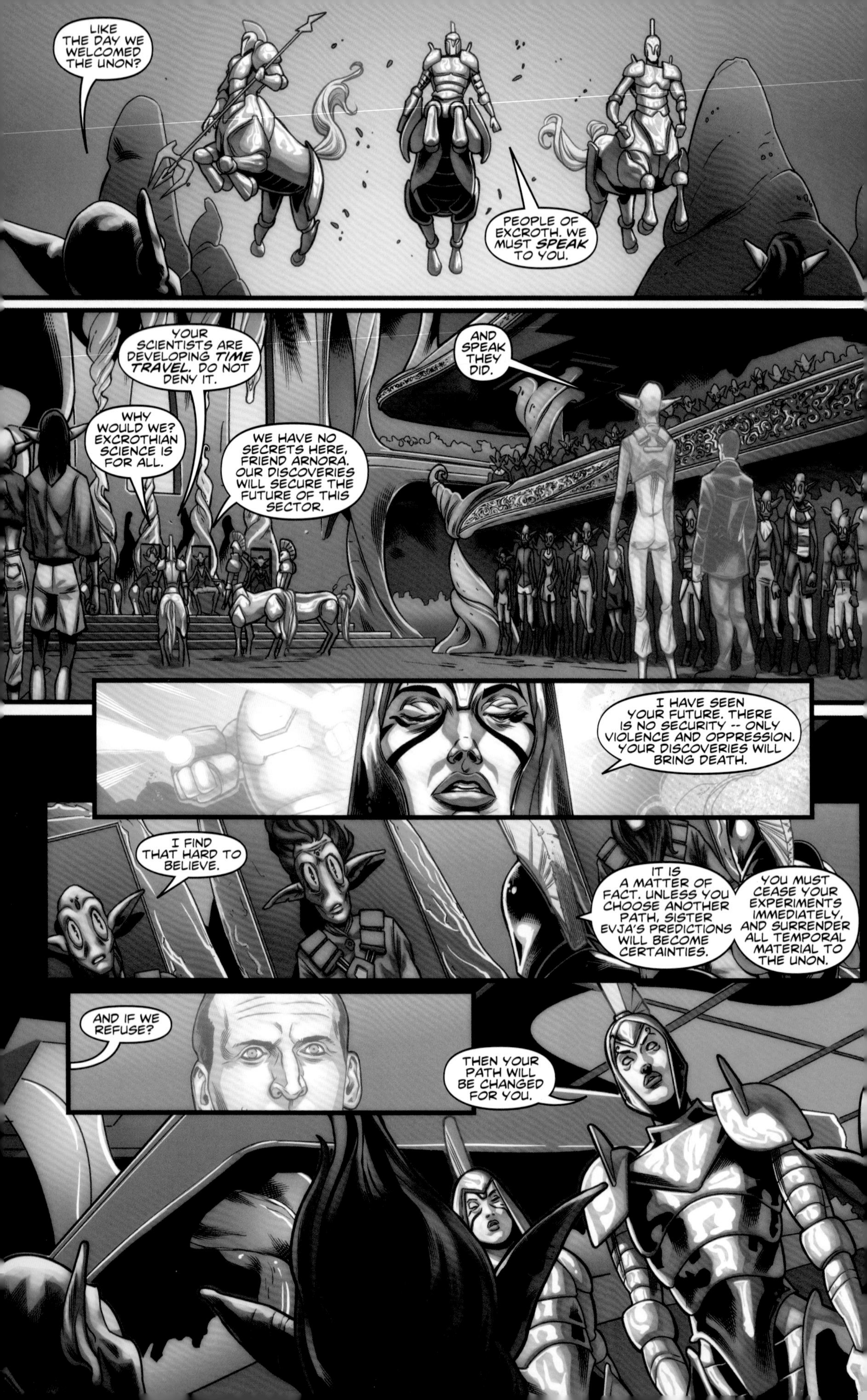
LIKE THE DAY WE WELCOMED THE UNON?
PEOPLE OF EXCROTH. WE MUST SPEAK TO YOU.
YOUR SCIENTISTS ARE DEVELOPING TIME TRAVEL. DO NOT DENY IT.
WHY WOULD WE? EXCROTHIAN SCIENCE IS FOR ALL.
WE HAVE NO SECRETS HERE, FRIEND ARNORA. OUR DISCOVERIES WILL SECURE THE FUTURE OF THIS SECTOR.
AND SPEAK THEY DID.
I HAVE SEEN YOUR FUTURE. THERE IS NO SECURITY -- ONLY VIOLENCE AND OPPRESSION. YOUR DISCOVERIES WILL BRING DEATH.
I FIND THAT HARD TO BELIEVE.
IT IS A MATTER OF FACT. UNLESS YOU CHOOSE ANOTHER PATH, SISTER EVJA'S PREDICTIONS WILL BECOME CERTAINTIES.
YOU MUST CEASE YOUR EXPERIMENTS IMMEDIATELY, AND SURRENDER ALL TEMPORAL MATERIAL TO THE UNON.
AND IF WE REFUSE?
THEN YOUR PATH WILL BE CHANGED FOR YOU.

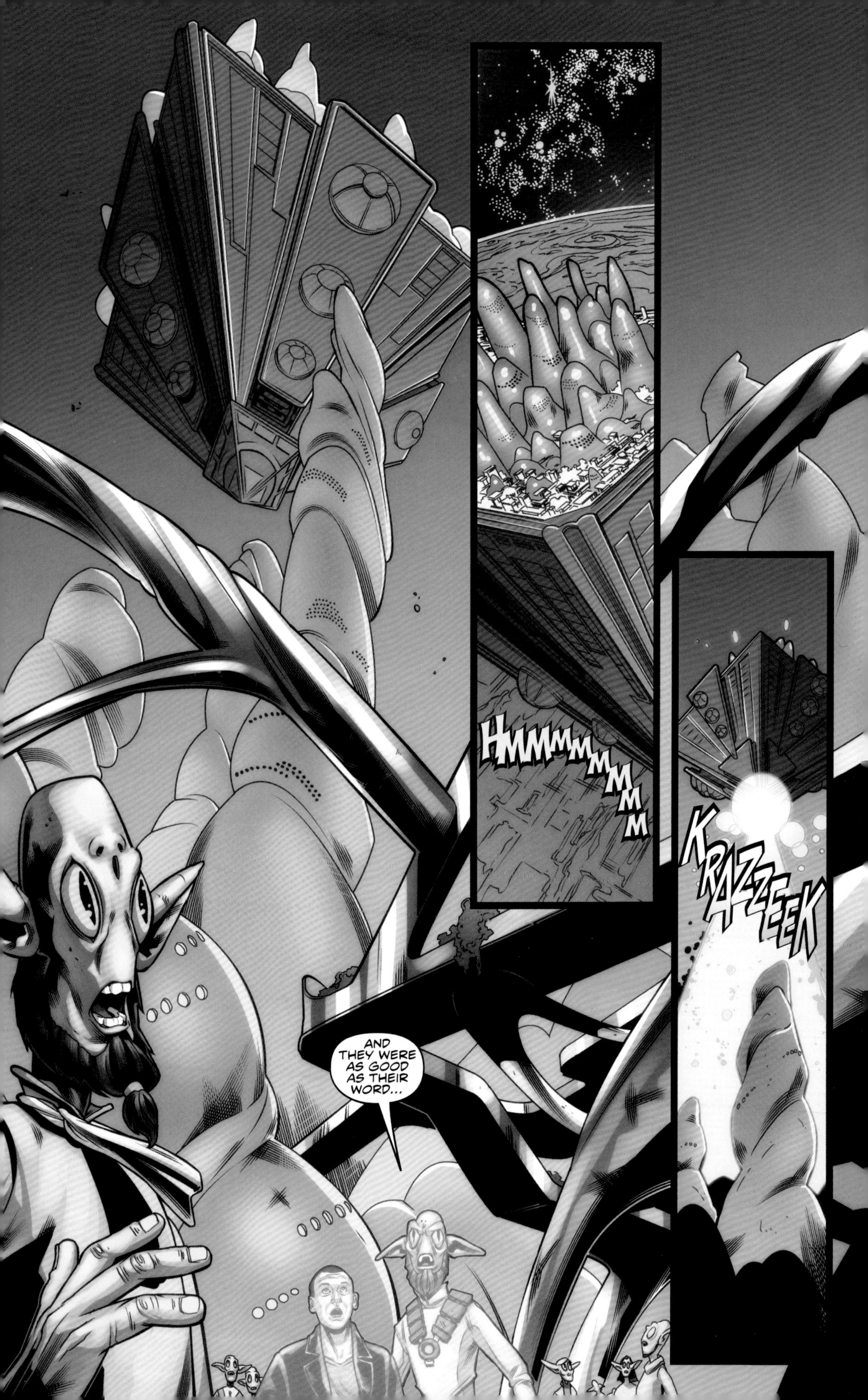
HMMMMMMMMM
KRAZZEEK
AND THEY WERE AS GOOD AS THEIR WORD...

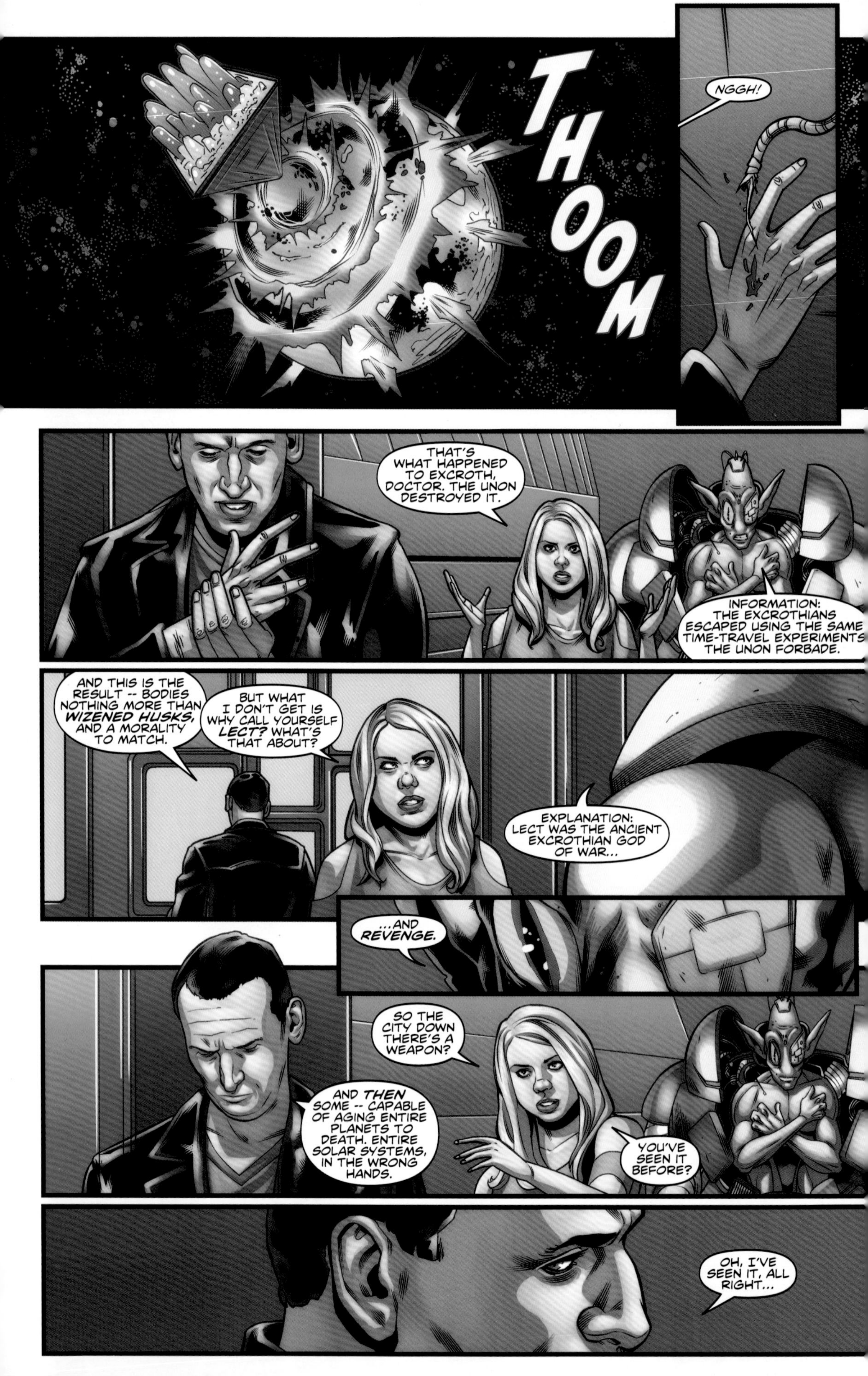
THOOM
NGGH!
THAT'S WHAT HAPPENED TO EXCROTH, DOCTOR. THE UNON DESTROYED IT.
INFORMATION: THE EXCROTHIANS ESCAPED USING THE SAME TIME-TRAVEL EXPERIMENTS THE UNON FORBADE.
AND THIS IS THE RESULT -- BODIES NOTHING MORE THAN WIZENED HUSKS, AND A MORALITY TO MATCH.
BUT WHAT I DON'T GET IS WHY CALL YOURSELF LECT? WHAT'S THAT ABOUT?
EXPLANATION: LECT WAS THE ANCIENT EXCROTHIAN GOD OF WAR...
...AND REVENGE.
SO THE CITY DOWN THERE'S A WEAPON?
AND THEN SOME -- CAPABLE OF AGING ENTIRE PLANETS TO DEATH. ENTIRE SOLAR SYSTEMS, IN THE WRONG HANDS.
YOU'VE SEEN IT BEFORE?
OH, I'VE SEEN IT, ALL RIGHT...

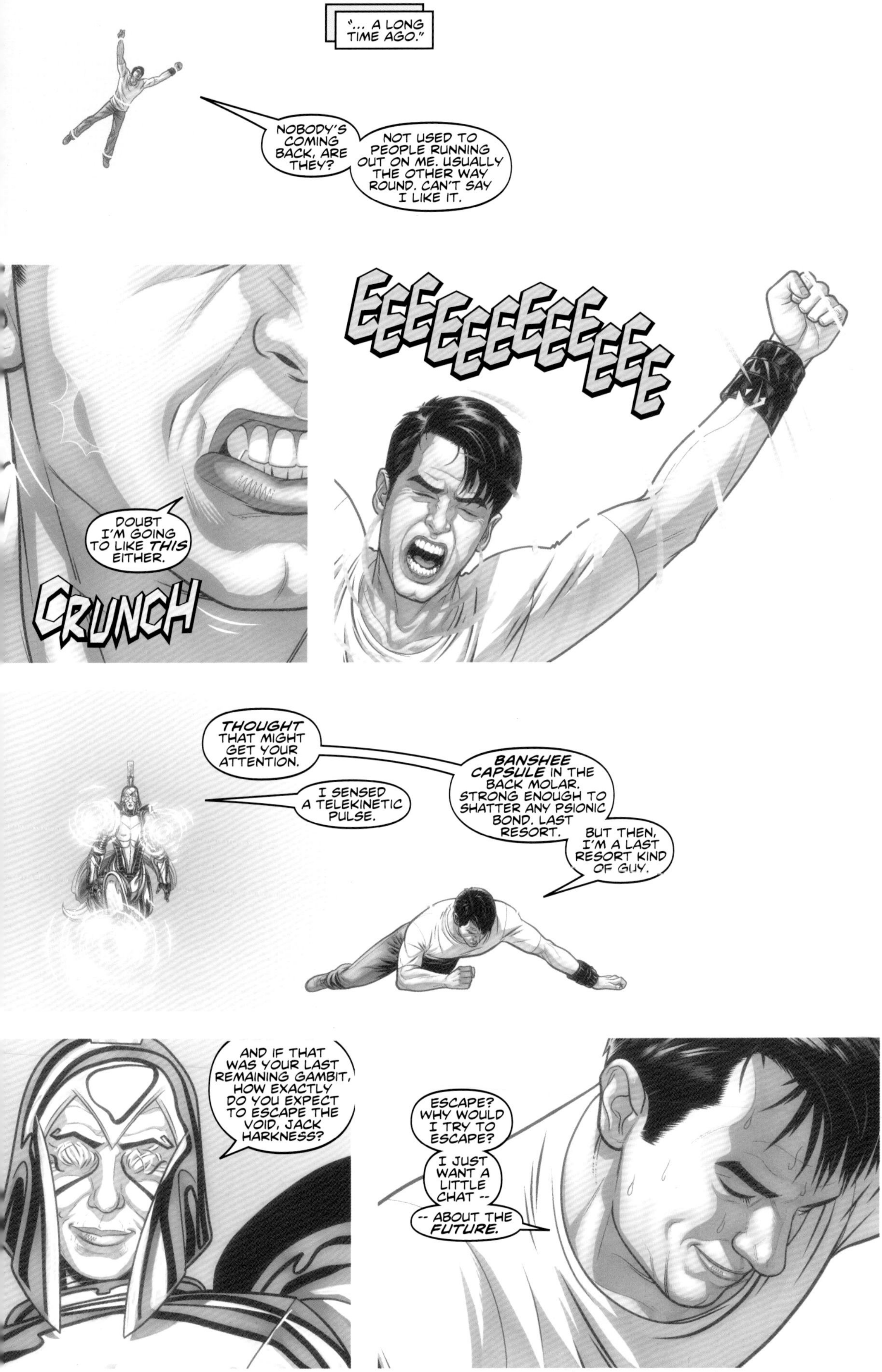
"... A LONG TIME AGO."
NOBODY'S COMING BACK, ARE THEY?
NOT USED TO PEOPLE RUNNING OUT ON ME. USUALLY THE OTHER WAY ROUND. CAN'T SAY I LIKE IT.
DOUBT I'M GOING TO LIKE THIS EITHER.
CRUNCH
EEEEEEEEEEEEE
THOUGHT THAT MIGHT GET YOUR ATTENTION.
BANSHEE CAPSULE IN THE BACK MOLAR. STRONG ENOUGH TO SHATTER ANY PSIONIC BOND. LAST RESORT.
I SENSED A TELEKINETIC PULSE.
BUT THEN, I'M A LAST RESORT KIND OF GUY.
AND IF THAT WAS YOUR LAST REMAINING GAMBIT, HOW EXACTLY DO YOU EXPECT TO ESCAPE THE VOID, JACK HARKNESS?
ESCAPE? WHY WOULD I TRY TO ESCAPE?
I JUST WANT A LITTLE CHAT --
-- ABOUT THE FUTURE.

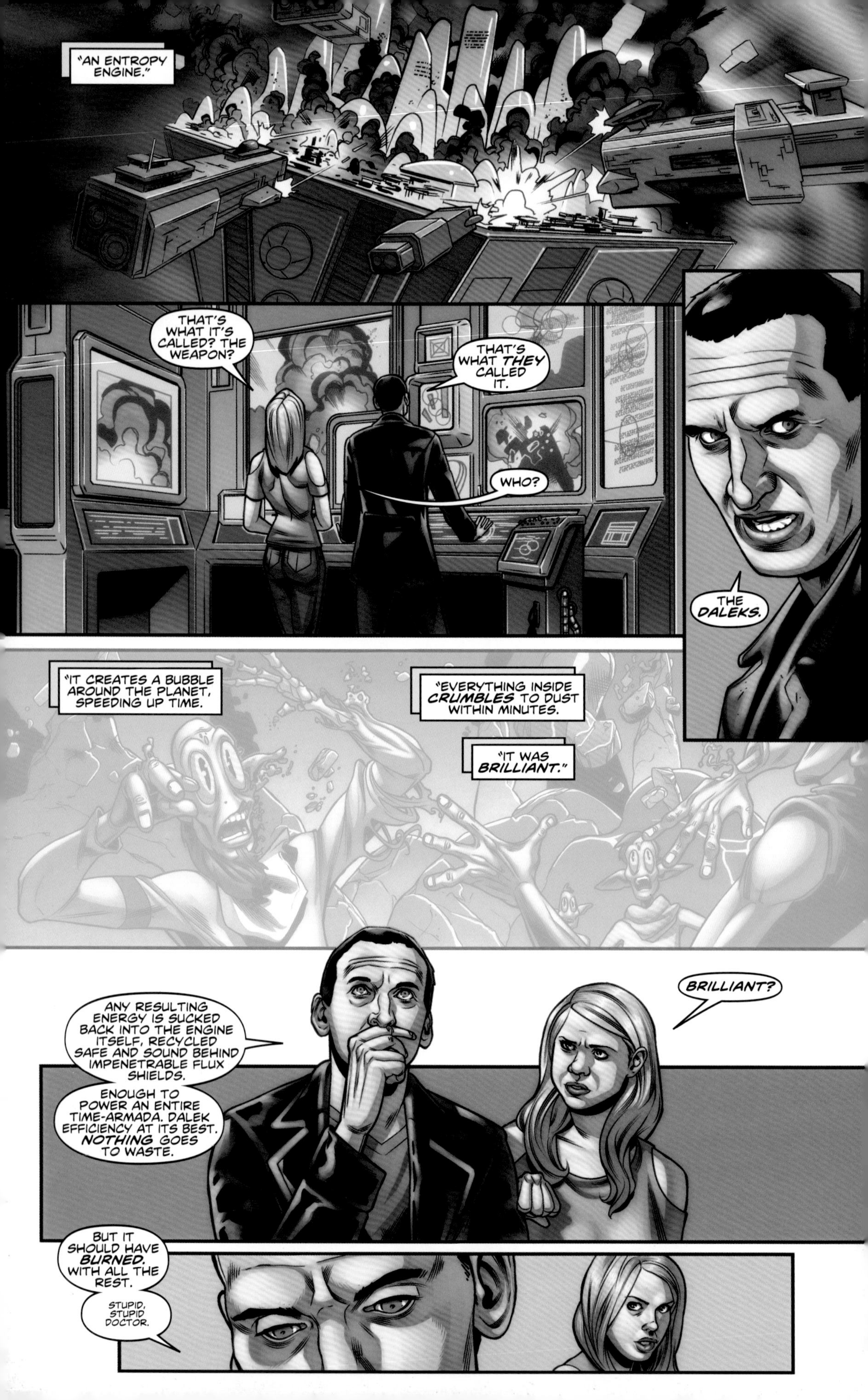
"AN ENTROPY ENGINE."
THAT'S WHAT IT'S CALLED? THE WEAPON?
THAT'S WHAT THEY CALLED IT.
WHO?
THE DALEKS.
"IT CREATES A BUBBLE AROUND THE PLANET, SPEEDING UP TIME.
"EVERYTHING INSIDE CRUMBLES TO DUST WITHIN MINUTES.
"IT WAS BRILLIANT."
BRILLIANT?
ANY RESULTING ENERGY IS SUCKED BACK INTO THE ENGINE ITSELF, RECYCLED SAFE AND SOUND BEHIND IMPENETRABLE FLUX SHIELDS.
ENOUGH TO POWER AN ENTIRE TIME-ARMADA. DALEK EFFICIENCY AT ITS BEST. NOTHING GOES TO WASTE.
BUT IT SHOULD HAVE BURNED. WITH ALL THE REST.
STUPID, STUPID DOCTOR.

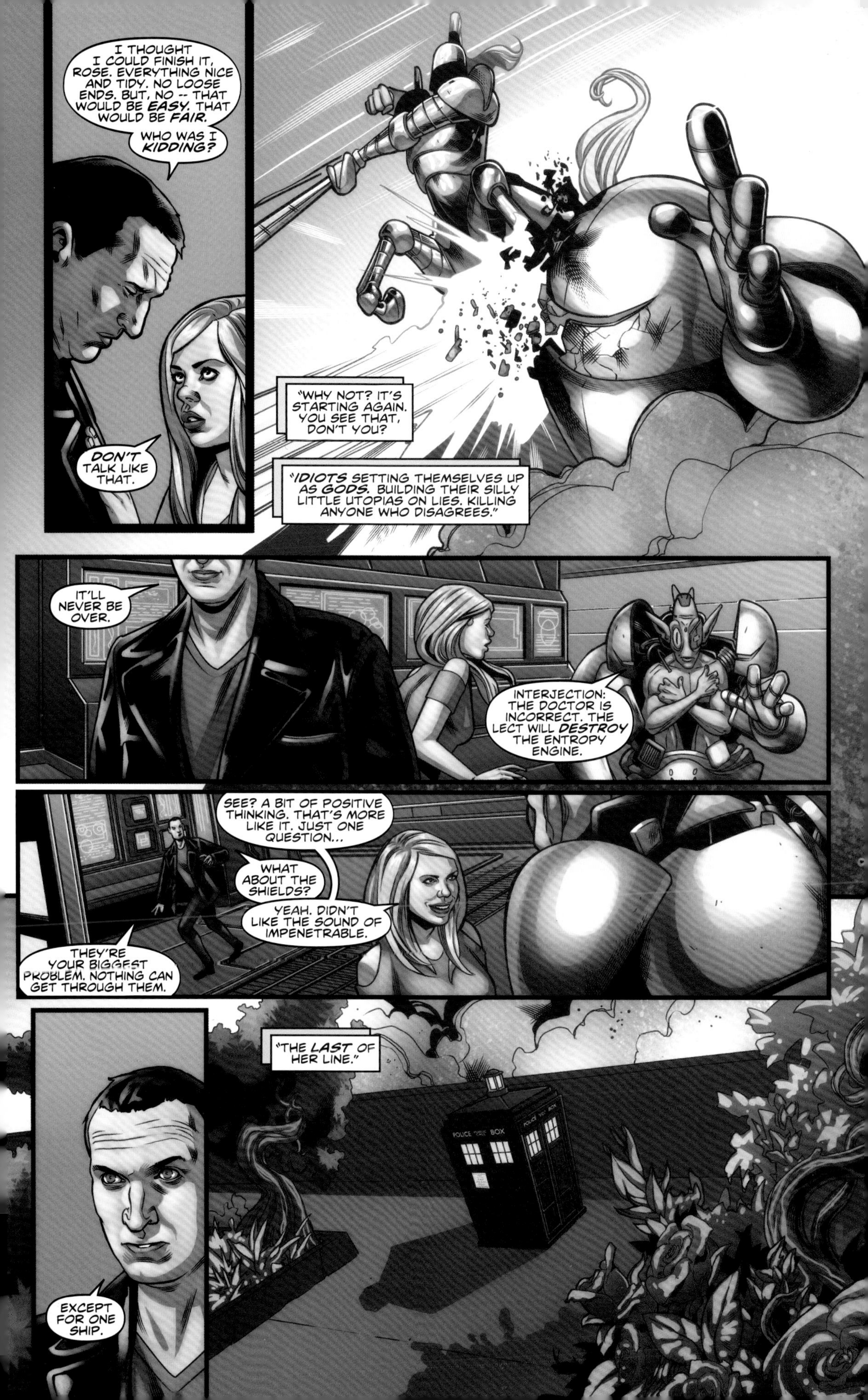
I THOUGHT I COULD FINISH IT, ROSE. EVERYTHING NICE AND TIDY. NO LOOSE ENDS. BUT, NO -- THAT WOULD BE EASY. THAT WOULD BE FAIR.
WHO WAS I KIDDING?
"WHY NOT? IT'S STARTING AGAIN. YOU SEE THAT, DON'T YOU?
DON'T TALK LIKE THAT.
"IDIOTS SETTING THEMSELVES UP AS GODS. BUILDING THEIR SILLY LITTLE UTOPIAS ON LIES. KILLING ANYONE WHO DISAGREES."
IT'LL NEVER BE OVER.
INTERJECTION: THE DOCTOR IS INCORRECT. THE LECT WILL DESTROY THE ENTROPY ENGINE.
SEE? A BIT OF POSITIVE THINKING. THAT'S MORE LIKE IT. JUST ONE QUESTION...
WHAT ABOUT THE SHIELDS?
YEAH. DIDN'T LIKE THE SOUND OF IMPENETRABLE.
THEY'RE YOUR BIGGEST PROBLEM. NOTHING CAN GET THROUGH THEM.
"THE LAST OF HER LINE."
EXCEPT FOR ONE SHIP.
POLICE PUBLIC CALL BOX

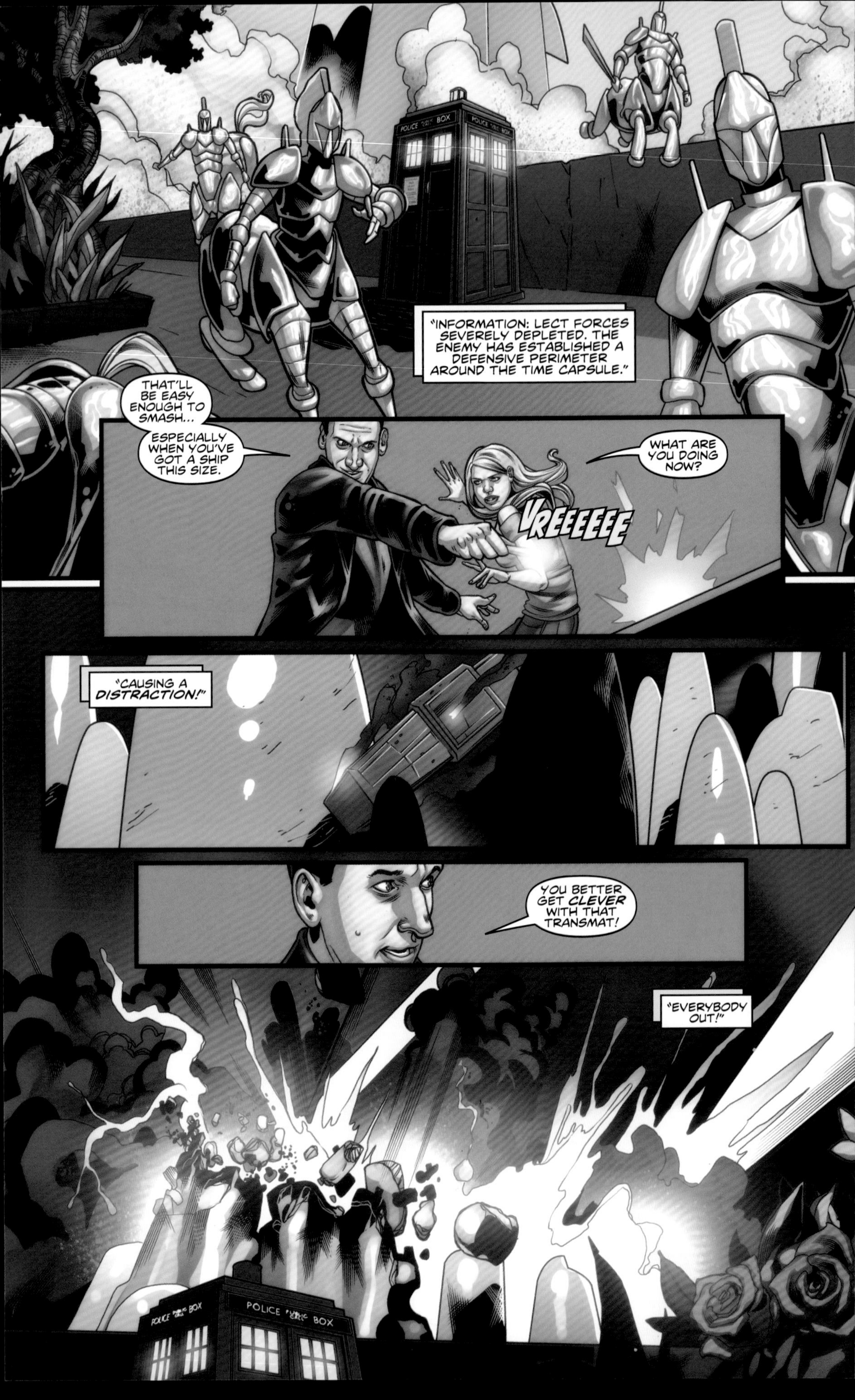
"INFORMATION: LECT FORCES SEVERELY DEPLETED. THE ENEMY HAS ESTABLISHED A DEFENSIVE PERIMETER AROUND THE TIME CAPSULE."
THAT'LL BE EASY ENOUGH TO SMASH...
ESPECIALLY WHEN YOU'VE GOT A SHIP THIS SIZE.
WHAT ARE YOU DOING NOW?
VREEEEEE
"CAUSING A DISTRACTION!"
YOU BETTER GET CLEVER WITH THAT TRANSMAT!
"EVERYBODY OUT!"
POLICE PUBLIC CALL BOX

THERE SHE IS.

THAT WAS A LITTLE *EXTREME,* WASN'T IT?

MEANS TO AN END.

AND THAT MAKES IT ALL RIGHT?

"*NOTHING* ABOUT THIS IS ALL RIGHT."

NO!

VWORP

"WHICH IS WHY WE HAVE *WORK* TO DO."

OR RATHER *HE* DOES.

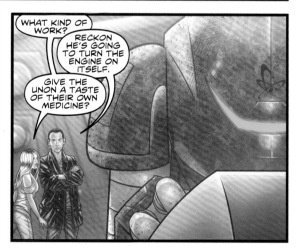

WHAT KIND OF WORK?

RECKON HE'S GOING TO TURN THE ENGINE ON ITSELF.

GIVE THE UNON A TASTE OF THEIR OWN MEDICINE?

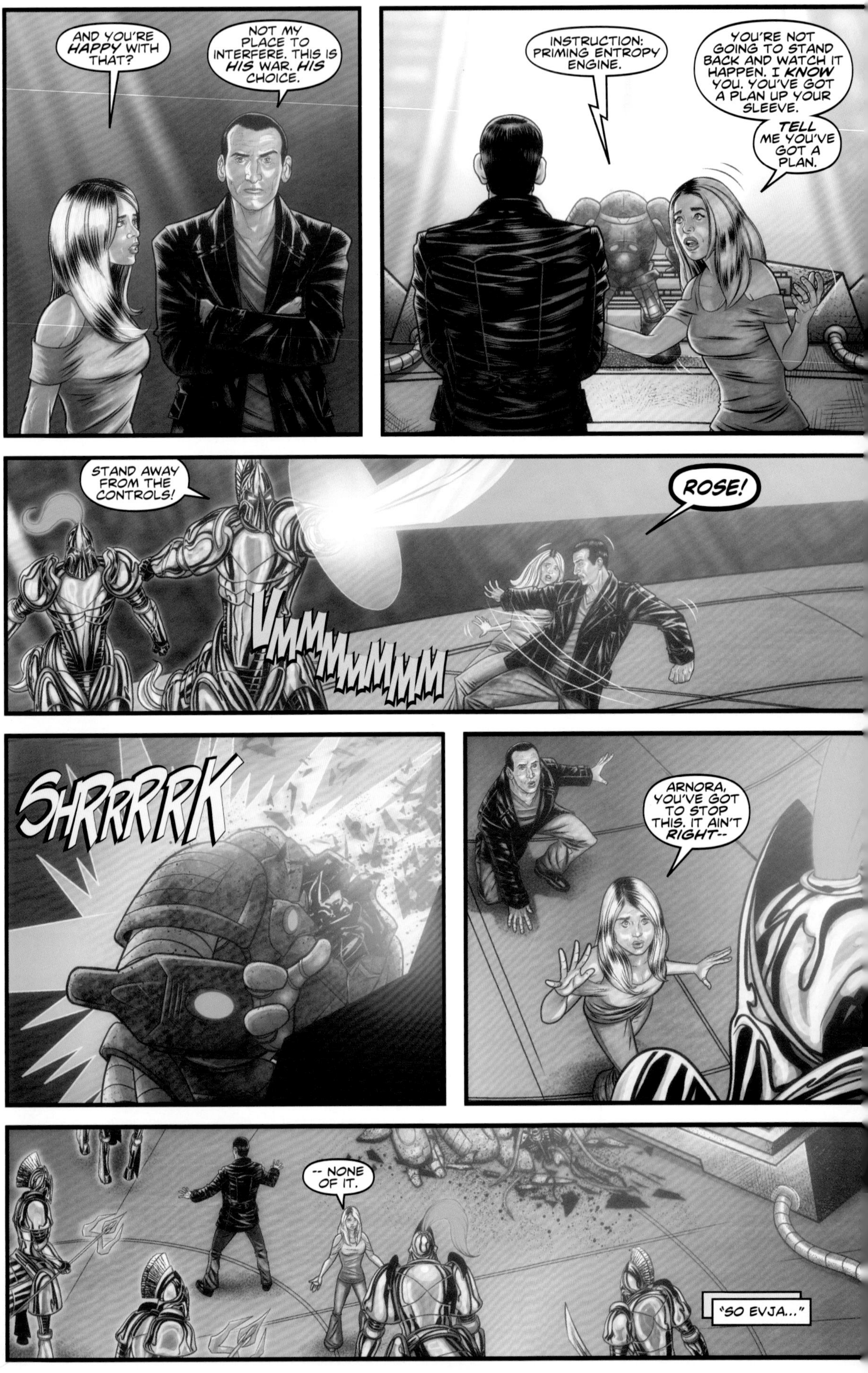

AND YOU'RE HAPPY WITH THAT?
NOT MY PLACE TO INTERFERE. THIS IS HIS WAR. HIS CHOICE.
INSTRUCTION: PRIMING ENTROPY ENGINE.
YOU'RE NOT GOING TO STAND BACK AND WATCH IT HAPPEN. I KNOW YOU. YOU'VE GOT A PLAN UP YOUR SLEEVE.
TELL ME YOU'VE GOT A PLAN.
STAND AWAY FROM THE CONTROLS!
ROSE!
VMMMMMMMM
SHRRRRK
ARNORA, YOU'VE GOT TO STOP THIS. IT AIN'T RIGHT--
-- NONE OF IT.
"SO EVJA..."

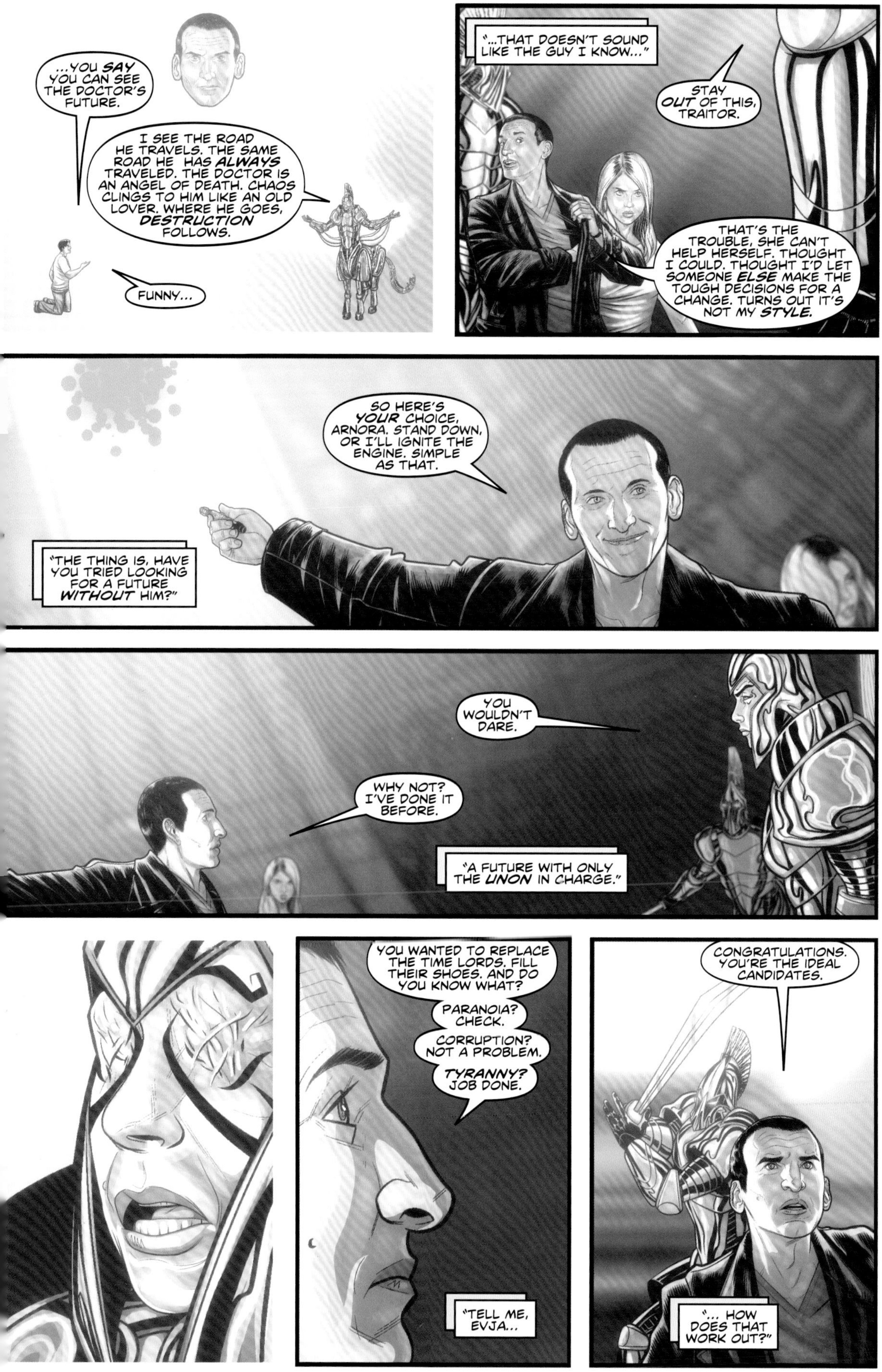
...YOU SAY YOU CAN SEE THE DOCTOR'S FUTURE.
I SEE THE ROAD HE TRAVELS. THE SAME ROAD HE HAS ALWAYS TRAVELED. THE DOCTOR IS AN ANGEL OF DEATH. CHAOS CLINGS TO HIM LIKE AN OLD LOVER. WHERE HE GOES, DESTRUCTION FOLLOWS.
FUNNY...
"...THAT DOESN'T SOUND LIKE THE GUY I KNOW..."
STAY OUT OF THIS, TRAITOR.
THAT'S THE TROUBLE, SHE CAN'T HELP HERSELF. THOUGHT I COULD. THOUGHT I'D LET SOMEONE ELSE MAKE THE TOUGH DECISIONS FOR A CHANGE. TURNS OUT IT'S NOT MY STYLE.
SO HERE'S YOUR CHOICE, ARNORA. STAND DOWN, OR I'LL IGNITE THE ENGINE. SIMPLE AS THAT.
"THE THING IS, HAVE YOU TRIED LOOKING FOR A FUTURE WITHOUT HIM?"
YOU WOULDN'T DARE.
WHY NOT? I'VE DONE IT BEFORE.
"A FUTURE WITH ONLY THE UNON IN CHARGE."
YOU WANTED TO REPLACE THE TIME LORDS. FILL THEIR SHOES. AND DO YOU KNOW WHAT?
PARANOIA? CHECK.
CORRUPTION? NOT A PROBLEM.
TYRANNY? JOB DONE.
"TELL ME, EVJA...
CONGRATULATIONS. YOU'RE THE IDEAL CANDIDATES.
"... HOW DOES THAT WORK OUT?"

DOCTOR! DOWN!

SKRRRRT

MISSED ME?

ARNORA. I'VE SEEN THE FUTURE. *OUR* FUTURE. SEEN WHAT WE WILL DO.

WE'LL REGULATE TIME. JUST AS WE PLANNED. BRING HEALING FOR ALL.

WHETHER THEY WANT IT OR NOT?

ENOUGH OF THIS. WE MUST REVERSE THE DAMAGE THE LECT HAS DONE. BRING THE ENGINE UNDER CONTROL.

FOOM

INFORMATION: OVER THIS UNIT'S DEAD BODY!

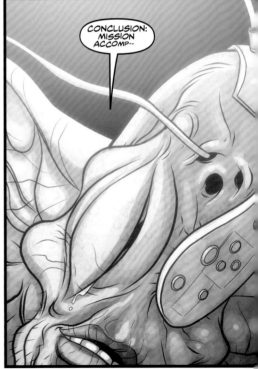

CONCLUSION: MISSION ACCOMP--

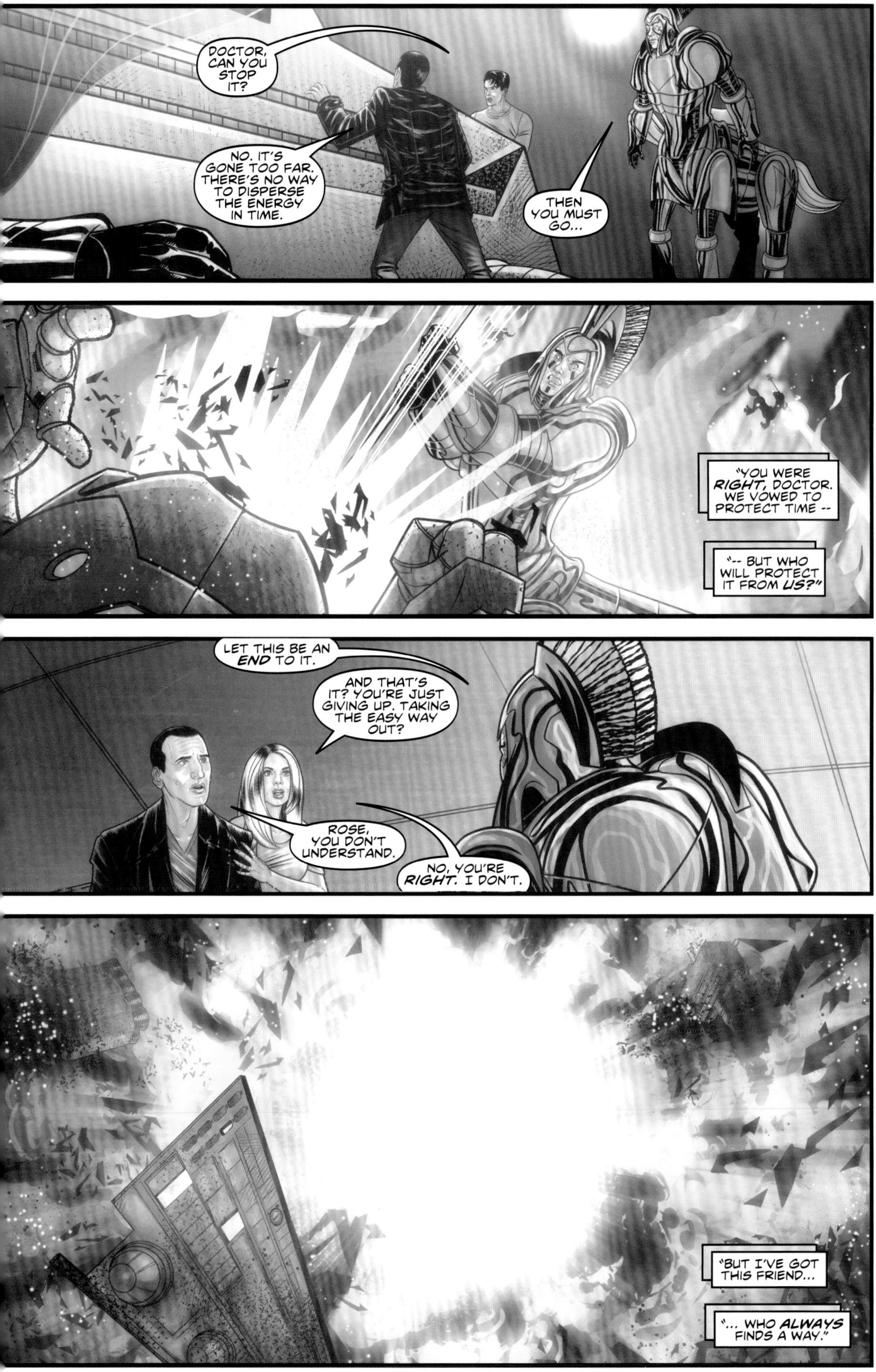
DOCTOR, CAN YOU STOP IT?
NO. IT'S GONE TOO FAR. THERE'S NO WAY TO DISPERSE THE ENERGY IN TIME.
THEN YOU MUST GO...
"YOU WERE RIGHT, DOCTOR. WE VOWED TO PROTECT TIME --
"-- BUT WHO WILL PROTECT IT FROM US?"
LET THIS BE AN END TO IT.
AND THAT'S IT? YOU'RE JUST GIVING UP. TAKING THE EASY WAY OUT?
ROSE, YOU DON'T UNDERSTAND.
NO, YOU'RE RIGHT. I DON'T.
"BUT I'VE GOT THIS FRIEND...
"... WHO ALWAYS FINDS A WAY."

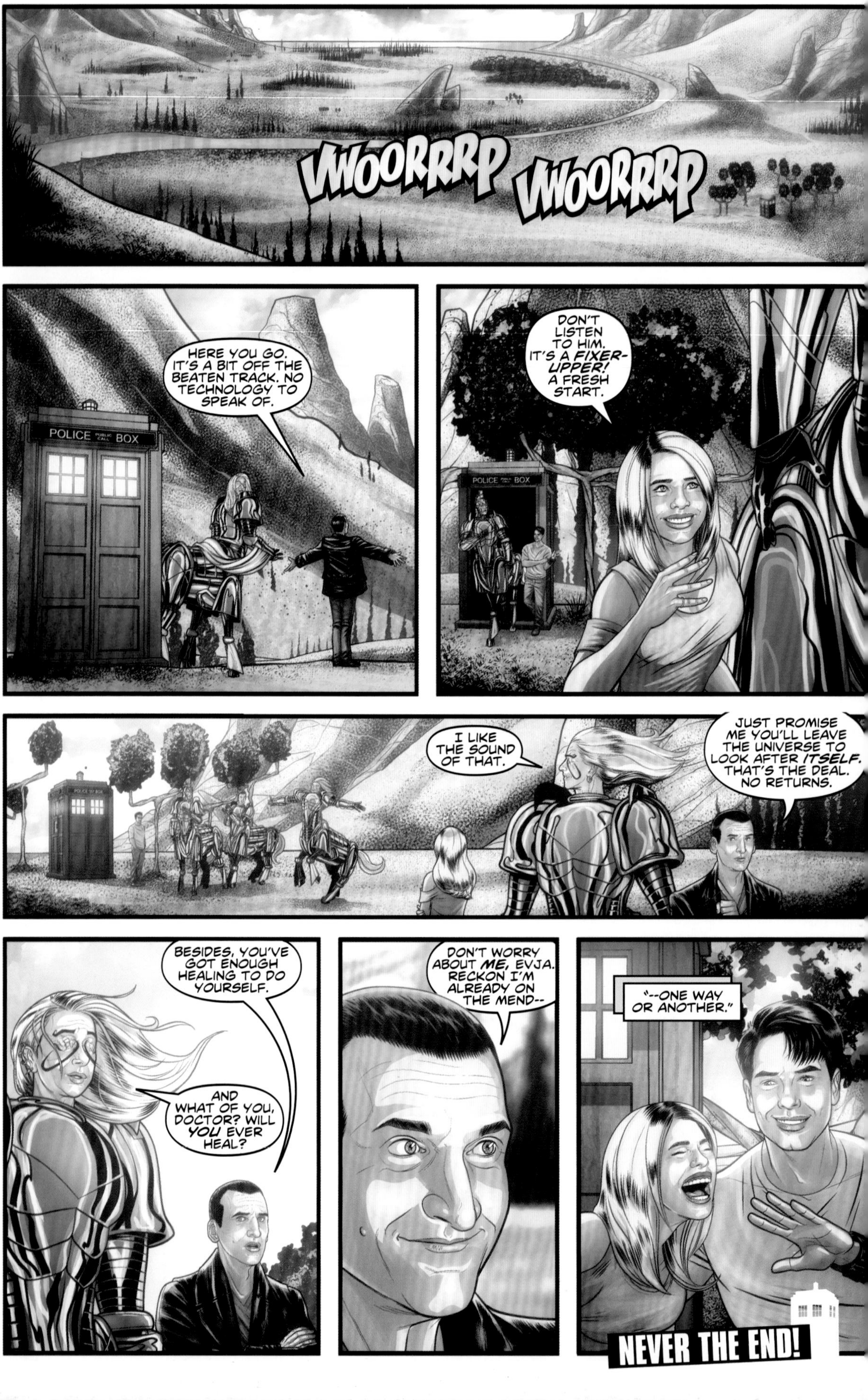

VWOORRRP VWOORRRP
HERE YOU GO. IT'S A BIT OFF THE BEATEN TRACK. NO TECHNOLOGY TO SPEAK OF.
POLICE PUBLIC CALL BOX
DON'T LISTEN TO HIM. IT'S A FIXER-UPPER! A FRESH START.
I LIKE THE SOUND OF THAT.
JUST PROMISE ME YOU'LL LEAVE THE UNIVERSE TO LOOK AFTER ITSELF. THAT'S THE DEAL. NO RETURNS.
BESIDES, YOU'VE GOT ENOUGH HEALING TO DO YOURSELF.
AND WHAT OF YOU, DOCTOR? WILL YOU EVER HEAL?
DON'T WORRY ABOUT ME, EVJA. RECKON I'M ALREADY ON THE MEND--
"--ONE WAY OR ANOTHER."
NEVER THE END!

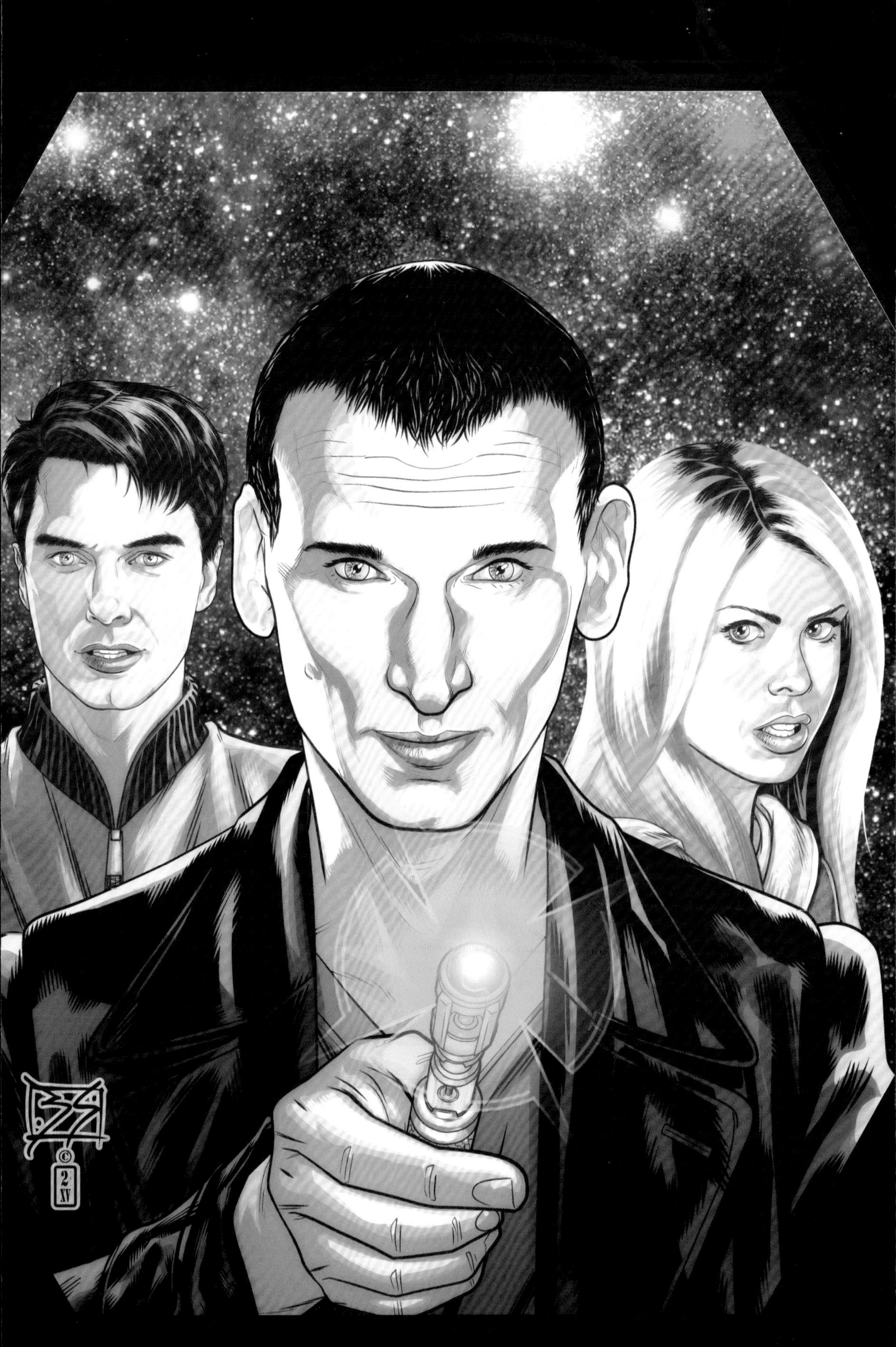

9D #1 Newbury Comics Cover: BLAIR SHEDD

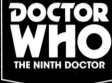

DOCTOR WHO
THE NINTH DOCTOR

COVER GALLERY

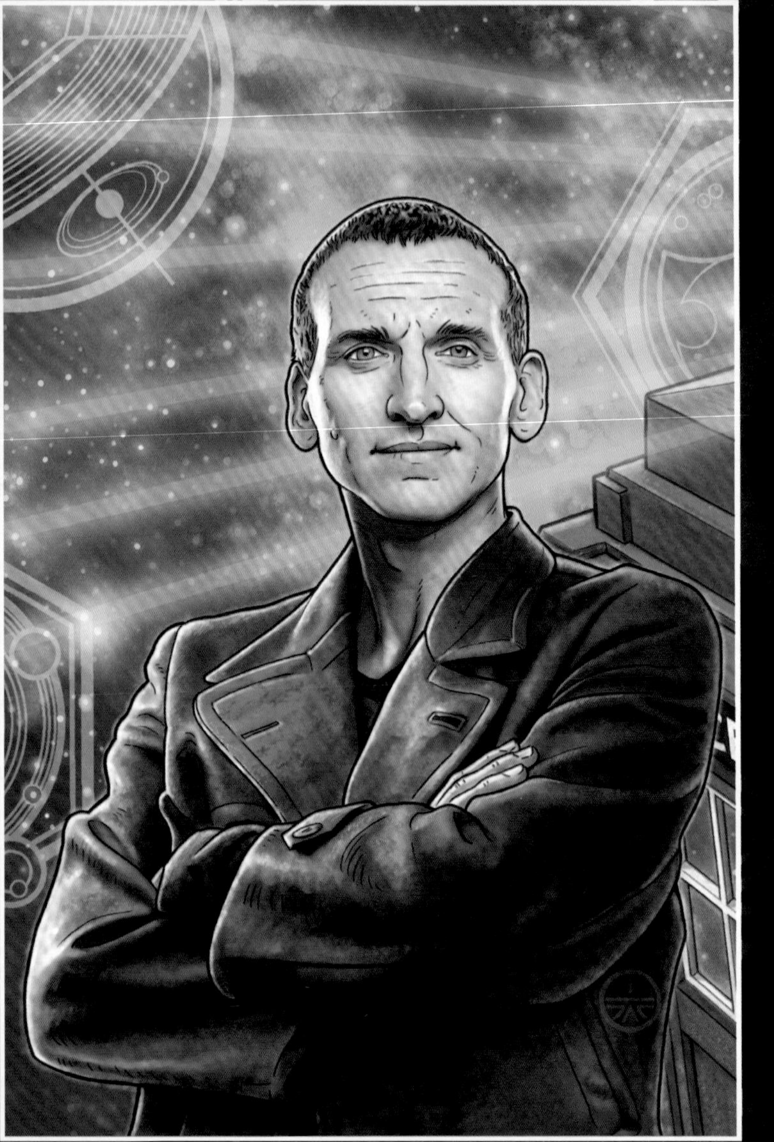

A

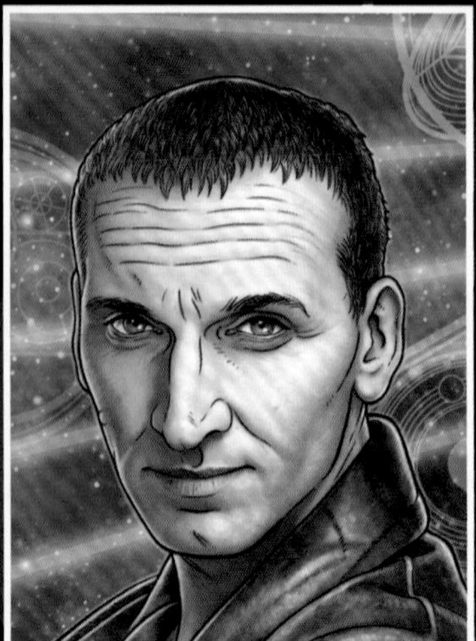

B

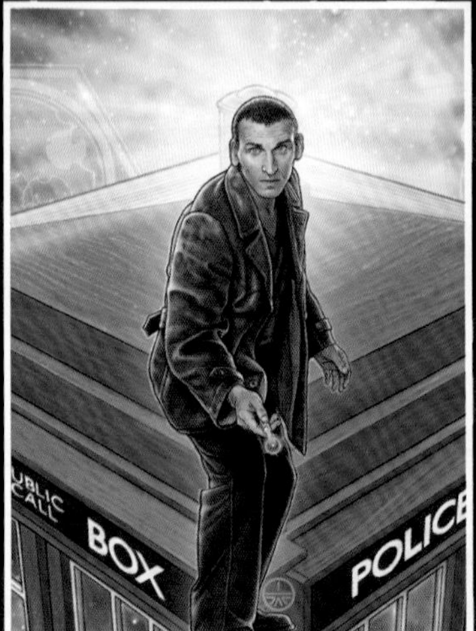
BOX
POLICE

C

ISSUES #1 - 3

A: #2 Hastings Cover – JEFF CARLISLE
B: #1 Hastings Cover – JEFF CARLISLE
C: #3 Hastings Cover – JEFF CARLISLE

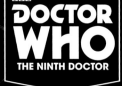

DOCTOR WHO
THE NINTH DOCTOR

COVER GALLERY

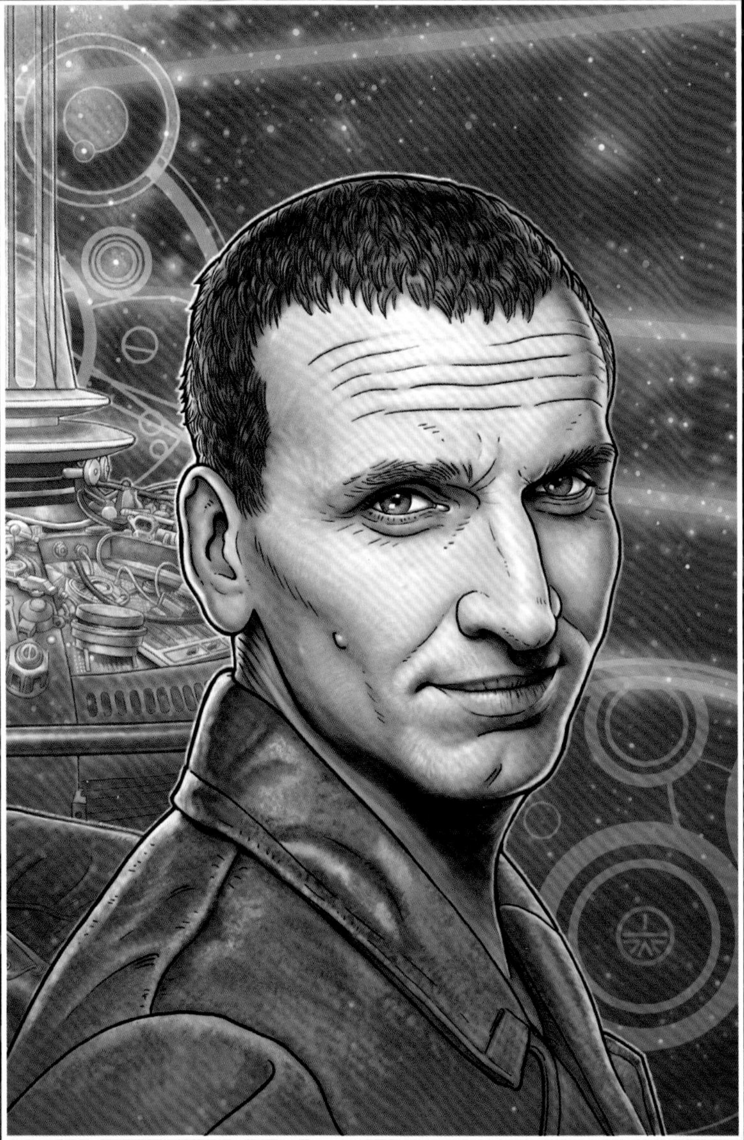

A

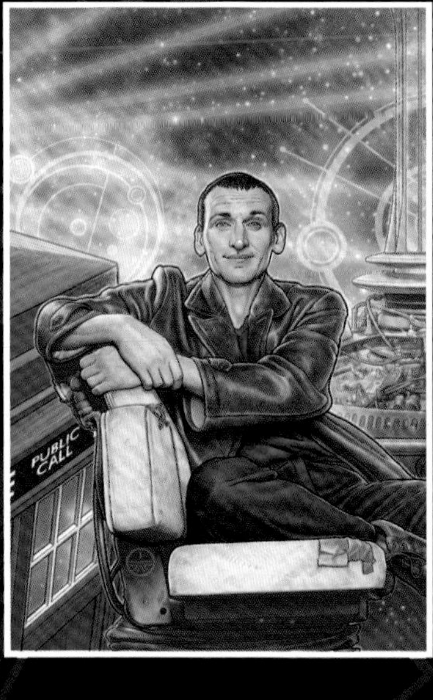

PUBLIC
CALL

B

ISSUES #4 - 5

A: #5 Hastings Cover – JEFF CARLISLE
B: #4 Hastings Cover – JEFF CARLISLE

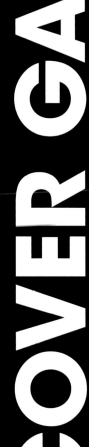

FOLLOW YOUR FAVORITE INCARNATIONS ACROSS THESE FANTASTIC COLLECTIONS!

DOCTOR WHO: THE TENTH DOCTOR
VOL. 1: REVOLUTIONS OF TERROR

BBC NEW ADVENTURES WITH THE TENTH DOCTOR
DOCTOR WHO
REVOLUTIONS OF TERROR
NICK ABADZIS • ELENA CASAGRANDE • ARIANNA FLOREAN

ISBN: 9781782761747
ON SALE NOW - $19.99 / $22.95 CAN / £10.99
(UK EDITION ISBN: 9781782763840)

DOCTOR WHO: THE TENTH DOCTOR
VOL. 2: THE WEEPING ANGELS OF MONS

BBC NEW ADVENTURES WITH THE TENTH DOCTOR
DOCTOR WHO
THE WEEPING ANGELS OF MONS
ROBBIE MORRISON • DANIEL INDRO • SLAMET MUJIONO

ISBN: 9781782761754
ON SALE NOW - $19.99 / $25.99 CAN / £10.99
(UK EDITION ISBN: 9781782766575)

DOCTOR WHO: THE TENTH DOCTOR
VOL. 3:THE FOUNTAINS OF FOREVER

BBC NEW ADVENTURES WITH THE TENTH DOCTOR
DOCTOR WHO
THE FOUNTAINS OF FOREVER
NICK ABADZIS • ELENA CASAGRANDE
ELEONORA CARLINI • ARIANNA FLOREAN

ISBN: 9781782763024
COMING SOON - $19.99 / $25.99 CAN / £10.99
(UK EDITION ISBN: 9781782767404)

DOCTOR WHO: THE ELEVENTH DOCTOR
VOL. 1: AFTER LIFE

BBC NEW ADVENTURES WITH THE ELEVENTH DOCTOR
DOCTOR WHO
AFTER LIFE
AL EWING • ROB WILLIAMS • SIMON FRASER • BOO COOK
GARY CALDWELL • HI-FI

ISBN: 9781782761730
ON SALE NOW - $19.99 / $22.95 CAN / £10.99
(UK EDITION ISBN: 9781782763857)

DOCTOR WHO: THE ELEVENTH DOCTOR
VOL. 2: SERVE YOU

BBC NEW ADVENTURES WITH THE ELEVENTH DOCTOR
DOCTOR WHO
SERVE YOU
AL EWING • ROB WILLIAMS • SIMON FRASER • BOO COOK • WARREN PLEECE
GARY CALDWELL • HI-FI

ISBN: 9781782761754
ON SALE NOW - $19.99 / $22.95 CAN / £10.99
(UK EDITION ISBN: 9781782766582)

DOCTOR WHO: THE ELEVENTH DOCTOR
VOL. 3: CONVERSION

BBC NEW ADVENTURES WITH THE ELEVENTH DOCTOR
DOCTOR WHO
CONVERSION
AL EWING • ROB WILLIAMS • SIMON FRASER • BOO COOK • WARREN PLEECE
GARY CALDWELL • HI-FI

ISBN: 9781782763024
COMING SOON - $19.99 / $25.99 CAN / £10.99
(UK EDITION ISBN: 9781782767435)

TITAN COMICS

For information on how to subscribe to our great Doctor Who titles, or to purchase them digitally, visit:

WWW.TITAN-COMICS.COM

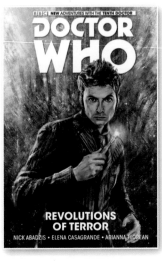

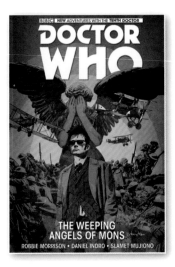

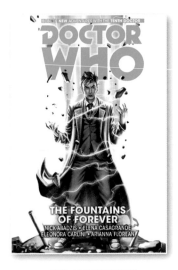

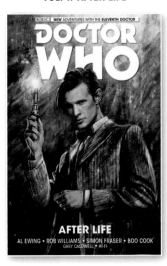

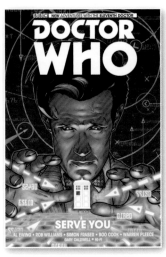

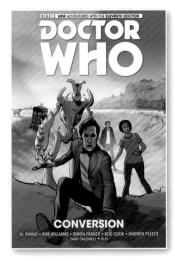

COMPLETE YOUR COLLECTION!

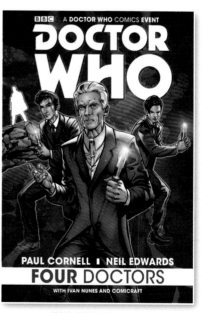

BIOGRAPHIES

Cavan Scott is a writer, editor and journalist. He is known for his comics writing on *Doctor Who: The Twelfth Doctor*, *Adventure Time* and *Power Rangers*, as well as his many novels, including the upcoming *Sherlock Holmes* and *Star Wars: Adventures in Wild Space* novels. He is also known for co-writing the bestselling *Who-Ology* book. He has written for over thirty magazines in the UK, and founded the award-winning *Countryfile Magazine*. He lives in Bristol with his wife, two daughters and an inflatable Dalek named Desmond.

Blair Shedd is an Amerian comic book artist who was educated at the Kubert school under Joe Kubert himself, subsequently forming oneGemini studios. An artist and writer, he has illustrated *Ghostbusters*, *Legends of Oz: Dorothy's Return*, *The Guild*, and many more. He lives in New England with his wife and three kids.

Rachael Stott is a comic book artist and illustrator based in London. As well as illustrating *Doctor Who* (becoming the new regular artist on the *Twelfth Doctor* ongoing series from January 2016), she has drawn *Star Trek* and the *Star Trek/ Planet of the Apes* crossover. She won the Best Newcomer Prize at the 2015 British Comic Awards.

Anang Setyawan was born in Temanggung, a small village in Java, Indonesia. He graduated from vocational high school and started working for a jewelry company, but soon realized that it was the wrong place for him, so quit his job to follow his dream of becoming a visual artist. He has been coloring professionally since 2011, and has worked on *Doctor Who* and *Sevara*.